DEMOCRATIZATION AND THE JUDICIARY

BOOKS OF RELATED INTEREST

The European Union and Democracy Promotion
The Case of North Africa
Edited by Richard Gillespie and Richard Youngs

Securitization and Democratization in the Mediterranean
Shifting Priorities in a Changing World
By Annette Jünemann

The Resilience of Democracy
Persistent Practice, Durable Idea
Edited by Peter Burnell and Peter Calvert

The Internet, Democracy and Democratization
Edited by Peter Ferdinand

Democratization and the Media
Edited by Vicky Randall

Opposition and Democracy in South Africa
Edited by Roger Southall

DEMOCRATIZATION AND THE JUDICIARY

The Accountability Function of Courts in New Democracies

edited by

SIRI GLOPPEN
University of Bergen

ROBERTO GARGARELLA
Chr. Michelsen Institute

and

ELIN SKAAR
Chr. Michelsen Institute

Routledge
Taylor & Francis Group
LONDON AND NEW YORK

First Published in 2004 by
FRANK CASS PUBLISHERS

Published 2005 by Routledge
4 Park Square, Milton Park, Abingdon, Oxon OX14 4RN
605 Third Avenue, New York, NY 10017

Routledge is an imprint of the Taylor & Francis Group, an informa business

British Library Cataloguing in Publication Data

Democratization and the judiciary
1. Democratization 2. Judicial power 3. Courts 4. Political questions and judicial power
I. Gloppen, Siri II. Gargarella, Roberto, 1964– III. Skaar, Elin
321.8

ISBN 13: 978-0-7146-5568-0 (hbk)
ISBN 13: 978-0-7146-8449-9 (pbk)

Library of Congress Cataloging-in-Publication Data

Democratization and the judiciary : the accountability funtion of courts in new democracies / edited by Siri Gloppen, Roberto Gargarella, and Elin Skaar.
p. cm.
Includes bibliographical references and index.
ISBN 0-7146-5568-6 (alk. paper) – ISBN 0-7146-8449-X (pbk. : alk paper)
1. Political questions and judicial power. 2. Democratization. 3. Latin American–Politics and government–1980– 4. Africa, Sub-Saharan–Politics and government–1960– I. Gloppen, Siri. II. Gargarella, Roberto, 1964– III. Skaar, Elin.
K3367 .D46 2004
340′.11–dc22

2003019752

This group of studies first appeared as a special issue of *Democratization*, ISSN 1351-0347, Vol.10, No.4 (Winter 2003) published by Frank Cass and Co. Ltd.

Contents

Introduction: The Accountability Function of the Courts in New Democracies

SIRI GLOPPEN, ROBERTO GARGARELLA and ELIN SKAAR

Courts are important for the working and consolidation of democratic regimes. They facilitate civil government by contributing to the rule of law and by creating an environment conducive to economic growth. They also have a key role to play with regard to making power-holders accountable to the democratic rules of the game, and ensuring the protection of human rights as established in constitutions, conventions and laws. These are central premises in contemporary democratic theory – assumptions that underlie political reform efforts throughout the world. What is the connection between these goals and what happens in actual practice?

Take the premise that in a democratic system, well-functioning and independent courts are central to making political power-holders accountable – that is, ensuring *transparency*; obliging public officials to justify that their exercise of power is in accordance with their mandate and relevant rules (*answerability*); and imposing checks if government officials overstep the boundaries for their power as defined in the constitution, violate basic rights or compromise the democratic process (*controllability*).[1] Do courts in new democracies play such a role? Under what circumstances are they most likely to develop a strong accountability function vis-à-vis the other branches of government – and is it always desirable to encourage them to do so?

The common concern motivating the authors contributing to this collection is the need for sober reflection on the accountability function of courts in new democracies – reflection based on sound empirical knowledge. The cases examined cover the experiences of African and Latin American countries. Few areas in the world seem to be more in need of judicial reform. Few areas have used so many resources and made so many efforts to reform their judiciaries. Notably, however, there has been very little theoretical reflection regarding why, when and how to carry out such reforms in these parts of the world. The fact that this volume dwells on African and Latin American experiences explains why the accounts pay so much attention to the accountability function of courts: in these areas of the world the survival of the rule of law seems to be fundamentally threatened by the constant attempts of the executive to expand its powers.

Most of our knowledge about the role of courts in a democratic system of governance is based on studies of the United States. How relevant is the US experience for the current situation of courts in Africa and Latin America? This question is explored in the first two studies in this volume.

Martin Shapiro examines the history of constitutional judicial review, both in the US and the European tradition. He finds little support for the current optimism regarding the positive effects of strong judicial review on democratic consolidation and social justice. These institutions have at best had limited success in their countries of origin, Shapiro argues, and there is even less reason to believe that they will succeed in new democracies which lack the social and political preconditions upon which the US and European courts built their institutional legitimacy.

Jennifer Widner takes a broader perspective when asking what the history of the United States can teach us about the process of legal reform. Based on her wide range of knowledge about the development of legal systems on two continents, Widner demonstrates how many of the problems currently experienced by African judiciaries closely parallel the experiences in early American legal history. Among the 'lesson to be learnt' emerging from her analysis is that the will to seek change in itself is not sufficient to build the rule of law. Her comparative perspective suggests that leadership, appropriate framing, a supply of ideas and institutional capacity all constitute crucial factors.

Studies of the political role of courts outside of the United States are scarce.[2] A central aim of this volume is to add systematic knowledge of how Latin American and African courts function within their political systems. It inquires of a number of countries whether the courts have sought to develop a strong accountability function, which strategies and resources they have engaged, and the extent to which they have succeeded.

In their studies Rodrigo Uprimny, Javier Couso, Theunis Roux and Siri Gloppen address these questions in light of recent experiences in Colombia, Chile, South Africa, Tanzania and Zambia respectively. Given the hyper-presidential nature of most of these regimes, particular attention is given to the ability of the courts to say 'no' to the executive and make it 'stick'.

Uprimny examines the efforts made by the Colombian Constitutional Court to control the executive's abuse of emergency powers, thereby illuminating the possibilities, limits and costs of judicial review in fragile democracies. His analysis of the gradual development of the court's jurisprudence regarding emergency powers, and how this is reflected in changes in the executive's practice of declaring a state of emergency, demonstrates how the Constitutional Court through its stepwise approach has managed to establish itself as a credible, albeit limited, check on the power of the executive.

In contrast to the Colombian Constitutional Court's efforts to develop its accountability function vis-à-vis the executive, Chilean legal history tells a story of judicial self-restraint, particularly with regard to legislative review. Javier Couso argues that the Chilean courts' refusal to exercise such powers should not necessarily be viewed in negative terms. Rather, he maintains, their cautious attitude may be explained as a strategic move aimed at preserving the autonomy and political independence of the judicial branch. This, he holds, should be seen as a major factor in explaining the relative strength of the legal system and the continuity of a culture of legalism in Chile, even under authoritarian rule. On the basis of the Chilean experience, Couso argues that too ambitious an agenda for courts in new democracies may lead to undue politicization and undermine the legitimacy of the courts and the foundation of the rule of law.

An inference that might be drawn from the Chilean case is that courts generally – and in new fragile democracies particularly – should abstain from engaging in judicial review based on social and economic rights, which profoundly affects political resource allocation. This is a domain often held to belong to the core of politics, outside the proper arena for judicial intervention. Theunis Roux's analysis of the jurisprudence of the South African Constitutional Court challenges the view that this should remain solely within the realm of politics. Through a close textual reading of the judgments in four significant cases recently decided by the court, Roux asserts that the court has skillfully challenged the conventional idea according to which political resource allocation should be immune from judicial scrutiny because the courts are not properly equipped and legally authorized to perform that task. Furthermore, he shows how the court has managed to use these cases to create legitimacy for itself with the new government, while at the same time succeeding in giving effect to certain social and economic rights.

Compared to most African and many Latin American countries, Colombia, Chile, and South Africa have well-developed and resourced legal systems. Siri Gloppen addresses the role of the judiciary in Tanzania and Zambia – very poor countries with much weaker and inadequately resourced courts. Gloppen critically examines the extent to which they have been able and willing to play a significant role in holding their governments to account. Finding that neither the Tanzanian nor the Zambian judiciary has developed a strong accountability function vis-à-vis the government, she addresses the question of why judges in the two countries rarely have challenged the government in politically significant cases. The focus is on three sets of factors that may explain why the judges behave as they do: the legal culture, the institutional structure and resource constraints judges operate within, and the social legitimacy of the courts.

The cases presented here illustrate the range of difficulties courts are facing in new democracies, relating to their lack of social legitimacy, lack of economic resources, and their political weakness, and the analyses show how this contributes to the problems they have experienced with regard to making the political branches accountable and ratify the enormous importance of ensuring this latter outcome: without properly tailored and sufficiently respected constitutional limits, the political branches, and the executive in particular, tend to interfere with the powers of the others branches.

The previous judgments push us towards a first and obvious conclusion concerning the value of having independent courts. Without independent courts, the whole idea of building the rule of law in new democracies appears debased.

Yet as many of the studies in this volume illustrate, matters are far more complicated than the foregoing conclusion. First, there is a question about means, namely, what it is necessary to do in order to build strong, independent, well-respected courts. One possible answer is that it requires wide efforts at institutional engineering or similar ambitious programmes. Martin Shapiro and Javier Couso, however, believe that the answer requires nothing of the kind. In their opinion, the quest for a more independent judiciary heavily depends on the very decisions of the judges: by properly using their powers and by carefully selecting the cases they address, judges could build their reputation and gain the necessary legitimacy. This strategic behaviour may require them to go first for 'routine' justice, rather than for 'spectacular' or 'dramatic' cases. Shapiro presents his view using examples from the United States and the European Union, while Couso takes Chile as his main example. Roux's analysis of South Africa shows, however, that what is strategic depends on the political context, and that judicial legitimacy may also be built through highly political cases.

In a different way, Rachel Sieder in her analysis of Guatemala also challenges the more traditional approaches to judicial reform. In her opinion, judicial reforms are condemned to failure if advanced from an institutionally focused approach. According to Sieder, these reforms need always to take account of the historical context within which understandings of 'law', 'justice' and 'rights' are shaped. Her main point is that institutions do matter, but only by understanding the role of law in long-run processes of state formation and the dynamic, inter-subjective nature of legal interactions can we begin to understand the specificities of socio-legal change.

Second, there is a normative question to answer. In effect, our previous conclusion, which emphasized the value of having independent courts, partially reproduces what Carlos Santiso calls the 'conventional wisdom' on judicial governance, namely, that the independence and autonomy of a judiciary are necessary prerequisites of the rule of law. According to this 'conventional wisdom', all democratic countries, and new democracies especially, need judicial independence as a condition for enhancing the 'legitimacy, credibility and reliability of the court system'. However, is judicial independence always good? And does judicial independence always produce these desirable outcomes?

Using Brazilian courts as his main example, Santiso advances negative answers to both these questions. Challenging the 'conventional wisdom', Santiso demonstrates that a too autonomous judiciary may become 'devoid of all accountability' and thus become 'a power above the law'. New democracies, he suggests, should be much more prudent before engaging in reforms aimed at increasing judicial independence, which can lead to undesired outcomes. To state this, of course, does not necessarily deny the value of having independent courts. What Santiso proposes, however, is that we reflect more carefully on such issues as how much independence is enough and how much is too much independence.

The study of Argentina by Roberto Gargarella in part supports Santiso's view. In Gargarella's opinion, the problem at stake is not so much that courts are too weak, both economically and politically (which, he admits, is obviously a serious problem). Rather, the problem is that judges were constitutionally granted the wrong powers. In a democratic community, he maintains, it should be seen as a problem that judges enjoy the final interpretative authority, that is, that they have the last word regarding the 'real' meaning of the country's constitution. The situation should be deemed even more problematic, he adds, when neither the people nor the political branches have any significant authority over the courts. According to Gargarella, this combination of ample powers granted to the court and few controls over its members represents an explosive formula for democracy – in particular for new democracies. The price for not recognizing these problems – an almost discretionary and too powerful judiciary, dangerously removed from the will of the people – can be found in several new democracies.

This collection represents the first expression of what the authors hope will develop into a broader co operative effort to investigate the role of courts in processes of democratization and social transformation. There is great need to continue and deepen these discussions on the basis of studies bringing out experiences from various parts of the world.

ACKNOWLEDGEMENTS

Earlier versions of the material in this volume were first presented at a workshop 'The Accountability Function of Courts in New Democracies', at the Faculty of Law, University of Bergen, Norway, 14–16 November 2002. The workshop was organised by the editors and Ole Egil Andreassen from the Faculty of Law (University of Bergen) and financed by the Chr. Michelsen Institute – University of Bergen Co-operation Fund.

NOTES

All the manuscripts in this collection were accepted for publication in July 2003.

1. See Guillermo O'Donnell, 'Horizontal Accountability in New Democracies', in Andreas Schedler *et al.* (eds), *The Self-Restraining State: Power and Accountability in New Democracies* (Boulder, CO: Lynne Rienner, 1999), pp.29–51.
2. Key works include C. Neal Tate and Torbjörn Vallinder (eds), *The Global Expansion of Judicial Power* (New York: New York University Press, 1997); Andreas Schedler, Larry Diamond and Marc F. Plattner (eds), *The Self-Restraining State: Power and Accountability in New Democracies* (Boulder, CO: Lynne Rienner, 1999); William C. Prillaman, *The Judiciary and Democratic Decay in Latin America: Declining Confidence in the Rule of Law* (New York and London: Praeger, 2000); Linn. A Hammergren, *The Politics of Justice and Justice Reform in Latin America: The Peruvian Case in Comparative Perspective* (Boulder, CO and London: Westview Press, 1998); Mark Ungar, *Elusive Reform: Democracy and the Rule of Law in Latin America* (Boulder, CO and London: Lynne Reinner, 2002); Maria Dakolias, *The Judicial Sector in Latin America and the Caribbean: Elements of Reform* (Washington, DC: World Bank, 1996); Michael Dodson, 'Assessing Judicial Reform in Latin America', *Latin American Research Review*, Vol.37, No.2 (2002), pp.200–220; and Jennifer Widner, *Building the Rule of Law in Africa* (New York: Norton Press, 2001).

Judicial Review in Developed Democracies

MARTIN SHAPIRO

The Success of Judicial Review: The United States' Experience

In the realm of constitutional judicial review, the question addressed here is success. How and when have constitutional courts succeeded? Success will be defined narrowly and positivistically in terms of when an exercise of constitutional judicial review has changed public policy in the direction the court wants public policy to go. Obviously implicit in this definition of success is the precondition that the court manages to establish and retain its power to exercise judicial review. What it does not contain is any substantive component such as changing public policy in a direction more favorable to 'human rights' or 'social justice'.

If the question is the success of judicial review, then the obvious starting point is the United States, which has the longest history of the greatest success, and carefully remembering the narrow way in which success is defined here. The US experience, however, is much misunderstood. Let me state it briefly. Throughout its history the US Supreme Court has been most successful in its federalism decisions where it has consistently supported nationalizing forces while placing sufficient constraints upon them to maintain its *bona fides* as a 'referee' between state and federal authority. Its most marked failure was the American Civil War (1860–1865), but that war constituted a massive failure of all American political, social and economic institutions. Aside from assuring its own institutional independence, the court has played a minor role in the separation of powers aspects of constitutional law. The constitutional relationship between Congress and the president has changed greatly over time. A massive set of institutions has evolved which do not fit into the separation scheme, such as the independent regulatory agencies. The presidency itself has changed enormously, becoming a large, bureaucratized institution. The relationship of the Senate to the House of Representatives has changed fundamentally. The constitutional relationship of the Congress to the president in matters of foreign and military policy have remained uncertain, indeed grown more uncertain. In all these matters the court has been almost entirely a spectator, occasionally asserting its authority but almost never exercising it. Finally, in the area of 'rights', or more properly preferred interests, the court developed a long, relatively successful record of defending property, and particularly corporate property, interests. It then succeeded in converting the institutional support it had built up defending the interests of the most powerful to support for its efforts to further 'individual' or 'human' rights, an effort that began tentatively at about the time of the First World War and reached a high point in the Supreme Court of Chief Justice Earl Warren in the first half of the 1950s.

Federalism

A further brief word about the three areas of US judicial review. As to federalism, the Supreme Court placed itself on the side of the winners. From its inception the most powerful social, economic and political interests in the United States favoured the growth of a national market. Technological developments, particularly the railroads, and economies of scale in steel and steel related industries, also favoured such growth. With a large number of states and a weakly disciplined Congress, the court was the best national agency available for policing state discriminations against out-of-state economic enterprise.

In more positive theoretical terms, any federalism is a kind of cartel in which members join because they perceive that if they all follow the same cartel rules they will all benefit more than if there were no cartel. It is in the nature of cartels, however, that if one member disobeys the rules while the others obey, the disobedient member will benefit more than it would if it obeyed. Thus in order to work over time cartels require a strong disciplinary mechanism that can spot disobedience by individual members and bring them back into line. Thus constitutional courts are likely to enjoy great success in their federalism jurisdiction. This is because when they intervene against a member state they will enjoy the political support not only of the federal government but of all the states except the offending one, because it is in the best interest of each state that all other states obey. Moreover where, as in the United States, individual parties have access to the constitutional court, the costs of policing the cartel largely are shifted to private parties and policing is more efficient. For instead of sporadic intervention by the central government or rival member states, the self-interest of thousands of economic actors is tapped continuously to monitor state actions potentially contrary to cartel rules, and bring them to the federal court's attention when the state action is adverse to the economic interests of the private enterprise.

Finally, in this whole activity the court is most often serving as the agent of the central legislature, policing the member states on its behalf while only occasionally limiting its powers.

It is probably not a coincidence, therefore, that the earliest successful constitutional review courts were those of federalisms, namely the United States, Canada and Australia, nor that the most successful 'new' constitutional review court is the European Court of Justice, a court primarily concerned with federalism which, through its reference procedure, provides for private as well as governmental access.

Yet cartel theory and the US federalism analogy ought not to be relied upon too heavily. Both depend on the member states perceiving continued membership as gaining them more benefits than would breaking up the federation or cartel. The original 13 American colonies all clearly perceived that a federal union was essential to their individual commercial and security interests and were soon joined by new member states that could not possibly have survived on their own. The voluntary entry of states into the European Union (EU) and the dominance of 'inter-governmental' EU institutional arrangements assures that the EU consists only of states that perceive themselves more advantaged by membership than non-membership. Where a federal constitution is imposed on localities that do not perceive continuation of the cartel as yielding more benefits than separation, the story may be quite different.

A federalism constitutional court is in an uncomfortable situation for two reasons. First, it is called upon to referee between two governments, a pygmy between two giants. Second, it is actually one of the limbs of one of the giants. The basic logic of courts is seriously eroded for such a court. One part of one of the parties is purporting to act as the neutral and independent third party resolver of the dispute between the two parties. If the member state loses it is likely to claim, quite rightly, that the central government has been judge in its own case. Federalism courts are protected from the second problem to the extent that the culture or cultures in which they operate have a well-developed myth of judicial independence and neutrality. Then constitutional judges can credibly say, 'Yes we work for the central government, but because we are judges, we are independent of and neutral toward that government in disputes between the central government and the member states'. As to the first problem, federalism constitutional courts can escape it only when the members of the cartel see a greater benefit in maintaining the cartel than in breaking it or alternatively where the central government has the means and the will to enforce court judgements adverse to the members.

In such formally federal states as Argentina, and in other quasi-federal states, where considerable autonomy has been granted to regions precisely because they are disaffected, we cannot be confident that either the logic of cartels or the myth of judicial independence and neutrality will be effective enough to insure the success of federalism constitutional courts.

Separation of Powers

As to separation of powers: that the US Supreme Court has done so little about separation of powers is notable. Theory might predict otherwise. Constitution makers who establish separation of powers within and between legislatures and executives may be seen as doing so to address a downside risk problem. Each of the various political factions among the constitution makers cannot be sure how they will fare in future elections under the new constitution. The more they fear that they may at least sometimes lose future elections, the more separation of powers they will prefer so that when and if they lose, their opponents will not have unlimited power to govern. Thus theory would predict a separation of powers constitution where future electoral competition is anticipated. And the very reason for the separation is to create conflict between the separated in order to inhibit excessive power wielding by electoral victors. Yet the constitution makers must fine-tune the conflict to avoid political paralysis. One mode of doing so is to provide conflict-resolving devices. Separation of powers constitutional judicial review is one obvious device, obvious because the main job of courts is conflict resolution.

All well and good as to why many constitutions provide for separation of powers and constitutional review of that separation. But putting it in the constitution does not necessarily mean that constitutional courts can or should do it. It is elections, or rather the fear of losing them, that drives separation of powers. In electoral regimes, elected politicians tend to become fixated, indeed we want them to be fixated, on the next election and on what happens between now and the next election. Serious separation of powers conflicts are likely to arise when different parts of government are in the hands of different political parties or coalitions. They are likely to occur not in the abstract but in the context of particular policy issues and the prospect of the only election elected politicians care about, the next one. A reviewing court is faced with two conflicting parts of government both more powerful than itself. It is an undemocratic entity called upon to intervene in a highly partisan, high-electoral-stakes, political controversy. In a polity that is democratic and election based, constitutional courts may well shy away from such conflicts no matter what the constitution says.

Only some separation of powers litigations really involve head-on confrontations between branches of government in the hands of different political parties. Moreover some litigation of this sort involves statutes or other actions composed of many parts, so that a court may give a little to one branch and a little to the other by striking down some provisions and upholding others. Along with relative inaction, the US Supreme Court has manufactured a basic constitutional separation of powers doctrine: each branch can interfere with the others but not too much.[1] This is surely a formula for judicial discretion but not necessarily for activism.

Most of the US constitutional norms of separation of powers have actually been worked out over long periods of time by a politics of mutual adjustment between the president and Congress. Almost none of them have really been established by the Supreme Court. In its early developmental history, the United States encountered very few situations where opposing political parties occupied opposing parts of government with opposing stances on major policy issues. Currently developing or new democracies that have adopted more or less rigorous separation of powers may not be so lucky. Russia certainly has not been. US experience is either neutral or negative as to whether separation of powers judicial review can be successful.

Rights Review

It is in constitutional rights review that US experience is actually most obscure even though it is sometimes taken as a guiding light. The great apparent success of the Warren Court in the enhancement of civil rights and liberties inspired a whole generation of American constitutional law scholars to an enormous enthusiasm for judicial review. Backed by various foundations and international bodies, they have been parading around the world pushing constitutional judicial review as the royal coach to rule of law and democracy itself. The American experience does not really justify their enthusiasm.

First of all, for about the first 130 years of its existence the Supreme Court did almost no rights business at all except the protection of property rights. It held early on that the Bill of Rights did not apply to the states.[2] And the states exercised nearly all the general powers of government that might engender violations of rights. Later the 14th Amendment did apply to the states, but the Court declined to fill its general language with specific rights except property rights. Only at the time of the First World War does the Court really enter the individual rights area, and the result is anti-free speech constitutional doctrine.[3]

Only after the Second World War, with a long history of successful review behind it, and with the rift with the 'political branches' occasioned by the Roosevelt administration's New Deal programme healed, does the Court move to elevated levels of rights protection. And the results are very mixed. The Court becomes and has remained a centre of political controversy. Its construction of a uniform national body of rights of the criminally accused engendered terrific political attacks, but it has been successful. The greatest political threat to the Court arose when it was seeking both the end of racial segregation and the protection of left-wing speakers against the red scare generated by the Cold War. Ultimately it actually gave up protecting reds as the cost of protecting blacks. In the course of doing so it gave constitutional approval to a US federal statute that blatantly violated the First Amendment and produced constitutional doctrine as unfavourable to free speech as it is possible to get in the face of the constitutional text.[4]

The Court's only great success in the speech area was its contribution to unleashing a tidal wave of pornography.[5] Its religion decisions, mostly about religion in the schools, not only inspired vocal political opposition but resulted in a massive amount of disobedience by local school authorities, although the Court ultimately was largely successful.[6] The Court's initial race decisions were massively resisted in the South and some of its later ones, on school busing, in some cities of the North as well. It is now quite fashionable, and no doubt correct, to argue that the Court cannot achieve major social change through its decisions alone. Yet almost immediately, and certainly over time, the Court has been successful in doing what courts can do. It has banished government policies of segregation established by law.[7]

The Court has also been successful in a major, democracy-enhancing, intervention into both state and federal elections law.[8] Its intervention in campaign financing law so far has rendered that law quite unworkable.[9] It has compromised on the death penalty. Its attempt to pull abortion policy out of politics has been entirely unsuccessful and has instead made the Court itself more of a political issue. It has refused to constitutionalize social or welfare rights.[10] And what is seen by rights enthusiasts as its current backsliding has led some of the new generation of American constitutional commentators to withdraw their enthusiasm for judicial review itself.[11]

Of course the post-Second World War political history of the Supreme Court can be read overall in one of two ways. One is that its rights initiatives have engendered great opposition and placed the Court squarely in the middle of partisan politics while achieving only very partial success. The other is that, in spite of political opposition, the Court has succeeded in achieving a number of major advances in civil rights and liberties. Whichever position one prefers, it is clear that the Court became active in defense of the rights of 'have nots' only after a very long historical development of its own legitimacy through judicial protection of the interest of 'haves', that its rights initiatives have been only partially successful, and that those initiatives have engendered substantial political opposition and the injection of judicial issues into partisan, electoral politics.

One final special note on American experience is in order. The enthusiasm of the World Bank, International Monetary Fund (IMF) and others for constitutional judicial review pretty much boils down to a way of assuring foreign investors that they will not be expropriated. The early history of the US Supreme Court provides some, rather mixed, support for such a hope. But even before the famous abandonment of property rights by the Supreme Court in 1937, the Court had sided with the government against property in the face of economic emergency. No clause is clearer in its specific, original intent than the abridgement of contract clause. Yet in the leading modern case the Court upheld a state statute that did precisely what that clause forbade, suspend creditors' contractual rights against a debtor.[12] It is notable that the attempt by the 'Chicago boys' (economists) to do in Chile what they have failed to do in the United States, that is, restore constitutional protection of property rights, has itself failed, and that the Hungarian Court too owes much of its popular support to its anti-IMF intervention.

It would be hard to conclude that the US historical experience ought to inspire great confidence that new constitutional courts in new democracies can achieve successful pro-rights interventions. On the other hand, American experience is historical experience, and history changes. As the Cold War ended two great secular religions have come to grip the world: environmentalism and human rights. The US Supreme Court leaned on the legitimacy it acquired by protecting dominant economic interests to move with some success into rights. New constitutional courts may be able to lean on the legitimacy of rights themselves to move to the defence of rights. It is precisely here that historical methods fail us because in no previous period have we experienced the contemporary global enthusiasm for rights.

European Review

The global enthusiasm for rights is no doubt one of the principal causes of the growth of European constitutional judicial review. There are two special cases. The initial enormous success of the European Court of Justice (ECJ) is rooted in federalism, not rights review. And judicial review was forced upon the French by their introduction of constitutional separation of powers. Of course both the ECJ and the Constitutional Council lately have been busy discovering constitutional rights in constitutions that did not actually contain them. Germany is a federalism, and the Italian constitution's provisions for judicial review were in part inspired by a need to acknowledge and protect Italy's autonomous regions. Both the German and Italian courts are, however, far more rights than federalism courts. The same can be said for Spain and other European additions to the constitutional judicial review list.[13] Everyone is aware of the belated and partial move of the United Kingdom in the same direction. The success of the European Court of Human Rights shows the degree to which judicial review is coupled with rights enthusiasm in Europe.

Hungary and Italy show a particular variant of rights review. In both, because of peculiarities in their transition to democracy, old bodies of law containing rights-hostile provisions remained in force and the capacity of normal legislative politics to undertake their massive revision was absent. In both, a constitutional court is established with the expectation that it will, piecemeal, case-by-case, purge the old law of its rights-threatening elements. In both instances the court has succeeded in doing so and thus cultivated its own legitimacy.

The central association of rights with European judicial review can be shown along quite a different dimension as well. While the success of the US Supreme Court undoubtedly has been a global beacon for judicial review, the model in Europe, both east and west, has been Hans Kelsen's.[14] That model is well known and can be briefly stated: (1) a separate constitutional court with exclusive jurisdiction, (2) access to that court for certain high government officials only, (3) abstract review, (4) review only of the constitutional boundaries between the various units of government. As a package, these four elements make sense. If only governmental boundary provisions are to be at issue, then a statute or other action by one part of government ought to be tested before it is enforced because what is at issue is whether that unit had the authority to do what it did in the first place. The boundary violation, and thus the breach of the constitution, occurs at the moment the statute is passed, not later when it is enforced. If the issue of concern is the invasion of the constitutional prerogatives of one part of government by another, then the principal officers of each are the parties best suited, and most highly motivated, to plead those issues. And, finally, if the only issues to be considered are those that pit one branch of government against another, and the parties are to be those parts of government themselves, then the cases are clearly not ordinary and are necessarily to a degree political. It follows that they ought to be handled by a special court with a special mode of judicial selection both to provide a more politically expert bench and to shelter the regular courts from political cases.

If, however, we strike out element (4) and substitute review of government boundaries *and* individual rights review, the coherence of the package falls apart. Damage to individual rights occurs not, or not only, when a statute or other government action is enacted, but later when it is enforced. More important, often we cannot accurately anticipate from the face of a statute what damage to individual rights its enforcement will ultimately entail. It may be only as it is enforced that its damage to rights becomes clear, and so it is only at that time and in that context that review may be effective. If individual rights are at issue then, not government officials but the individual bearers of those rights are the appropriate parties. And if specific violations of the rights of particular individuals are to be the issue, such issues are most likely to arise not separately but rather entangled in 'normal' litigation, where each individual will plead all the rights he can think of whether constitutional, statutory or contractual. Thus, 'regular' courts must somehow handle constitutional rights claims along with other rights claims.

Because every one of the European states that adopted the Kelsenian model has either initially or subsequently also moved from pure boundary to boundary plus rights review, European review is now in something of a muddle. The most extreme Kelsenian state is France. And so, in France today, a citizen whose constitutional rights have been violated by a promulgated statute cannot go to the Constitutional Council for redress. However, he can go to an ordinary French court, express the same right as a right protected by the European Convention on Human Rights, and get redress under the French statute domesticating the convention. He may do so because his rights claim at that point is statutory, not constitutional, and therefore appropriate to individual litigants in regular courts employing concrete review. Other European states have also clung to the separate constitutional court but provide for some individual access and concrete review. Most European states and the EU provide for a reference procedure under which constitutional issues raised in regular courts may be referred to the constitutional court. For reasons that cannot be explored here, the reference procedure over the long haul will end up creating constitutional jurisdiction in the regular courts and transforming the constitutional courts from the sole constitutional courts into merely the highest constitutional courts.

My point here, however, is not the somewhat incoherent and evolving nature of European review institutions but rather that European enthusiasm for rights is so great that while purporting to follow Kelsen, Europe has actually abandoned the key anti-rights elements of the Kelsen model. And it has done so in spite of Kelsen's dire warnings that rights were too political for even separate constitutional courts to handle.

Moreover rights review in western Europe has been successful and is contemporary. Although member states had an option, individual access to the European Court of Human Rights now exists for all member states. While being careful about a 'margin of appreciation', the Court has engaged in some substantial interventions and has been relatively successful. Initially without concrete treaty provision on rights, the European Court of Justice first injected some rights into the free movement clauses, but subsequently announced free-standing rights and has been backed by subsequent treaty amendments. It is noteworthy that one of the primary purposes of the 'pillar' architecture of the later treaties was to limit ECJ review in the area of justice and home affairs, but most of the third pillar has now been moved to the first with enlarged, if still somewhat constrained, review. The treaty changes chart the struggle between pro- and anti-rights review forces, and the 'pro' forces have been winning.[15]

The English have now adopted a very constrained and not quite constitutional rights review, but a rights review none the less. Viewing German, Italian, Spanish and French constitutional review together, it is certainly possible to argue that European constitutional courts are now engaged in a constitutional dialogue with their legislatures that is more successful, that is to say it leads to more judicial influence on public policy, than present in the United States.[16] The major vehicle for that dialogue may be abstract review in which courts more or less signal to the legislatures what statutory language they will accept. But, at least outside of France, more or less American-style concrete review, either through direct individual access, or by reference, also is generating 'leading cases', vetoes of statutory provisions and constitutional jurisprudence to which legislatures must take heed.

Abstract vs Concrete Review

The issue of abstract versus concrete review attracts much rather abstract debate.[17] The EU reference procedure sheds some more concrete light. In the early years of the nineteenth century, Supreme Court Chief Justice John Marshall was compelled by the absence of explicit judicial review provisions in the constitution to adopt concrete review. We have already noted the particular advantages of concrete review for judicial protection of individual rights. It has an enormous political advantage as well. A judicial declaration that a statute is unconstitutional is likely to come a considerable time after its passage. In two-party systems with weak party discipline such as the US, and in multi-party systems, legislation typically is a coalition product. Very often the coalition that initially passed a statute cannot be rebuilt some years later to confront a delayed judicial veto. Or, in a two-party strong party discipline system, the other party may be in control of the legislature by the time the constitutional court vetoes legislation passed by its opponents. The chance of direct confrontation with the legislature is even further diminished in separation of powers systems with multiple veto points where it is difficult to pass any legislation including statutes responding antagonistically to judicial vetoes of earlier ones. Moreover, as public choice analysts advise us over and over again, so long as the reviewing court chooses any interpretation of an enacted statute that any winning coalition in the legislature might have voted for, it may alter the actual statute for which the coalition that actually formed actually voted.[18] Of course this delayed veto weakens the potential for legislative–judicial dialogue which is arising in western Europe, but it is that very dialogue that highlights the political character and democratic dubiousness of judicial review.

Moreover concrete review can, and in the Marshall Court did, avoid some direct confrontation with other branches in another way. Marshall's review was expressed in conflicts of law terms. When confronted by two conflicting laws that would determine the outcome of a case, a judge, any judge, must choose to follow one. Where one is a higher law, that is a constitutional provision, and the other is a lower law, that is a statute, the judge must choose the higher law and thus refuse to follow the statute. In this form judicial review is not a command to the legislature and/or the executive which they can choose to disobey. Instead it is a command only from a higher court to itself and lower courts not to enforce a particular statute. Courts are likely to obey other courts, particularly when they gain power themselves by accepting the duty to choose imposed upon them. And in a great many instances, it will be state courts that initially declare state laws unconstitutional or decline to enforce them because they have been declared unconstitutional.

The EU reference procedure, which contains elements of both concrete and abstract review, offers similar advantages. Because reference is the product of concrete litigation, it tends to extend the time interval between legislation and judicial response just as American review does and with the same political advantages. And because under the reference procedure the ECJ addresses itself only to other courts, only other courts are called upon to obey it. In reference cases where the ECJ finds a national law incompatible with the treaties, it is the national referring court, not the ECJ, that actually refuses to follow the statute. Moreover, as in all concrete review, the actual case may involve very small stakes and so receive very little media attention, obscuring the dramatic legislative–judicial confrontation that is potential in all constitutional veto cases. It is probably not a coincidence that nearly all the cases by which the ECJ has 'constitutionalized' the treaties, and thus extended its own review powers, have been reference cases.

Rights, Majorities and Democracy

With or without abstract review, however, rights review has the greatest anti-majoritarian dimension. In separation of powers review, the court places itself between two contenders both of whom claim majority backing. In federalism review both state and central government also claim majority support, albeit of different majorities. Rights review, almost by definition, pits legislative majorities representing electoral majorities against some interest that has lost in the majoritarian legislative arena.

To the extent that we perceive 'rights' as simply particular interests that seek a preferred legal position over other interests, surely rights business is legislative in character. It is the legislature that is supposed to do interest balancing and aggregation. Of course one can be a positivist, and even a majoritarian positivist, and still support rights judicial review. Preferences for certain interests may have been posited by the constitution itself, and the constitution may have been a product of majority will. Indeed it may well have been that a majority for the constitution could only have been achieved by the embedding of rights in its text. This position may also be expressed in terms of a majority self-consciously recognizing that it has both short-term policy interests and long-term interests in rights, and assigning the pursuit of one to the legislature and the protection of the other to constitutional courts. Or a natural law or human rights position may be taken in which majorities are seen as properly constrained by rights of some higher or deeper source than positing.

Majorities of the moment are nonetheless politically powerful entities. And rights, no matter how defined or sourced, are favoured interests. Strong voices against rights review as anti-majoritarian have been raised on both sides of the Atlantic by distinguished minds that favoured separation of powers review.[19] Rights review almost always places courts on the side of the less politically powerful against the more politically powerful. And rights review often involves a court seeking to stop the government from doing what it wants to do rather than choosing which part of government must give way to which other.

Rights review thus raises most accurately the basic political problem of all judicial review. Review undeniably has an anti-majoritarism aspect, one which is emphasized by abstract review of recent legislation but does not go away even for concrete, delayed review. On the other hand, successful review may be entirely dependent on competitive electoral democracy. It would be nice even to be able to say that we face a 'chicken and egg' problem concerning review and democracy, but I do not think we do. It may well be possible to have democracy without review as in the UK and the French Third and Fourth Republics. It is almost certainly impossible to have successful review in the absence of a party-competitive electoral democracy.

This claim may be supported either historically or in terms of positive political theory. We do not know of any state without electoral democracy that has had successful review. From a theoretical perspective we should expect to find successful judicial review when the majority of the moment expects to be displaced by a different majority at some future time. Under this condition the current majority will accept adverse judicial review limiting its own powers, and particularly whatever power it has to stymie the succession of an alternative majority, so that it itself may subsequently make use of review to limit the powers of subsequent majorities and preserve the conditions that allow its own subsequent return to power. It is difficult to imagine, in terms of self-interest, why a party or group enjoying the prospect of a continuous future monopoly of political power should choose to accept adverse judicial review.

Only two exceptions are easy to conceive. One is foreign pressure. The EU in effect makes rights review a condition for admission. The World Trade Organization and IMF have both pressured national regimes in that direction, and one could imagine them making it a precondition. Yet ultimately international financial interests are unlikely to care about any rights except property rights, and the protection of foreign property rights against dominant domestic political powers, whether one party or democratic, is hardly likely to be a winning hand for the judiciary.

The second exception to positive political theory's claim is that the party or faction controlling a non-competitive elections state will be itself so ideologically committed to rights and so self-conscious of the short-term temptations to violate them that it will establish review and subsequently accept adverse review. Past experience, however, is that one-party states may proclaim their love of rights, and even institute judicial review, but not acquiesce to adverse constitutional rights review. A benevolent, rights-dedicated, one-party state is a theoretical possibility, and indeed China might claim to be an example. But so far we have not encountered such a state, at least not one that has lasted in that condition for any substantial length of time.

If constitutional review, including rights review, can only flourish in democratic states then the potential tension between rights review and majoritarianism must be acknowledged, and indeed has been acknowledged in the new polities where judicial review has been successful. In some of those polities constitutional courts may have imposed rights review as a necessary cost to the 'political' branches of using the courts to operate constitutional federalisms. The United States, Canada and the EU are principal examples. Elsewhere genuine consensus on rights, together with the expectation of competitive elections, may be enough, especially for polities constitutionalized or reconstitutionalized only recently when rights have become such a dominant ideology. Yet successful rights review is likely to be the most difficult for courts to pull off because of its openly anti-majoritarian thrust. Thus it may require the highest level of judicial political-strategic skills. A central strategic political skill in democracies, of course, is compromise. So we should expect that, even in a mature democracy, let alone a new or transitional one, judicial enforcement of constitutional rights frequently will be compromised, in both senses of that word. Moreover we should expect the most compromises where constitutional courts enjoy only marginal perceived legitimacy. Because rights review is about the most obviously political thing courts do, such review poses strong threats to the public perceptions of neutrality and independence on which all courts depend for their perceived legitimacy. So we would expect constitutional courts that have only weak legitimacy themselves to be extremely modest in their rights review or to lose their legitimacy entirely by being too bold.

Of course various judicial strategies may be used to soften or disguise judicial anti-majoritarianism. The constitutional court may choose to protect specific rights claims that actually enjoy majority popular support which, for one reason or another, is not translated into legislative majorities. It may announce relatively bold rights doctrines that it hopes will take popular hold over time while not using those doctrines actually to constrain particular government acts very much.

However politically skillful a constitutional court may be, ultimately successful rights review depends upon majorities being sufficiently ideologically dedicated to rights that they will accept judicial, rights-based, vetoes on what they want to do, and accept that, in order to defend rights, courts should enter politics. Indeed the hope must be that popular support for rights will be so great that the citizens will blind themselves to the political nature of rights review and instead see such review as the ultimate manifestation of judicial neutrality and independence.

While this kind of dedication to rights today is, in a sense, global, it is not likely to be at the highest level in new or developing democracies, particularly those just emerging from violent political conflict and/or where ethnic or other parochial loyalties remain high. Even in such places as the

United States successful rights review would appear to depend upon deft judicial strategies, strategies that will often involve ignoring some rights holders in order to protect others. And each successful judicial intervention in favour of rights will involve a delicate calculus of trading popular belief in the political neutrality of courts for whatever popular support for the substance of the right protected the court can elicit. Each such intervention reminds everyone of the majoritarian issue inherent in rights review.

This necessarily sketchy survey of judicial review in developed democracies indicates that the United States and the European Union show a very successful record of federalism review, that rights review in the United States has been far less successful than it has often been presented as being, but that the recent strong development of rights review in Europe gives some hope in that direction, although the inherent dangers of rights review posed for courts in democratic states counsels caution for courts in developing democracies.

Administrative Review

If all constitutional review, except perhaps federalism review in truly voluntary federalisms, is quite dangerous for courts, it may be worth examining an alternative, namely administrative review. To do so it is useful to look at 'the rule of law', a concept both narrower and wider than 'rights'. The initial or primitive notion of the rule of law was that government must act only according to law, not on the basis of arbitrary or discretionary, particularized decisions of government officers. Or, from a slightly different angle, governments must obey their own laws until they choose to change them. Such rule of law does not necessarily depend on the existence of a competitive, more than one-party, electoral democracy, nor on deep allegiance to rights. It may depend only on the determination of a centralized authoritarian regime with no interest in rights that lesser and local government officials be strictly subordinated to higher, central officials. If the law-making is centralized, and it is easy for the centre to make new laws, then rule of law judicial review becomes one of several methods for maintaining centralized discipline over subordinate government officials. Far from generating direct judicial confrontation with the dominant political power, democratic, majoritarian or otherwise, such judicial review presents the judges as allies of, indeed as loyal subordinates of, those holding the core law-making powers. Moreover the overall impact of such review is likely to be an increase in the efficiency of the political regime as a whole. To the extent that the regime itself has introduced procedural rules that enhance the quality of government decision making, rule of law review improves the efficiency of both democratic and non-democratic regimes. Today's global concern with procedural rules that guarantee transparency of and wide participation in government decisions is partially driven by democratic concerns, partly by rights concerns but also partly by efficiency concerns. *Glasnost* and *perestroika* were enthusiasms of the late Soviet and post-Soviet phases, in large part because secret, closed government decision making came to be perceived as producing poor decisions. Decisions tested by open, public participation bring more information and ideas to the decision-making process and more understanding of the potential costs of and barriers to implementation.

Here again we have little choice but to look to past experience in older democracies to help us make guesses about future developments in newer ones. The United States experienced major new developments in administrative law in the last half of the twentieth century.[20] Largely initiated by courts, but supported by Congress, administrative law evolved a set of rules that sought to maximize transparency and participation in government decision making. This evolution was driven by pluralist democratic beliefs and was sometimes expressed in a rhetoric of 'group rights'. It has also raised serious concerns about the efficiency costs of pushing judicially enforced procedural rights too far, of making the transaction costs of government decisions too high. Nonetheless, few question that increased transparency and participation have, quite apart from any democracy gains, resulted in better researched, better reasoned, better pre-tested government decisions. The current concern is to find ways to cut back on the strategic, self-serving behaviour of participants not to cut back on the transparency and participation itself. The writer has argued elsewhere that the EU is currently moving in the same transparency and participation direction.[21]

Conventional courts are a hierarchically organized communications channel. Appeal is an obvious mode of sending centralized commands (laws) downward from highest to most local courts. Appeal is also a very significant means through which the centre receives information from the bottom *that it is otherwise unlikely to receive.* What goes up is not what local authorities want to go up but what losing parties want to go up. Appeal does not involve summarization, but rather the movement upwards of many slices of local life. And appeal emphasizes not success but failure. Appeals cases tend to be 'trouble cases', slices of life where things are not going well or even routinely but badly. To the extent that the actual courts meet the model of courts, this is an independent channel of information upward. Moreover, to the extent that the courts enforce rule of law, appeals will channel upwards incidents of failure of local government officials to obey orders (laws) from the top and also serve as an independent means of enforcing commands from the top on local officials.[22]

Precisely because rule of the law in the narrow sense is a regime-supporting device, in some contexts it may harm human rights. The highly correct *Rechtstaat* judges of Hitler's Germany come to mind. And more generally the Germanic *Rechtstaat* concept reminds us that the identification of law or right with rule or state perversely may serve to lend the prestige and perceived legitimacy of law to terrible regimes. In the Soviet Union the great legal scholar of socialist legality, Vishinsky, was one of Stalin's satraps. Nevertheless the narrower rule of law can be an enormous judicial resource for holding regimes accountable. To tell a terrible regime that it must rule by law may generate terrible laws. But in many contexts to hold government to actions authorized by law serves individuals. Guarantees that subordinate government officials will act lawfully rather than arbitrarily and/or corruptly may be of more immediate importance to more individuals than guarantees of freedom of speech or religion. That a local government officer may not arbitrarily withhold a licence to participate in a street market or permission to tap into a public water pipe, or unlawfully detain a son or destroy a fruit tree may be the most immediately important aspect of government accountability for most citizens. Courts to which such persons may resort to check such practices may be more important than constitutional courts.

And crucially, courts which step forward to enforce the accountability of officials not to constitutional rules but simply to law may protect individuals under the guise of serving dominant government authority, be it authoritarian or majoritarian. Such courts protect individuals without provoking confrontations with the politically most powerful. And to the extent that they do thwart government initiatives, they leave government the option of enacting new laws rather than destroying courts.

In short, statutory judicial review by administrative courts may, particularly in new or developing democracies, offer greater immediate prospects of rendering government accountable and protecting individual interests than does constitutional rights review by a constitutional court. Such courts may successfully restrain arbitrary government action precisely because they are perceived as serving rather than opposing government. The most frightening prospect of all may be a totalitarian dictatorship served by a legally disciplined and thus efficient bureaucracy. In emerging democracies, however, the creation of a legally disciplined bureaucracy often may be a move toward more democracy *and* more individual rights.

All this is particularly true if administrative law globally is increasingly moulded by concerns for greater transparency and participation.[23] Judicial review under such administrative law simultaneously serves democratic accountability of government and individual rights, and does so not necessarily at the cost of government efficiency but even with efficiency benefits.

Finally, if we begin with statutory or administrative law judicial review guided by and in the name of rule of law in the narrow sense, then we may be providing a useful building block for constitutional rights review either openly or under the guise of administrative review. It has been typical of modern jurisprudential developments that a broader, substantive rights dimension has been insinuated into the narrower conception of rule of law. Today when we speak of rule of law we treat not only government obedience to law but also legal guarantees of individual rights as inherent in the concept. We move from the narrower notion that government must rule by general laws rather than by particularized, arbitrary actions to the notion that such general laws must themselves be respectful of rights. We treat the demand that government act lawfully rather than arbitrarily as the first step in protecting individuals but then see the second step, that the laws themselves must guarantee rights. The move from step one to step two is not logically necessary but it is historically confirmed. That is, holding government accountable to law and by law may be seen as an end in itself quite apart from any programme of substantive rights protection. But certainly in the course of the last century substantive rights have actually become the central focus of rule of law discourse.

If courts in an evolving democracy begin by emphasizing narrower rule of law jurisprudence – one that purports to enlist the courts in the service of government – then they can hope for a fairly high degree of success in creating government accountability or protection of individuals against arbitrary government action now, while also establishing foundations for building more confrontational constitutional rights review later.

One difficulty, of course, is that most states that have instituted constitutional judicial review do so through a separate constitutional court. The two-step process envisioned here would require that the administrative courts and/or regular courts act first and only later the constitutional. What would constitutional courts do in the meantime? Indeed if they held back from active review in the early years, wouldn't that very early passivity tend to inhibit subsequent activism? Some national constitutional courts might engage in federalism and/or separation of powers review now and defer rights review till later. Others might begin early to strike down discrete executive or administrative acts on constitutional grounds but initially avoid vetoing statutes. Although not all constitutions contain US-style 'due process' clauses, most contain one or more clauses that would enable a constitutional court to strike down an unlawful executive act or decision as unconstitutional on procedural grounds. Such executive acts might be found unlawful (and thus unconstitutional) because they violated procedural requirements provided in the statute. Such decisions would actually be administrative judicial review, but constitutional enough to fall within the jurisdiction of separate constitutional courts.

In other instances constitutional courts could find that particular executive actions violated constitutional rights provisions. Then in interpreting the statutes purportedly authorizing the executive action, they could reason that surely the legislature in its statute had not intended to authorize executive violation of such rights. Thus under a proper interpretation of the statute at issue the particular executive action was legislatively unauthorized and thus was unconstitutional, not under the national constitution's rights provisions but under its separation of powers provisions or those defining the scope of executive authority. In doing so, of course, a constitutional court would also be giving forewarning of what statutory commands to the executive it might find unlawful, if they were made so explicitly that they could not be turned aside by judicial interpretation based on the judicially presumed unwillingness of legislatures to violate constitutional rights. Such constitutional decisions would be cast in the narrower discourse of rule of law that is about compelling executives to obey statutes. Such decisions would prepare the way for a subsequent move to the wider rights-endowed rule of law, while avoiding early, open, direct, explicit confrontations with majority law-making. Such review would assure legislative majorities that the constitutional court was working for them rather than against them.

Many such decisions against the executive could also be made in 'soft' procedural ways. The executive decision might have been valid if the executive had followed proper procedures in reaching it, had more adequately justified it or had sought and received legislative authorization for it. Such soft review constitutes a suspensive rather than final judicial veto and so is less confrontational even to the executive.

There may well be a number of new democracies in which majority and general popular support for individual rights is sufficiently great that courts successfully may veto legislation on constitutional rights grounds. There may well be a number of new democracies, however, in which courts can be more successful in rendering government accountable for rights protections by initially confining themselves to narrow rule of law based invalidations of executive action, particularly by subordinate or local officials, in which the courts may present themselves as allies rather than opponents of the law-making and/or highest executive authorities. The two-step nature of 'rule of law' would facilitate subsequent successful judicial movement from a more modest to a more activist protection of individual rights.

NOTES

1. See *Morrison v. Olson*, 487 US 654 (1988).
2. *Barron v. Baltimore*, 7 Pet. 243 (1833).
3. See *Gitlow v. New York*, 268 US 652 (1925).
4. Cf. *Brown v. Board of Education*, 347 US 483 (1954).
5. See *Roth v. United States*, 354 US 476 (1957).
6. See *Wallace v. Jaffree*, 472 US 38 (1985) and cases cited there.
7. See Charles Black, 'The Lawfulness of the Segregation Decisions', *Yale Law Journal*, Vol.69 (1960), pp.421–67.
8. *Reynolds v. Sims*, 377 US 533 (1964); *Wesberry v. Sanders*, 376 US 1 (1964).
9. See Albert Lowenstein, 'A Patternless Mosaic: Campaign Finance and the First Amendment After *Austin*', *Capital University Law Review*, Vol.21 (1992), pp.381–422.
10. See *San Antonio Independent School District v. Rodriguez*, 411 US 1 (1973).
11. See e.g. Mark Tushnet, *Taking the Constitution Away from the Courts* (Princeton, NJ: Princeton University Press, 1999).
12. *Home Building and Loan Assoc. v. Blaisdell*, 290 US 398 (1934).
13. See Alec Stone Sweet, *Governing with Judges: Constitutional Politics in Europe* (Oxford: Oxford University Press, 2002).
14. Hans Kelsen, 'La Garantie Jurisdictionnel de la Constitution,' *Revue de Droit Public*, Vol.44 (1928), pp.197–24.
15. See Charter of Fundamental Rights of the European Union, OJ 364/1 (18 December 2000).
16. Stone Sweet, *Governing With Judges* (note 13).
17. See Martin Shapiro and Alec Stone Sweet, *On Law, Politics and Judicialization* (Oxford: Oxford University Press, 2002), ch.6.
18. See Robert Cooter, *The Strategic Constitution* (Princeton, NJ: Princeton University Press, 2000).
19. Cf. Kelsen with Learned Hand, *The Bill of Rights* (Cambridge, MA: Harvard University Press, 1958).
20. See Richard Stewart, 'The Reformation of American Administrative Law', *Harvard Law Review*, Vol.88 (1975), pp.1667–1813; Martin Shapiro, *Who Guards the Guardians* (Athens, GA: University of Georgia Press, 1988).
21. Martin Shapiro, 'The Giving Reasons Requirement', *University of Chicago Legal Forum*, Vol.1992 (1992), pp.179–221; Martin Shapiro, 'The Institutionalization of European Administrative Space', in Alec Stone Sweet, Wayne Sandholtz and Neil Fligstein (eds), *The Institutionalization of Europe* (Oxford: Oxford University Press, 2002), pp.94–113.
22. Martin Shapiro, *Courts* (Chicago: University of Chicago Press, 1981), pp.49–56.
23. Martin Shapiro, 'The Globalization of Judicial Review', in Lawrence Friedman and Harry Scheiber (eds), *Legal Culture and the Legal Profession* (Boulder, CO: Westview Press, 1996), pp.119–37.

How Some Reflections on the United States' Experience May Inform African Efforts to Build Court Systems and the Rule of Law

JENNIFER WIDNER

The ambition of this collection is to examine the contribution of courts to the rule of law and governmental accountability. By 'rule of law', scholars and policy makers usually mean that (1) government officials and others act in accordance with the letter of the law, (2) people accused of crimes or civil infractions under the law receive due process, and, more controversially, (3) the laws themselves accord with some universal standards of justice, often captured in United Nations covenants. We typically think that accountability improves when rule of law exists. That is, members of the public may be able to make officials responsible by challenging infractions in courts able to provide a fair hearing. Citizens may also block laws that conflict with principles stated in constitutions by triggering judicial review of legislation. If elections provide citizens one way to remove politicians who engage in malfeasance or fail to manage collective resources competently, the courts provide an alternative avenue for such action between campaign periods.

This happy state of affairs does not materialize automatically, of course. Judicial independence is an important background condition: the contribution of courts to the rule of law is higher when judges are not subject to partisan influence in particular cases. Effectiveness is another element. It is all very well and good to have independent courts, but congested dockets and poor training can create injustice through delay and create opportunities for the manipulation of outcomes short of intimidating or buying a judge. Public awareness is a third factor. It is perfectly possible to have independent and effective courts that do little to enhance governmental accountability because citizens are unaware that they may challenge the constitutionality of legislation or bring grievances against public officials to the judiciary for resolution.

This essay differs from others in this volume because it asks how court systems capable of holding public officials accountable evolve. Although its main purpose is to inform the way we understand this process in Africa and other parts of the developing world, the analysis tries to make general points by way of a short, idiosyncratic excursion through United States judicial history. The challenges that many countries face today are very similar to those encountered in the period of the westward expansion in the United States. It is all too easy to forget that the American government once lacked effective control over territory and over its own agents in the judiciary. Recapturing this experience provides some useful insights and cautions for contemporary policy makers. The purpose is to provoke more careful reflection about the propositions and prescriptions we often entertain with respect to developing countries, neglecting the lessons of a related and not so distant past.

The Big Picture

A simple theory about the relationship between courts and the rule of law might posit that as income to be derived from trade, production or innovation increases, the incentive to build effective mechanisms for dispute resolution also rises. That is, seeing they can improve profits, private entrepreneurs push public officials for fair and efficient ways to resolve disagreements about contracts or employment. Appropriate institutions eventually materialize, shaped by the available technology and by politics. This story accords with the broad-brush account in Douglass North's writing about 'the rise of the western world'.[1] But this simple proposition leaves out the most interesting part of the story.

How people convert incentives, like the prospect of greater profit, into social action and institutional change is really what is of interest in practical policy making. We want to know more about the 'politics' that remain a black box in the standard economists' account of the rule of law. One theory currently in vogue posits that independent courts arise when political party systems are highly competitive. Under these conditions, the story goes, no party would want incumbents to be able to change the outcomes of court decisions in ways that undermined ability of the opposition to compete for office or easily and selectively reverse rules for which important constituents have lobbied. Thus, they opt to delegate dispute resolution to independent courts and take steps to guarantee that independence. They may also invest in improving court capacity so that delay cannot be used strategically to accomplish the same nefarious ends as a breach of independence. This argument is plausible on its face. Ability to use office in order to win judgements that barricade others from the corridors of power is a worry to opposition parties everywhere. Some recent studies claim to find strong empirical support for the proposition.[2]

The problem with such accounts is that they accord rather poorly with the history of most countries that have fairly high levels of judicial independence and judicial capacity today and they don't always appear to help us understand intra-regional variation. Elsewhere the writer has proposed an alternative argument, which contends that (1) the starting points for building independence tend to be idiosyncratic and highly contingent, (2) through their ability to shape procedural rules and to project legal norms to the larger community, judges themselves have played important roles in making short-term delegation of authority from a quixotic executive more enduring, and (3) regional and international bodies can be helpful in providing protection or surveillance of reform-minded courts, in the short run.[3]

The purpose of this analysis is to look still more closely at important aspects of explanation. Although the case used to illustrate the theoretical points is the United States, the point is not to suggest that reform in developing countries must follow American paths. Presumably there are many routes to successful change depending on local circumstances. Rather, the aim is to show that reform requires more than an incentive to seek change. Leadership, appropriate framing, a supply of ideas, and institutional capacity all matter too. Rarely do these things come together at the same moment, although happy conjunctions are more likely to occur in some political systems than in others. Change happens slowly, in fits and starts, with the benefits realized only after the ingredients are all assembled. Whether it is possible to sustain the impetus for reform while the pieces come together may depend heavily on the existence of organized civic groups and the links between the members of these groups and those in power. Thus, the essay tries to provide an antidote to the analytically elegant but overly simple models often purveyed. It also suggests that a better understanding of the complexity of the relationships we want to understand, as well as their strategic character, opens up possibilities and potentially creates a basis for hope in parts of the world that seem inhospitable to current objectives.

The Setting

The performance challenges that developing country judiciaries confront now are similar to those that American courts faced during the nineteenth century. If we could block out names and dates, it would be hard to distinguish a contemporary account of justice system performance in Africa or Latin America from the complaints that filled pamphlets and political speeches in nineteenth-century America.

At the time, the United States shared some geographic characteristics common in Africa now. Much of the population was concentrated in a few cities on the Atlantic coast. Vast territories to the west were thinly populated, and it was both difficult and expensive to maintain a state presence there. Police and 'justice' operated beyond the direct control or scrutiny of central authority. Judges rode circuit to hear cases in outlying areas and often swept into town with lawyer-friends and marshals in tow, sacrificing the appearance, if not the reality, of the separation of powers.

Partisanship entered into the courts in several ways. For at least the first 30 years of the life of the American court system, several prominent judges gave political speeches from the bench. There was little agreement among elected officials on the need for independent courts, although the demand for such had featured in revolutionary-era writing. The courts were in ill repute generally, and the Supreme Court met in a noisy room underneath the stairs of the capitol building, so unimportant in the country's political life did it seem.

Court performance left much to be desired. Some problems originated in the law itself. Procedures were archaic and cumbersome. In the late 1800s, appeals on procedural grounds were common, and the ratio of reversals to affirmations ran about 5:1, exposing the courts to charges that they dealt mainly in technicalities, not justice, and opening them to fierce criticism.[4] The absence of pre-trial discovery rules meant that 'trial by ambush' prevailed, as it does in many developing countries today. That is, instead of exchanging information before trial, lawyers constantly produced new witnesses and evidence at trial, and their opponents demanded frequent continuances to respond, causing delay. Statutory limits on the jurisdiction of courts also created difficulties. In inflationary periods, Congress failed to adjust the limits on amounts-in-controversy that lower courts could hear, flooding the upper courts with petty civil suits instead of leaving these cases for resolution at the lowest levels. Congestion interfered with fairness.

Senior judges had no power to 'manage' their courts. Chief justices had little authority to move judges with low workloads to congested courts in order to relieve their over-worked brethren and reduce delay. There were no court administrators who could manage case flow. Clerks were usually elected officials who used their powers to benefit their supporters. Corruption naturally entered the picture as a result. In New York, the site of some of the earliest agitation for reform, the 'Tweed ring' bought judges and law enforcement. Railroads also purchased decisions in some of the state courts.[5] Similarly, on the frontier the appearance of fairness suffered from the occasional, spectacular scandal, the case of Judge Roy Bean being one of the best known.[6]

Frontier justice suffered a number of other difficulties familiar in developing countries today. The challenges of building an organizational presence and of ensuring accessibility were considerable. Low population density meant that courts were geographically dispersed. Although justices of the peace were usually within a single day's travel for most people, the superior state courts and the federal courts usually lay at a considerable distance. Witnesses had to make long journeys and sometimes failed to show up, forcing continuances or adjournments. Today the equivalent problem in African countries is a major source of public criticism.

Inconsistency in the application of the law was a severe problem, because few really knew what the law was. On the frontier, it was hard to find copies of either the statutes or the law reports, which contained the decisions that constituted binding precedent and were an integral part of the law in common law countries. Early colonial governments had subsidized private printers to produce these, but the system fell on hard times after the Revolution, and it wasn't until the very end of the 1800s that extensive publishing of reports began again, possibly fueled by an increase in the number of lawyers in the country. The situation has parallels in the collapse of law reporting in Africa from 1980 until about 1995.

Finding judicial talent was a severe problem. Service in remote areas was unpopular with many, especially because the pay was low.[7] At mid-century, at the lower levels of the judiciary, most of the men who served had little or no legal training. Only about 45 per cent had formal schooling beyond basic reading and writing skills.[8] They relied on 'Justice of the Peace' manuals, one of the first mass-produced legal documents in the new United States. In several parts of Africa magistrates have similarly found themselves forced to rely on their school notes or on abridged versions of the law that donors helped to organize and publish.

Despite all of these flaws, the few systematic studies available suggest that most of the people who occupied these positions performed adequately, mastered basic legal principles, and offered quick, cheap dispute resolution at about $11 per case.[9] For simple, run of the mill cases, the arrangement seems generally to have worked. As economies grew more complicated, change grew necessary, as it is in Africa and Latin America today.

The beginning of pressure for change initially took the form of popular grumbling about law and lawyers. Lawyers were in the forefront of the American Revolution. But both before and after independence, the legal profession and the courts were also objects of attack. In the early years of the republic debt collection was one of the main tasks lawyers carried out, and debt collection won few admirers. Capturing popular sentiment, in 1808, author George Watterston published a tract, *The Lawyer, or Man as He Ought Not to Be*. Although lawyers' reputations improved in the 1820s, dissatisfaction resurfaced in the middle decades, so that by the end of the century even the leaders of the emerging profession argued that the integrity of practitioners had seriously collapsed. Complaints about delay, corruption and bad law appeared in newspapers and publications such as the *Green Bag* and the *World's Work*. In the 1920s, Moses H. Grossman, a former judge, reported lawyers' concern that three-year delays in the courts would soon lead to revolt.[10] The *American Law Review* opined that populism had filled 'the bench with political partisans, the minor legal offices with political hacks, and the bar with an indiscriminate herd of camp followers'.[11]

All of these descriptions resonate with citizens of developing countries today. Interviews with ordinary people, lawyers and magistrates turn up the same sorts of comments. But what explains the lower incidence of such problems in most US courts now, compared to several decades ago? And can we learn anything from the American attempt to address these sorts of problems historically?

The American Experience with Judicial Reform, 1835–1940

In the United States, grievance built up for some time before small episodes of reform began to metamorphose into sustained, broad-based collective action. Bar associations, organized by people who had improvement of the judicial system as an important ambition, formed only in the 1870s, and their activities and membership were fairly limited until the turn of the century. Other civic associations focused on the legal system gradually appeared thereafter. The major procedural reforms and management innovations[12] took place in the 1920s and 1930s, or 60 to 70 years after fervour for reform had first made itself felt.

It is instructive to consider why the intensity of reform increased when it did and why reformers experienced varying levels of success.

Leaders Are Not Always Available When Needs Arise

There is no necessary relationship between grievance and action. It takes energetic and savvy leadership to mobilize support for reform. Not only must the people at the forefront of the movement understand the problems the courts and their users confront, they also need to know how to win the attention of the people who can make a difference: elected politicians, senior judges and opinion-makers. The capacity to spend time planning, consulting, and lobbying is also critical. And people who have these kinds of knowledge and skills, plus time, are rarely in abundance. Therefore, an understanding of successful reform must include an account of the supply of leadership, a subject on which western political scientists are notoriously reluctant to hypothesize.

In the American case, the intensity of reform activity grew at the very end of the nineteenth century and into the first decades of the twentieth century. Why did it do so then when, at least on the surface, no one individual could benefit from the work he or she invested in trying to move reform ahead? The timing of change may provide some clues:

- High volumes of railroad litigation and increasing numbers of disputes that affected people across state boundaries brought greater awareness of the variety in substantive law and judicial performance within the United States. Comparison bred ferment, but more to the point, the complexity of handling legal cases that crossed jurisdictional boundaries highlighted the problems in the system.
- More practitioners could support themselves comfortably than had been true earlier. Many of the people who became leaders of the reform movement were from well-to-do families, had steady incomes from representing railroads, or were beneficiaries of economic expansion. With financial comfort came more leisure for civic pursuits. Even if the supply of potential leaders was constant throughout the nineteenth century, the capacity to act was not.
- Participation in professional associations and scientific organizations was more acceptable than it had been earlier. Just after the Revolution, egalitarian sentiment militated against the creation of bar associations or movements that might reproduce privilege. Lawyers and lawyers' library societies were targets of public disfavour. But by the 1870s, the tide had turned.

The attitude toward mixing law and politics had also shifted. As the nineteenth century progressed, lawyers began to draw more distinctions between law and politics. They sought to portray themselves as neutral technicians, partly to distance themselves from earlier, post-revolutionary criticism that they were merely the agents of a corrupt, moneyed elite. This image also described the new roles elite lawyers had assumed: roles which emphasized drafting, negotiation and counsel over courtroom advocacy.[13] Yet law work inevitably focuses attention on legislation and on the political world. Leadership of independent commissions and civic groups met the need to exert influence without seeming partisan.[14] It made participation in reform more palatable to some, while others continued to seek political office in order to make a difference.

As a result of these changes, legal reform provided an avenue for younger men of ambition to advance. The reformers often came from distinguished legal families and had to struggle to make their own mark. They likely grew frustrated with a system that privileged knowledge of the intricacies of arcane procedural codes: knowledge best acquired over time. Corruption also lessened the appeal of law as a career open to talent. Thus, younger elite lawyers had incentive to invest in reform, they had somewhat greater means than many of their predecessors, and organizing fellow practitioners on behalf of reform had grown more acceptable.

The genesis of the American Bar Association was a case in point. In the mid-1870s, there were seven small city bar associations in existence and eight state bars. Most were not very active. The Bar Association of the City of New York had been in existence only a few years, inspired by the fight against the 'Tweed ring' and corruption. There was no national bar, nor was there a national movement for legal and judicial reform. In late 1877, 38-year old Simeon Eben Baldwin, then the dean of the four-person faculty of the Yale Law School, attended a meeting of the American Social Science Association, a reform-minded body that included jurisprudence as one of its four departments. Out of that meeting he appears to have hatched the idea of a national law association that could promote uniformity of legislation, help raise standards of legal education, and promote sensible reform of the courts.

Although he practiced law on the side, Baldwin found time to persuade the Connecticut bar to permit him to organize a national meeting. He sent out letters to try to obtain the support of distinguished practitioners and ensured that prominent reformers were on his list of founders. He approached the prosecutors of 'Boss Tweed' and the 'Whiskey ring', a president of a civil service reform association, and the man who had re-written the Pennsylvania criminal code.[15] Once he had these men on board, he wrote to 100 other lawyers to persuade them to attend a meeting in Saratoga, New York, a popular summer resort town.

Over the next half century, other societies with related functions began to emerge. For example, the American Judicature Society, the enduring organization centrally preoccupied with judicial system reform, got its start at the University of Michigan law school in 1913. Would-be reformers joined forces with a lumber magnate who had lost a contract case as a result of a corrupt southern state judge. In return for suggesting removal of the case to federal court (where the litigant subsequently won), the reformers received financial support for a new organization that would focus public attention on court reform.

Status and Numbers Matter

Although calls for judicial reform grew throughout the nineteenth century, change occurred only sporadically through much of the period. One of the reasons for the slow response was that some lawyers profited from the archaic procedures others wanted to abolish. To make a living, a lawyer could either collect more fees for handling drawn-out cases or increase the volume of cases he handled. Relatively few lawyers outside commercial centers could hope to increase the volume of business significantly, and they had invested heavily in learning the elaborate procedural codes many courts used. Even for major litigants, such as the robber barons, manipulating procedure to delay a competitor was often more important than efficient dispute resolution. As late as 1906, 20 years after the creation of the American Bar Association (ABA), Roscoe Pound's speech on the 'Causes of Popular Dissatisfaction with the Administration of Justice' was considered so controversial that the ABA leadership refused to print copies and referred the proposals the speech contained to a committee for deliberation sometime in the future.[16]

It took a critical mass of well-placed reform-minded elite lawyers to overcome the objections of fellow practitioners. The stature of reform advocates, coupled with other changes in the political landscape and in the character of disputes, made it less acceptable for professionals to oppose the cause of reform. Judicial reform became an important cause among literati and important public figures. William Howard Taft brought the issue centre stage in the 1908 presidential campaign, declaring that 'the greatest question now before the American public is the improvement of the administration of justice ... both in the matter of its prompt dispatch and the cheapening of its use'.[17] Others took up the refrain. For example, in 1912 the former president of Harvard, Charles W. Eliot, exhorted the Massachusetts bar to accept the need for change, citing problems of delay, contentiousness, poor attorney preparation, excessive numbers of appeals and retrials, and other challenges.[18] It grew less and less acceptable for lawyers to object to the changes proposed to solve these problems.

The Supply of Ideas and Practical Proposals is not Guaranteed

A reform movement usually has to do more than grumble to be successful. Most policy-makers and politicians lack the time to develop concrete proposals and deliberate carefully about their pros and cons. Movement leaders who can generate and package ideas are more likely to have an impact than those who do not. But developing ideas takes time, and few practitioners had spare time in the 1800s.

The American judicial reform experience depended heavily, though not exclusively, on the rise of the law school. For decades after the Revolution, one became a lawyer in the United States simply by reading. There were no admissions requirements. There were no real law schools and those that called themselves law schools lacked coherent curricula. But by the late

1800s, universities were beginning to develop law programmes. In lieu of working in the office of another lawyer or reading law on one's own, a student could participate in group study, still loosely organized, at one of a handful of new programmes.

The new institutions altered the possibilities of reform. Law teachers had to prepare lectures and write books. They could justify time spent in careful analysis of statutes and decisions from a variety of jurisdictions. Their need to schematize material for their students meant they were more likely to chafe at inconsistencies and idiosyncrasies than others were.

The presence of law teachers in the new reform movements was remarkable. A large proportion of the people who showed up to the first organizational meeting of the ABA in Saratoga were law teachers.[19] Soon thereafter, the ABA leadership issued explicit calls for law teachers to develop opinion on broad legal issues.[20] In 1901, James Barr Ames, the dean of the Harvard Law School, pronounced that judges could never hope to be serious scholars, but 'the professor, on the other hand, while dealing with his subject in the lecture room, is working in the direct line of his intended book'[21] Law teachers had an interest in playing this role, but so did law schools, then new, often on fragile footing in their respective universities, and bent on finding a clear way to express their mission.

Law schools also provided shelter for would-be reformers. In 1906, when Roscoe Pound's address on the need for judicial reform left the ABA leadership chagrined, Northwestern University's law school and the University of Chicago offered Pound a base from which he could prepare practical proposals for solving the problems he had identified in his speech.[22] The University of Michigan allowed the American Judicature Society to work from its basement, in the early 1900s. The University's president, Harry B. Hutchins, observed in his 1913 commencement address, 'If some of the thinking that in recent years has gone into legal manipulation on behalf of great interests had been devoted to judicial reform and to reconstruction of both substantive law and procedure ... much of the criticism to which courts and the profession have been subjected would have been avoided.'[23]

Whose Ideas Matter Depends on Access and on Having the Right Networks

Legal reformers in the United States included prominent politicians in their ranks, and that meant that the ideas central to the movement often had a receptive audience in the White House and the Congress. Herbert Hoover sat side by side with Charles Evans Hughes and an array of reform-minded lawyers at the initiation of the American Arbitration Association. William

Howard Taft had a long history of involvement in the reform movement. The ideas were not imposed on them. They had helped to carry them forward.

Crises Can Help Create Opportunity

The fifth lesson of the American experience is that crisis can create opportunity. The federal courts came under attack in the early part of the twentieth century because judges used powers of judicial review to strike down statutes designed to regulate labour practices. For much of the nineteenth century the power of judicial review John Marshall had created in *Marbury v. Madison* remained mostly unused in the federal courts. But at the end of the century and in the early 1900s, the Supreme Court began to use the power to strike down laws, and it did so in a way that favoured the interests of business over workers. The famous 1905 case of *Lochner v. New York*, coupled with the nullification of federal child labour statutes, galvanized organised labour into action.

In 1912, Wisconsin's Senator LaFollette argued that 'the judiciary has grown to be the most powerful institution in our government ... Evidence abounds that, as constituted today, the courts pervert justice almost as often as they administer it. Precedent and procedure have combined to make one law for the rich and another for the poor. The regard of the courts for fossilized precedent, their absorption in technicalities, their detachment from the vital, living facts of the present day, their constant thinking on the side of the rich and powerful and privileged classes have brought our courts into conflict with the democratic spirit and purposes of this generation.'[24]

President Theodore Roosevelt ultimately took up the cause. The 'progressives' called for popular sovereignty and restriction of the courts. Later the American Federation of Labor (AFL), strengthened during the First World War, called for an end to judicial review. It helped to trigger a national movement to permit popular recall of judges and of judicial decisions.

Within the bar, the movements for judicial recall and an end to judicial review met with considerable opposition. The ABA cited several reasons for standing fast against these popular demands and focused particularly on threats to judicial independence and on the risk that recall would undermine the ability of the courts to protect minority opinion from the tyranny of the majority. Lawyers commissioned surveys of public opinion to better pinpoint the source of public dissatisfaction and used the results to argue that people wanted better performance but thought insistence on more stringent standards of appointment preferable to recall. The influence of these opinions spilled over into the public arena. The 1924 election focused partly on policy toward the courts.

Although no more than six states ever adopted recall measures and the appeal to end judicial review generated few important political allies, these debates placed the performance of the judiciary squarely on the public agenda. The reform movement lawyers had launched years earlier gained momentum. Supreme Court Chief Justice William Howard Taft used the furore to move ahead with his own agenda. He reached out to allies in the press and in the bar both to defeat the more radical reform bid and to advance his own reform proposals. At the urging of the bar and of influential members, Congress began to enact a series of statutes that gave the federal courts more power to handle the workload effectively.

Radical reform proposals lost support, partly as a result of wavering progressive leadership, but also partly because of actions taken by the court itself. Signs of a changing jurisprudence and better drafting of new bills meant that the Supreme Court began to exercise its powers of judicial review in a manner more in line with popular opinion.

Framing and Timing Make a Difference

The recall movement failed, while its twin, focused on enhanced effectiveness, persisted. Why? The answer appears to rest partly with the congruence between the cultural heritage of the political elite and the norms embedded in alternative proposals. Progressive leaders thought courts were important and worried about upsetting the separation of powers and system of checks and balances.[25] They grew unwilling to support the more radical calls for change. The ideas of the mainstream reform movement were more palatable, given the values of most legislators and pundits at the time.

Similarly, the introduction of the Commerce Court at the federal level in the late 1920s met with failure. The record of the Supreme Court at the time led people to believe the court would be under the thrall of big business. Although there was no strong evidence that it was so, its future was tainted, and it eventually collapsed.

Civic Organizations Keep Issues on the Agenda, and Experience Abroad Can Provide a Push

The movement for judicial reform in the mid-1800s received a push from abroad, and it was sustained in part by an increasingly dense network of specialized civic associations. Judicial reform and law reform were both on the agenda in England at roughly the same time they surfaced in the United States. In 1869, a year before the creation of the New York City Bar Association and the decade that saw the creation of the ABA, England had created a royal commission to inquire into the operation of its courts. Earlier proposals for procedural reform and changes in substantive law had traveled back and forth between the two countries. Although the proposals were not always apposite, the appearance of a 'wave' of change provided ideas, reinforcement, and perhaps a certain cachet to judicial reform that it had not enjoyed earlier. By the end of the 1800s, many American states had set up judicial reform commissions, and the ABA had created a committee to think about the subject. The founders of the American Judicature Society were explicitly motivated by the example of the English judicial reform movement.[26]

The increasing density of civic organizations dedicated to judicial reform helped sustain the movement over decades and created both a watchdog capacity and a source of ideas. Almost 70 years elapsed between serious reform legislation passed and the time David Dudley Field made some of the first proposals to clean up the system and 50 years elapsed between the legislation and the founding of the bar association movement. Although reform was on the public's mind, the foundation of very strong, stable civic associations helped keep the issues and proposals at the forefront and centre.

Courts Must Have the Organizational Capacity to Reform

Capacity to implement proposals does not arise spontaneously. American reformers were intent not only on promoting procedural change, more stringent selection procedures, and better management but also the ability for courts to put changes into effect. Change proceeded in phases, beginning with the legislation that created circuit courts of appeal to relieve pressure on the justices of the supreme court, vesting rule-making authority in the judiciary, and creating an administrative office for the US courts. The administrative office came into being in 1939, many years after it was first proposed by reforms in the ABA. Provision for legislative liaison materialized in 1948, and it was not until 1967 that capacity for research and education was put in place. The creation of management capacity at the state court level proceeded slightly more rapidly.

Judicial Reform and Alternatives to Courts go Hand-in-Hand

In discussions of the rule of law in developing countries today, it is common to hear policy makers counterpose assistance to judicial reform and the creation of alternative forums for dispute resolution. To paraphrase, 'If the courts do not work, then we should invest instead in the creation of new institutions.' But in the American experience, the development of the courts and of alternatives generally went hand-in-hand. Many of the same people most active in changing civil procedure and developing better court management were also involved in promoting private commercial arbitration and specialized forums to handle particular kinds of cases.

The interest in alternatives to courts, or in specialized courts, had several sources. As in many developing countries today, the legal culture at American independence stressed the desirability of settling disputes without resort to lawyers or courts. Many of the religious communities that settled in the territory during the 1600s emphasized settlement of conflicts through negotiation and disapproved deeply of those who sought the help of law.[27] These systems broke down as populations in the colonies grew more diverse and interaction expanded. But trust in law and lawyers remained low.

More important, merchants had their own tradition of private arbitration, which they brought with them, too. In England, trade guilds had responsibility for resolving commercial disputes, and merchants decided disagreements that occurred in markets and fairs. Only in the 1690s did England's state courts begin to play a role, and initially, that role was mainly to record the settlements merchants had effected, which coincidentally gave the state courts an opportunity to collect a fee and raise a little revenue. Many of the colonists had rebelled against the intrusion of the British government on their lives and favoured the practices with which they were more familiar. Arbitration was also the practice in the Netherlands, and New York City, originally New Amsterdam, became home to the first arbitration tribunal in the Americas in 1647.

Chambers of commerce provided arbitration services in the early years. Stock exchanges began to provide similar forums as merchants began to organize them. For example, the Philadelphia Stock Exchange, organized in 1790, provided for arbitration, as did others, later. Laws of many states and territories stipulated that disagreements about trespass, fence keeping and taxes would be subject to arbitration.[28]

These ideas never disappeared, and reformers drew on them as the need and opportunity arose. For the poor, court congestion meant that reconciliation, or conciliation, held out some promise as a means for resolving disputes. Conciliation services developed in conjunction with crowded small claims courts. In most regions of the country it remained relatively unpopular, at least until succeeded by modern mediation services.

Labour arbitration attracted interest in the late 1800s as violent clashes between workers and businesses heightened anxiety that a society fresh from war over slavery might plunge into a new kind of conflict. Voluntary associations such as the Chicago Civic Foundation tried to find Christian alternatives to violence and found them in arbitration. There was talk of borrowing compulsory arbitration statutes from New Zealand, the first country to enact them. Labour groups worried that underlying inequalities might put workers at a disadvantage in these proceedings but gradually grew more receptive, especially after stronger unions emerged in the twentieth century.[29]

Commercial arbitration expanded during the early 1900s. The conditions that supported its success reappeared with the increasing organization of industrial sectors in the 1920s.[30] Just as organization made it possible to promulgate codes of ethics for different industries, so did it facilitate private dispute resolution within particular lines of business. Delay in the courts made these services attractive to entrepreneurs, but the privacy of the proceedings helped too.

But in business, although the space for arbitration remained large and use of arbitration expanded, the courts remained an important feature of the legal landscape. Surveys of firms at the turn of the century suggested that arbitration was sometimes a tool for extracting information, prior to a legal suit, and that where delays in the courts were low, entrepreneurs preferred to use the courts.[31] In less organized trades, new areas of economic activity or transactions between new types of actors, arbitration was not always feasible or desirable.

The same people who championed court reform were also leaders in the movement to expand alternative dispute resolution. For example, the impetus for reform of arbitration in the 1920s came from the bar of New York, the bar of New York City and the Chamber of Commerce of New York, working in concert. Charles Evans Hughes and other distinguished lawyers and businessmen organized to create the Arbitration Society of America, which organizes a 'People's Tribunal' to support quick settlement of civil disputes. An alternative association, which excluded lawyers, formed in 1925.[32] The two organizations merged to form the American Arbitration Association in 1926 – appropriately after arbitration of the differences of opinion between lawyers and businessmen.[33]

Drawing Lessons

Change does not take place in the same way in different periods or places. The possibilities alter with shifts in economic and social structure, with the incentives political institutions create, with the availability of models and with new ideas. There is no such thing as a theory to guide us in all times and countries. Nonetheless, reformers everywhere face the same basic challenges: leaders must appear, they must have a way to support themselves and their ambitions through the reform process, and opportunity must arise. It is worth reflecting on four issues with particular relevance for court-watchers in developing countries today.

Where are the Leaders? What Helps a Would-be Reform Leader Assume Responsibility?

Latent leadership may exist in developing countries, as it did in the United States. Many lawyers around the world have stuck their necks out to secure change. But in some places latent leaders do not begin to take the steps necessary to build pressure for reform. And the American example may suggest some reasons why. First, the economic pressures many lawyers in developing countries face are such that it is hard to invest in activities that will not return an income. The demand for legal services in many places is not strong enough to make law a viable vocation for very many. Latent leaders may have less incentive to invest as a result.

Second, in many countries the legal and judicial communities are small. The likelihood that a reformer will appear before a given judge is quite high. And lawyers worry about their ability to win decisions on their merits after having said something in public that might have offended a member of the bench. Conversely, magistrates comment that they are disinclined to impose sanctions for delay because they might soon find the lawyer so sanctioned a colleague or a superior. The American lawyers had some greater benefit of anonymity as a result of their geographical dispersion and the higher volume of court business even in a single urban area. But they also sought to detach extracurricular ambitions from courtroom practice by speaking as a group, and that is something not all developing country legal reformers have done.

Is There a Clash of Big, Organized, Economically Central Interests to Keep the Issue on the Public Agenda?

In the American case, businesses and workers both focused on the courts as central to their ability to resolve disputes effectively or to the balance of power between social groups. That clash of titans kept judicial reform on the agenda in a democratic system. But in many parts of the developing world, non-competitive political regimes keep these interests from being heard, and often natural constituents like business and labour in the US case, are not much in evidence.

Interests are often as much a matter of ideas – of what people come to think is important or of how they define their identities – as they are material. Latent constituencies for more effective courts exist in developing countries, especially among the candidates sponsored by new opposition political parties and among new firms that lack the patronage connections of their older counterparts. But they do not always see the relationship between their interests and the judiciary. Where important constituents are not in evidence, funding for courts gets little priority.

Are there Concrete Proposals Available and Are They Acceptable Within Local Discourse?

New law school faculty became an important source of reform plans in the United States, supplemented extensively later by think tanks or law-focused non-profit organizations such as the American Law Institute, the American Judicature Society, and the bar associations. In developing countries, law faculty sometimes play a similar role, but the collaboration between reformers and the international community often gives recommendations a foreign feel and means they lack the concreteness or specificity required to make them work locally. It is not that borrowing is bad. Everywhere the history of law is partly the history of transplants. But what is too often missing is the local deliberation and fine-tuning that make for appropriation rather than imposition. The African Economic Research Consortium (AERC) is a partial solution to the analogous problem in the field of economics. An AERC-equivalent for law might go far in the effort to boost the supply of ideas.

Is There Internal Capacity to Carry Out Reform?

One of the biggest differences between the American experience and developing countries today lies in restructuring the internal management of court systems so that chief justices and their deputies are not overwhelmed by reform demands. Over a period of decades, reformers and reform-minded senior judges in the United States worked to obtain changes in rules and institutional design to free up the labour to make the courts work. By contrast, developing country reform initiatives generally give no heed to the problem of centralizing responsibility in a single person, usually the chief justice, and his or her small staff. Implementation of other changes is slow, uneven and often of poor quality, as a result. Thus, human capital *per se* is often not the limiting factor in judicial reform. Sensible strategies for dealing with time-demands on the judges managing change are.

Do these reflections mean that our existing theories about judicial independence and effectiveness have little to contribute to our understanding of changes taking place around the world today? Do competitive party systems have nothing to do with the creation of independent judiciaries? Clearly not. Under the right conditions, party competition creates an incentive to delegate authority to independent courts. Its more important function may be to create a bulwark against the dismantling of such courts. But party competition is certainly not a sufficient condition for courts to exercise their accountability function, and it is quite possibly not a necessary condition either. Successful efforts to build independent, effective courts people will use to make officials accountable all encounter some shared challenges, however, including the need to reduce points of potential interference, enhance monitoring within the judiciary itself, and build a popular following. But we also must be mindful of the important roles of leadership, timing, ideas, framing, networking and internal capacity. Too often donor-inspired reform programmes ignore these elements of institutional change, without which the US courts would not be what they are today and without which not much progress toward accountable government will take place in Africa, Latin America or Asia. Moreover, Americans have much to learn from current experiences abroad. Eternal vigilance is the price of liberty, as one American patriot proclaimed. Human nature being what it is, lapses in the horizontal accountability courts provide will take place in the best of circumstances. There is plenty of room for an exchange of lessons across national boundaries as across time.

ACKNOWLEDGEMENT

Parts of this essay were written while the author served as a visiting scholar at the World Bank and she thanks the Bank for its sponsorship.

NOTES

1. See Douglass C. North and Robert Paul Thomas, *The Rise of the Western World* (Cambridge: Cambridge University Press, 1973) for this argument, and Bruce Bueno de Mesquita and Hilton L. Root (eds), *Governing for Prosperity* (New Haven, CT: Yale University Press, 2000) for a more recent view.
2. See William M. Landes and Richard A. Posner, 'The Independent Judiciary in an Interest Group Perspective', *Journal of Law and Economics*, Vol.18, No.3 (1975), pp.875–901.
3. A more precise and elaborate form of this argument appears in Jennifer Widner, *Building the Rule of Law* (New York: W.W. Norton, 2001).
4. Lawrence Friedman, *History of American Law* (New York: Simon and Schuster, 1973), p.346.
5. John A. Matzko, 'The Best Men of the Bar: The Founding of the American Bar Association', in Gerard W. Gawalt, *The New High Priests: Lawyers in Post-Civil War America* (Westport, CT: Greenwood Press, 1984), p.78.
6. There is an abundant literature on this colourful character, as well as a Judge Roy Bean Society. For a synopsis of the man's life and times see Elizabeth Gibson, 'Judge Roy Bean, Law West of the Pecos', <http://www.suite101.com/article.cfm/3439/23580>, 3August 1999 (accessed 18 February 2003).
7. These historical observations come mainly from John R. Wunder, *Inferior Courts, Superior Justice* (Westport, CT: Greenwood Press, 1979), Gordon Morris Bakken's several books on law on the frontier, and Friedman (note 4).
8. Wunder (note 7).
9. Wunder (note 7).
10. Jerold S. Auerbach, *Justice Without Law?* (New York: Oxford University Press, 1983), p.106.
11. As quoted in Matzko (note 5) p.78.

12. The first systematic use of pre-trial conferences took place in civil lawsuits in Detroit in 1929.
13. Wayne K. Hobson, 'Symbol of the New Profession: Emergence of the Large Law Firm, 1970-1915', in Gawalt (note 5), p.3.
14. On this subject see also Friedman (note 4) pp.152–3.
15. Matzko (note 5) p.87.
16. Michael Belknap, 'From Pound to Harley: The Founding of AJS', *Judicature*, Vol.72, No.2 (1988), pp.80–84.
17. William G. Ross, *Muted Fury: Populists, Progressives, and Labor Unions Confront the Courts, 1890–1937* (Princeton, NJ: Princeton University Press, 1994), p.78.
18. Ibid., pp.76–7.
19. Matzko (note 5) p.87.
20. William C. Chase, *The American Law School and the Rise of Administrative Government* (Madison, WI: University of Wisconsin Press, 1982), pp.17–18.
21. Ibid., pp.18–19.
22. Arthur L. Harding, 'Professor Pound Makes History', in A.L. Harding (ed.), *The Administration of Justice in Retrospect: Roscoe Pound's 1906 Address in a Half-Century of Experience* (Dallas: Southern Methodist University Press, 1957), p.14.
23. Belknap (note 16) p.82.
24. As quoted in Ross (note 17) p.15.
25. Ross (note 17) p.60.
26. Belknap (note 16), pp.78–91 passim.
27. Auerbach (note 10) p.47.
28. Frances Kellor, *Arbitration and the Legal Profession* (New York: American Arbitration Association, 1952).
29. Auerbach (note 10) p.65.
30. Ibid. p.101.
31. Kellor (note 28) pp.16–17.
32. Auerbach (note 10) p.108.
33. Ibid. p.113.

The Constitutional Court and Control of Presidential Extraordinary Powers in Colombia

RODRIGO UPRIMNY

There are strong theoretical and empirical arguments in favour of the thesis that the rule of law is essential for democratic consolidation and economic development. The existence of an independent judiciary capable of controlling government abuses is an essential element of the rule of law. So it is important to improve our understanding of the factors that enable courts to fulfil properly this key function in precarious democracies. In that context, this study analyzes certain aspects of the efforts of the judiciary in Colombia to control government.

In Colombia, there have been several attempts by various courts or judges to hold the government, or at least some government officers, to account. For instance, the Council of State has stated, on numerous occasions, that the Colombian government must pay monetary compensation to certain citizens owing to violations of their human rights by the military or police. Also, the Constitutional Court has tried to reduce impunity in cases of human rights abuses by narrowly interpreting the legal competence of military justice to investigate military and police officers. This is significant because, according to human rights groups, the *esprit de corps* and the direct participation of the public forces in the internal armed conflict have ensured that the military justice system has not punished the military and police personnel involved in these crimes. Furthermore ordinary judges and the Constitutional Court have tried to eliminate abuses and inhuman conditions in the prisons. There are other examples of judicial involvement of a similar nature.

In spite of an array of judicial efforts to develop some form of executive accountability, this inquiry focuses on just one point: the attempts by the Colombian Constitutional Court to control the abuse of presidential extraordinary or emergency powers in the last decade. Three reasons explain this choice: the intrinsic importance of this subject, the centrality of the Constitutional Court in Colombian politics, and the originality of the Colombian experience in this field.

First, this subject is significant not only for Colombia but also in theoretical and comparative terms, because the abuse of governmental extraordinary powers is a permanent threat to democratic consolidation.

Second, during the past ten years, the Constitutional Court's leading role in Colombian political life has been acknowledged not only by those who support its efforts but also by its fiercest critics.

Third, one of the most important and original interventions of the Constitutional Court has been its efforts to restrict the president's use of state of siege measures. This is no mean feat in a country like Colombia, where emergency powers have been improperly utilized for several decades, even to the extent of putting at risk the maintenance of the rule of law.[1]

The study has four parts. The first part shows the importance of judicial control of emergency powers, that is, the judicial checking of those constitutional powers given to the government in serious or war-like crises. The second part describes some features of Colombian politics and the legal system that are important to understand the context of Constitutional Court intervention. The third part examines how the Constitutional Court has endeavoured to control presidential emergency powers. Part four evaluates how this has been possible and the effects of such judicial involvement. Based on the Colombian experience, the essay concludes with a short theoretical reflection on the possibilities and limits of judicial review as an instrument to avoid the abuse of emergency powers in a developing democracy.

The Dilemmas of Emergency Powers: Rule of Law, War-like Crises, Emergency Powers and Judicial Review

War-like crises that threaten the very existence of the state or the continuity of social organized life pose a difficult dilemma for the rule of law, especially in emergent or precarious democracies. The dilemma can be explained as follows. If society does not authorize governmental extraordinary powers to face the crisis, it will face two dangers: either the regime could collapse or, more probably, the government, without the possibility of resorting to legal extraordinary powers to face the crises, will act illegally, provoking in consequence a breakdown of the rule of law.

It therefore seems necessary that constitutional regimes recognize the existence of emergency or extraordinary powers to address this kind of crises. The essence of these powers, which some scholars call 'constitutional dictatorship', is that they temporarily increase governmental faculties and authorize the restriction of certain constitutional guarantees and personal fundamental rights in order to defend the constitutional order and reestablish normality.[2] This seems necessary for the continuity of the rule of law. But the dilemma emerges because in a lot of cases, these extraordinary powers, conceived to preserve democracy, have been an instrument used by authoritarian governments to distort democracy and undermine the rule of law. This has been especially true in Latin America, where emergency powers have been used as a pretext for systematic human rights violations by antidemocratic regimes.

Constitutional regimes and legal scholars have responded to this dilemma in different ways, which may be classified in three main groups. Some argue that, because of the danger of abuse of emergency powers, we had better not incorporate these kinds of regulations in constitutional regimes.[3] Other scholars claim that such a response is unwise and counterproductive because it stimulates constitutional breakdown. They conclude that political realism recognizes the need for sweeping extraordinary governmental powers to face serious crises. Finally, there is a middle position, adopted by international human rights law, asserting that emergency powers must be recognized but that they need to be strictly regulated and controlled, in order to prevent governmental abuses or extralimitations.[4] According to this third position, some regulations are important. It is necessary to stipulate what kinds of crises allow for the use of emergency powers. Governmental powers should be enumerated, and the legitimacy of their use should depend on conformity to some principles, like the principles of necessity and proportionality. Consequently, political and judicial controls should be established and strengthened.

This constitutional dilemma obviously has implications for judicial review of presidential decisions in war-like crises.[5] Some argue that judicial review is impossible because the use of extraordinary powers in serious crises falls within the realm of pure necessity and, therefore, cannot be subjected to any judicial scrutiny. This is clearer if judicial control operates throughout ongoing crises. In this situation, judges tend to abdicate judicial responsibilities because of security concerns. They are unable to stop executive self-aggrandizement, because they perceive their own institutional and personal restrictions with respect to successfully responding to and overcoming profound social crises. Emergency powers are then, seen as political questions that are not justiciable.

By contrast, other scholars argue that constitutional crises should be controlled by the judiciary as any other issue, no matter the intensity of the crisis. And recently, yet others, like Robert Burt, have tried to depart from these two opposing views. Instead, they stress the importance of the teaching role of judges as an alternative theoretical paradigm to explain and justify judicial review of extraordinary executive powers. In this paradigm, judges function as 'special interest advocates'. According to Burt,

> This alternative – a third way to understand the judicial role – is not to conceive judges as the final authority responsible for balancing the demands of legal regularity against the claimed need for enlarged executive authority to protect the society's essential security. Instead this alternative sees judges in effect as 'special interest advocates' on behalf of the rule of law rather than as final decision-makers.[6]

In Burt's approach, the fact that judicial review in times of crisis is not final has the paradoxical effect of strengthening the judicial role in these situations. This because judges feel they can act more freely, knowing that their judgements can have some political effect, depending on the prestige of the judiciary, but at the same time knowing that it is not the last word on vital security issues.

Discussions of the judiciary's role in controlling extraordinary powers in constitutional crises are at the same time difficult and important, because they are related to central problems of democratic consolidation. The significance of these debates is greater in precarious or emergent democracies, such as Colombia, for at least two related reasons. First, these regimes are usually very vulnerable in economic and political terms, and prone to face serious crises in which emergency powers appear to be necessary. Second, the dangers of abuse of these extraordinary powers are greater in these regimes, precisely because of the fragility of the rule of law. So, in emergent democracies, governmental extraordinary powers seem to be more necessary but also more dangerous than in consolidated democracies. The question that follows is, could judicial control be a useful instrument to reduce the dangers of emergency powers in emergent democracies? Or, on the contrary could the judiciary's involvement in these very complex situations be, if not impossible, at least dangerous, because it may either undermine judicial legitimacy or obstruct political measures to resolve the crisis? The Colombian experience usefully explores this dilemma. To understand the real meaning of the judicial attempts to control emergency powers in Colombia, it is necessary briefly to present some background to the Colombian political and legal systems.

A Democracy in Permanent Emergency: Colombia's Legal and Political Systems and the Abuse of Emergency Powers

Colombia has long been a somewhat strange and paradoxical country. It is one of the oldest formal democracies in Latin America and has a long established tradition of civilian government, in a region in which military rule has been very common. According to the English historian Malcom Deas, 'This republic has had more elections, under more systems, than any other Latin American or European country'.[7] For example, its previous constitution (of 1886) lasted for more than 100 years, with only some very short interruptions to civilian rule, and Colombia has had more or less fair elections at least sine 1830.

Also, Colombia has had a relatively independent judiciary, at least since 1958. It was one of the first countries in the world to establish a system of judicial constitutional control or judicial review, which has been more or less respected by political actors for the last 100 years. Law, especially constitutional law, has thus played an important role in Colombian politics. Besides, until very recently, Colombia was seen as economically and politically stable, at least according to Latin-American standards.

However, Colombia has not really been a consolidated democracy, due to three important shortcomings. First, for long periods at a time, Colombia has faced high levels of violence, not only political violence, but also in the ordinary life of citizens. The homicide rate over the last two decades has been about 70 per 100,000 inhabitants – one of the highest in the world. For the last three decades, Colombia has suffered armed conflict, which has increased in intensity and cruelty.

Second, civilian rule and economic and political stability have not led to social and economic democratization. Colombia has exclusionary policies, resulting in a society with deep inequalities and oligarchic rule.[8] For instance, the 20 per cent with the highest incomes receive in total 26 times more than the poorest 20 per cent. The Gini coefficient of 0.564 is one of the highest in Latin America, which in turn is one of the world regions with the greatest inequality.[9]

Third, and related to the two previous factors, Colombia has experienced a very serious human right crisis, especially since the end of the 1970s. Initially, the largest problems were arbitrary detentions, torture and unfair sentences. Subsequently, in the 1980s, violations against life became the main concern, given the abrupt increase in massacres, disappearances, torture and murders. For instance, according to the Colombian Commission of Jurists, for the last 15 years, an average of at least ten persons have died every day for politics-related reasons. About four of these ten were victims of war operations, and six murdered by right wing paramilitary forces, leftist guerrilla groups, drug lords or military or police officers.[10]

These features make it difficult to define Colombia's political regime. It is not really a consolidated democracy, due to its widespread violence, human right abuses and deep social inequalities. Nevertheless, Colombia is neither a dictatorship nor a simple façade democracy. Popular elections are held periodically to elect governmental representatives. Judicial controls and other constitutional checks and balances are more or less effective, at least in some parts of the country. For instance, in March 1987, a Supreme

Court decision declared that it was unconstitutional for military courts to investigate and punish civilians. Since that date, not a single civilian has been judged by military courts.

Besides this complex combination of authoritarian and democratic traits, Colombia's state formation has been historically very precarious. State institutions have never really been in command of all Colombian territory, some parts of which traditionally have been controlled by private actors. In recent years, the increase in the armed conflict and the major economic crisis that started in 1997 have aggravated these problems of state formation. According to some interpretations, while Colombia is not yet a failed state, it is a collapsing state.[11]

Analysts have found it difficult to classify this ambiguous political system, which is both stable and precarious, and also democratic in some respects, yet antidemocratic and authoritarian in others. Some call it a 'restricted democracy' or 'oligarchic democracy', whereas others name it a 'besieged democracy'. Yet others prefer to talk about a 'precarious democracy' or a 'semi-democratic regime'. Of course, these different expressions presuppose different analytical approaches and have different political and academic implications.[12] Let us dwell on the presidential emergency powers, institutionalized as a 'state of siege' regime by the Constitution of 1886, which has been one of the key elements in explaining the particular evolution of Colombian politics and its legal system. With the 1886 declaration, the president acquired the possibility of promulgating special decrees with force of law (*decretos legislativos*) to restrict some constitutional liberties and to legislate on matters related to public order alteration.

This state of siege regime was created for the purpose of addressing crises alone. However, in practice, it became an ordinary instrument of government, in at least three different senses. First, Colombia has lived under this regime most of the time. Colombia was under state of siege for more than 30 of the 42 years from 1949 to 1991. Second, large and very important legal reforms were adopted by means of siege decrees, which were then legalized by Congress.[13] In short, the president became a de facto legislator. Last, but not least, the almost permanent state of siege has placed deep restrictions on constitutional liberties. During the 1970s, many social protests, like workers' strikes, were suppressed by extraordinary assertions of executive power; freedom of association, movement and expression were encroached upon continuously. Besides, executive decrees adopted during the states of siege not only increased punishments and created new felonies and misdemeanours but also severely undermined 'due process' guarantees. This is particularly true for the period between 1965 and 1987, when military judges were allowed to investigate and punish civilians. At the end of the 1970s, about 30 per cent of the felonies established in the Criminal Code were under the competence of courts martial.[14]

In sum, the abuse of state of siege powers made Colombia a democracy under permanent emergency. This phenomenon has had fundamental implications for the nature of Colombia's political and legal systems. In particular, it has blurred the distinction between legality and illegality and between democracy and authoritarianism. Colombia was not a military dictatorship but was not a well functioning democracy either, because civilian governments constantly abused the emergency powers.[15]

In 1991, Colombia adopted a new constitution, replacing the 1886 Constitution. The 1991 Constitution was not the product of a triumphant revolution. Rather, it grew out of a very complex historical context, as an attempt to come to an agreement to broaden democracy in order to confront violence and political corruption. Under these circumstances, certain political and social forces that had previously been excluded from competing for office played a notable role in the Constituent Assembly. These included representatives of demobilized guerrilla groups, and indigenous and religious minorities. Thus, of the 70 members of the Constituent Assembly chosen by popular vote in December 1990, 19 came from the Democratic Alliance-Movement 19 April (AD-M19), two from the Patriotic Union,[16] two indigenous, two non-Catholic Christians, and two representing students and children. Furthermore, three delegates came from guerrilla groups that demobilized only after the elections, while the assembly was actually in session.[17] This meant that over 40 per cent of the members of the Constituent Assembly did not belong to the Liberal and Conservative parties, which until then had dominated Colombian electoral politics. Many saw this as the end of the two-party system of political domination. Furthermore, because of the voting system, which required qualified majorities, and in the absence of a clearly dominant group, all the Assembly's delegate groups had to seek consensus and organize dialogue and transactions in order to reach decisions. Within this framework, many of the delegates identified the following as the main problems contributing to the crisis: exclusion, the lack of participation and weakness in protecting human rights. This explains some of the ideological orientations in the 1991 Constitution, namely, the broadening of participation mechanisms, the imposition of social justice and equality duties upon the state, and the incorporation of a new constitution that is rich in rights and new judicial mechanisms for their protection. The 1991 Constitution is therefore not, in Teitel's words, 'backward looking', but, rather, 'forward looking' in that, beyond codifying the existing power relations, this legal document also projected a model of the society yet to be built.[18]

Because of the abuse of the state of siege in the past, the new 1991 Constitution tried to limit extraordinary governmental powers. It defined more precisely the situations where the president is permitted to declare a 'state of exception'.[19] It further stipulated temporal limits for its use, and also incorporated normative limits to governmental powers, especially specific prohibitions (such as the ban on the use of military justice to try civilians) and the principles of proportionality and subsidiarity. According to these principles, the government could only take measures specifically linked to the causes of the disturbance that were strictly necessary to reestablish normality. Besides, these measures must be in accordance with the gravity of the crises and can only be used if ordinary instruments of government are insufficient (See articles 213 and 214 of the constitution.)

The account so far raises the following key questions. First, what has been the role of judicial review in relation to the abuse of emergency powers in Colombia? Second, what has been the effect of the new constitution in this area? These questions are addressed in the next section.

Judicial Attempts to Control Presidential Emergency Powers

State of siege measures were subjected to judicial review by the Supreme Court, which was the organ that exercised constitutional judicial review under the 1886 Constitution. The 1991 Constitution established a Constitutional Court that took charge of the task of controlling the constitutionality of legislation and emergency decrees. It is helpful to compare the activities of these two tribunals related to the control of governmental extraordinary powers in order to understand the peculiarities of Constitutional Court intervention.

The Evolution of Judicial Control over Emergency Powers in Colombia

To understand the evolution of judicial control over emergency powers in Colombia, it is important to keep in mind that the president can adopt two different kind of decisions. First, he can declare a 'state of siege' (under the 1886 Constitution) or a 'state of exception' (under the 1991 Constitution) in order to acquire emergency powers. After this act, he can use the emergency powers to promulgate decrees that restrict liberties, or to legislate in certain matters. Two questions are important here. First, to what extent is the declaration of a state of siege or a state of exception a political question that is, or alternatively is not, beyond judicial review? Second, once the president has acquired emergency powers, what has been the scope and intensity of judicial control over the concrete measures taken by the government?

Scholars who have tried to answer these questions agree that it is possible to distinguish three different periods of judicial review of emergency measures.[20] From the reestablishment of electoral democracy in 1958 after a short military regime to the beginning of the 1980s, judicial review was very lenient. First, the Supreme Court decided that the president's evaluation of public order was in a certain sense a 'political question' that could not be judicially controlled. So, the Supreme Court achieved only formal control of the decree of declaration of a state of emergency; it simply verified if the decree was signed by the president and the members of his cabinet, but refused to examine whether there was crisis severe enough to justify the government acquiring emergency powers. The result was not only that governments assumed emergency powers during minor crises but also that states of emergency extended well beyond the time-span of these situations. Just one example: in May 1965 the government declared a state of siege because of a student protest in Medellín against the American invasion of Santo Domingo. The student demonstration was quickly brought under control, but the state of emergency lasted for over three-and-a-half years.

The Supreme Court declared the constitutionality of almost all state of siege decrees, even when the measures had nothing to do with the crises, or restricted very severely constitutional liberties and 'due process' guarantees. For instance, the Supreme Court accepted that courts martial could try and punish civilians accused of political crimes. A snapshot review of some of the limitations of fundamental rights upheld by the Supreme Court shows the leniency of judicial control during this period. For instance, Decree 2686 of 1966 established police surveillance on those suspect of subversive activities, authorized censorship on writings that were considered an apology for crime, and imposed a five-year prison term on those who supported subversive activities. Decree 1129 of 1970 banned any meeting of more than three persons. Decree 70 of 1978 authorized, according to its critics, some kind of a secret death penalty because it excluded from criminal investigation any crime committed by the police or the army in operations developed against kidnapping, extortion or drug trafficking. Finally, Decree 1923 of 1978, known as the Security Statute, was more or less a copy of similar legislation adopted by Argentina, Brazil and Chile during their military dictatorships.

During the second period from the beginning of the 1980s until the enactment of the 1991 Constitution, judicial review by the Supreme Court became marginally more stringent. This tribunal maintained the doctrine that the declaration of a state of siege was subject only to formal control, but was stricter on the judicial scrutiny of the concrete measures taken by the government during the state of emergency. For instance, the Supreme Court declared void numerous decrees because they did not have any link with the facts presented by the government as the cause of disturbances to public order.[21] More importantly, the Supreme Court overruled some of its precedents in order to give a stronger protection to due process. In this context, perhaps the most important decision was that of March 1987, which declared unconstitutional the possibility that civilians were tried and convicted by courts martial. This was a significant change in that the use of military justice to investigate civilians had been one of the key elements of the previous state of siege practice.

In the third period, beginning with the enactment of the 1991 Constitution and up to the present, judicial control on emergency measures has become stronger, because the constitution not only now recognizes new fundamental rights but also poses stricter regulations on the use of emergency powers. In this context, the new Constitutional Court has been more strict in its judgments on government measures taken during any state of emergency. According to García Villegas, only nine per cent of state of siege decrees were declared void by the Supreme Court between 1984 and 1991, whereas 34 per cent of Internal Commotion Decrees were nullified by the Constitutional Court between 1992 and 1996.[22] The most dramatic change was perhaps the new legal doctrine regarding the control of the declaration of a state of emergency. After issuing its first opinion on that subject (Judgement C-004/92),[23] the Constitutional Court decided that from now on this presidential act would be subject not only to 'formal' control but also to 'material' or 'substantial' control, meaning that it was the duty of the court to analyze if the crisis was severe enough to justify the declaration of a state of emergency.

The next section concentrates on the efforts of the Constitutional Court to exercise a 'material' control of the declaration of a state of emergency, which is the most controversial and arguably the most interesting aspect of Colombian judicial review.

Efforts of the Constitutional Court to Exercise 'Material' Control of the Declaration of a State of Emergency

The doctrine of material control entered Colombian constitutional practice quite smoothly. The reason was perhaps that the court strongly emphasized this new legal doctrine the first time it had to analyze a declaration of a state of emergency. However, the tribunal did not seem to apply this judicial standard in the first few cases related to a declaration of a state of emergency.

Judgement C-004/1992 was the first time the court controlled a declaration of a state of emergency. It was a state of *social* emergency, something the framers of the constitution had devised to meet very serious economic crises or natural catastrophes. The reasons invoked by the government were general social unrest and a threat of strike by some police officers because of low wages. The government argued that emergency powers were necessary to urgently increase the wages of police officers and other state servants in order to avoid a possible strike. In this Judgement C-004/92, the court vigorously defended a quite strict material control of a state of emergency declaration. It stated that in these situations, the president (1) had to prove the facts on which he relied, and (2) that he had very little discretion to evaluate if these facts really constituted a crisis serious enough to justify the assumption of emergency powers. The court further stated that, (3) according to the subsidiarity principle, the president had to show that ordinary instruments of government were insufficient to face the crisis. The court concluded that if (1) either the facts were not proven, or (2) the presidential evaluation about the gravity of the crisis was wrong, or (3) the government had legal instruments to face the crisis, then the declaration of the state of emergency would be void. In short, the court in this opinion established a rigorous standard of review. However, it was quite lenient in its application to the particular case because, as a dissident justice underlined, it was not at all clear that there was a danger of a serious strike. It was less clear that had such a strike gathered pace there would have been grave consequences. Finally, it was not at all clear that the government was deprived of ordinary legal instruments to deal with the situation.

An examination of the first four declarations of states of emergency, summarized in Table 1, shows that the approach and style of Judgement C-004/92 were not unique. In a certain sense Judgements C-556/92 and C-031/93 were in keeping: they dealt with the first two declarations of Internal Commotion, and in its opinions the court established somewhat stringent judicial standards, but did not apply them to the cases under review.[24] So, as Ariza and Bareto had stressed, in the first two years, the new 'material' control was, in a certain sense, just 'rhetorical', in that the court talked about a rigorous theoretical standard, but did not apply it strictly to the situations under judicial scrutiny.[25]

In consequence, during this rhetorical phase, the doctrine of material control did not exert a real and direct control over abuses of presidential emergency powers. Nevertheless, it had two positive effects. First, the doctrine of material control was more or less accepted within the court and even by the government. For example, in these four decisions, there was not a single dissident opinion on the doctrine of material control. Second, the acceptance of the new doctrine had some influence on the subsequent declarations in the following years. On the next occasions, the government felt compelled to better justify a new declaration of a state of emergency, by

TABLE 1
DECLARATIONS OF STATES OF EMERGENCY IN COLOMBIA AFTER THE 1991 CONSTITUTION

Date and Decree	Nature	Facts invoked by the government	Court's decision
Decree 333 of 24 Feb 1992	Social Emergency	Social unrest and threat of strike by the police	C-04/92. Upheld
Decree 680 of 26 April 1992	Social Emergency	National electricity crises due to a severe drought	C-447/92 Upheld
Decree 115 of 10 July 1992	Internal Commotion	Threat of an immediate release of dangerous prisoners	C-556/92 Upheld
Decree 1793 of 8 November 1992	Internal Commotion	Guerrilla attacks and threats, and general increase in violence	C-031/93 Upheld
Decree 874 of 1 may 1994	Internal Commotion	Threat of an immediate release of dangerous prisoners	C-300/94 Void
Decree 1178 of June 9 of 1994	Social Emergency	Earthquake and avalanches	C-366/94 Upheld
Decree 1370 of August 16 of 1995	Internal Commotion	General increase in violence and criminality and guerrilla attacks	C-466/95 Void
Decree 1900 of November 2 of 1995	Internal Commotion	Violence, terrorist acts and assassination of the political leader Gómez Hurtado	C-027/95 Void partially and upheld partially
Decree 80 of January 13 of 1997	Social Emergency	Crisis in payment balance, revaluation of the national currency and fall in central bank reserves	C-122/97 Void
Decree 2330 of Nov 16 of 1998	Social Emergency	Crisis in financial and banking system	C-122/99 Void partially and upheld partially
Decree 195 29 Jan of 1999	Social Emergency	Earthquake	C-216/99 Upheld
Decree 195 1 Aug of 2002	Internal Commotion	Terrorist attacks, generalized guerrilla threats against many mayors and very high violence	C-802 /02 Void partially and upheld partially

Source: Author's analysis of decrees and court's decisions.

explaining more exactly what were the facts that warranted calling the situation a crisis. A comparison of Decree 115 of 1992 and Decree 874 of 1994 is instructive on this point because they dealt with a similar problem, namely, the threat of an immediate release of dangerous prisoners. But the content of the decrees was very different. The first was very poor in its justification, whereas the second tried to explain that this declaration was in conformity with the standards set by the court.

One obvious question arises: why was this doctrine of material control, which constituted a radical departure from the attitude of the Supreme Court in the past, so easily accepted, at least in those first years? A possible explanation is that these first steps of the court – very bold in the theory and doctrine, but quite timid and hesitant in the concrete decision – eventually provoked an ambiguous consensus. On the one hand, those who were very critical of state of siege abuses in the past might have seen the court's decisions as a step in the right direction. They might have begun to hope that in the future the court would apply its doctrine and strike down declarations of state of emergency. On the other hand, potential critics of this kind of judicial control might have believed that the court's interest remained rhetorical only. In that context, they might have thought that this could be useful even for the government, because this 'material' control increased the legitimacy of using presidential emergency powers, as long as it remained rhetorical.

This situation also shows the ambiguity of judicial control in general and specifically of judicial review of emergency measures. Judicial participation in these areas can always be an effective instrument of control or just a mechanism of legitimating de facto decisions. Accordingly, some scholars have been quite critical of Constitutional Court decisions in those years. Ariza and Barreto for instance argue that this rhetorical control has increased the prestige of the tribunal without really strengthening the control over emergency powers. In the end, this kind of judicial involvement reinforces emergency powers because the rhetoric of material control legitimates the declaration of a state of emergency without really limiting governmental powers, precisely because of the rhetorical nature of the judicial review.[26]

In the course of the next years, the tension between effective control and legitimation increased and the ambiguous consensus discussed above gradually dissolved, because the court decided to exercise a more rigorous and effective material control over emergency powers

In the next two years, the court struck down two declarations of Internal Commotion, one by President Gaviria (1990–1994) in 1994 and another by President Samper (1994–1998) in 1995 (see Table 1). It is important to underline that the reasons presented by the government to justify these declarations of Internal Commotion were similar to those adduced in the first two declarations in 1992, which had been upheld by the court. Decree 115 of 1992, upheld by Judgement C-556/92, talked about the perils of a massive release of dangerous prisoners. The same fact was invoked by Decree 874 of 1994, though Judgement C-300 of 1994 nullified this declaration. Similarly, Decree 1793 of 1992 justified the Internal Commotion because of guerrilla attacks and a general increase in violence. Judgement C-031/93 accepted these criteria. But similar reasons were rejected by Judgement C-466/95, which declared void decree 1370 of 1995. Some critics attacked the court because they saw this change as a serious inconsistency. But the court and its supporters justified the apparent change in two ways. First, the facts were not identical. Second, and more importantly, they argued that 1992 was still a transitional year (the new constitution being enacted in 1991), and this should be taken into account in the analysis of emergency powers.

These two decisions of 1994 and 1995 that struck down the declarations of Internal Commotion were accepted by the government but severely criticized by both presidents. Then the real discussion over the legitimacy of this material control began. The court received strong support from trade unions, human rights organizations, several leaders of new political movements, and some scholars, who defended this kind of material control as a necessary instrument to really control emergency power abuses in Colombia. But the court was also fiercely attacked by government officials, the business elite, many leaders of the traditional political parties, and some scholars. They argued that this judicial involvement was a form of judicial dictatorship, which made it impossible for the government to control public order. These divisions could be found even inside the court itself. For Judgement C-300/94 had been adopted by a 6–3 vote, and three justices explicitly rejected the material control doctrine. In Judgement C-466/95, four justices abandoned this doctrine.

The reactions against the court were not only theoretical. First, President Samper tried to put pressure on the court. Judgement C-466/95 struck down Decree 1370 of 1995, which declared the Internal Commotion, adopted on 18 October 1995. Less than two weeks later, after the assassination of Alvaro Gómez, a former presidential candidate and a well known member of the political elite, the government declared once more a state of Internal Commotion, for very similar reasons to the ones invoked in Decree 1370 of 1995. The challenge to the court was hard to resist, Gómez's assassination being strongly condemned by almost all the political forces. Everyone felt that if the court did not accept this new declaration, a constitutional reform would be proposed very quickly to make it impossible for the court to exercise this kind of material control ever again. But, if the court decided to uphold this new declaration, it would be strongly criticized for being inconsistent and for not being capable of resisting political pressures. In this complex situation, the court took a middle way. Judgement C-027 of 1996 established that this new declaration of Internal Commotion was partly void and partly constitutional. The court said that the facts adduced in decree 1370 of 1995 and reproduced in this new declaration of Internal Commotion were not sufficient to justify a state of emergency. In this aspect, the court maintained some coherence with its previous decision. Nevertheless, the court accepted that Gómez' assassination, coupled with threats to murder other political leaders, were facts serious enough to validate the use of emergency powers.

The other attack on the Court was even more direct. Several political leaders, together with President Samper, proposed an amendment to the constitution in order to eliminate the power of material control, but for a number of reasons too complex to describe here the amendment was not adopted.[27]

As Table 1 illustrates, the court has continued to exercise this kind of material control. Its decisions appear to have made a major impact. For example, in spite of a very difficult public order situation, Colombia's President Pastrana (1998–2002) decided not to declare an Internal Commotion state. Nevertheless, controversy over the judicial intervention of the court still rages. Thus, for instance, President Uribe (2002–06) has not only declared a state of emergency but also has proposed amending the constitution. One of his proposals is the suppression of the material control developed by the court. At the same time, the court, after a change of several of its justices, is strongly unified in defending its power of material control. Thus in Judgement C-802 of 2002 it upheld Uribe's declaration of Internal Commotion, with all nine justices agreeing on the doctrine of material control, even though they acquiesced in a less stringent standard of review.

Evaluating and Interpreting the Constitutional Court's Efforts

This section tries to explain what factors made material control possible and evaluates the real impact of the Constitutional Court's decisions.

How was Material Control Possible?

Bearing in mind that some comparative studies on judicial institutions underline that the courts and the law tend to be conservative and to reflect and protect the dominant interests, what elements could explain the Constitutional Court's efforts to control governmental abuses? This development seems more difficult to understand in a country like Colombia, enduring years of violent conflict and with a precarious democracy.

To answer this question, it is important to note that this 'material' control of emergency powers is not an isolated doctrine of the Constitutional Court but is part of a more general trend of this institution, which has developed a progressive activism in several fields. The court has been vigorous not only in its attempts to control emergency powers abuses but also in its intention to protect the rights of individuals and disadvantaged groups. The court's efforts have been wide ranging, not just in respect of the sheer number of rulings and the variety of subjects that it has addressed,[28] but also because it has, to a certain degree, taken Colombian society by surprise with its progressive orientation. So, the question about the control of emergency powers can be situated within a larger inquiry: what has made this progressive activism of the Constitutional Court possible? While there are no simple answers, some legal, institutional and transitional elements might help explain this evolution.[29]

The Constitutional Court was created under the new constitution approved in 1991. However, Colombia already had a long tradition of judicial control over constitutionality. Going back to at least 1910, the Supreme Court of Justice was granted binding authority to rule on a law's constitutionality. In consequence, when the Constitutional Court began operating in 1992 the Colombian legal and political culture was already very familiar with judicial review, to the point that few in the Colombian judicial community thought it strange that the court had the power to annul governmental decrees or laws approved by Congress. The court could therefore act vigorously, without fear that the executive branch or the political forces would decide to shut it down, as has happened in other countries where the first task of a constitutional court has been to secure legitimacy for its role.

Second, the procedural design has helped this active intervention, because the Court automatically had to respond to any emergency measure adopted by the government. Besides, in the other fields, access to constitutional justice is very easy and not too costly. For instance, the 1991 Constitution created the *tutela*, by virtue of which any person may, without any special requisites, directly request that a judge intervene to protect his or her fundamental rights. It is relatively easy for citizens to transform a complaint into a legal issue that the constitutional justice system must decide upon and within quite a short period of time. And, as has been demonstrated in comparative legal studies, with greater access to the courts comes greater political influence for the courts.[30]

Third, the procedural design of constitutional justice also confers enormous legal power on the court. In practice, thanks to its ability to annul, for constitutional reasons, other judges' decisions, the Constitutional Court has gained prominence as a super-court that lords over the other high courts. This fact also facilitates the court's activism in that comparative sociology demonstrates that there tends to be more judicial activism in countries where most of the authority is concentrated in a single supreme court, such as in the United States. There is a marked contrast with other countries like France where this power is distributed among different courts and jurisdictions.[31]

Fourth, the Constitutional Assembly of 1991 and the president at that time saw the Constitutional Court as one of the most important institutions of the new constitutional order. It was given considerable financial and technical support to develop its activities.

Beyond these legal and institutional elements, two political factors have stimulated the court's activism: the crisis in representation, and the weakness of Colombia's social movements and opposition parties.

Colombian's disenchantment with politics has led certain social sectors to demand answers from the judicial branch to problems that, in principle, should be debated and resolved by means of the people's participation in the political sphere. This phenomenon is not exclusive to Colombia.[32] But, in the case of Colombia, the weakness of the mechanisms for political representation runs deep, for which reason there is greater temptation to substitute judicial for political action. On many occasions, what has taken place is not that the court has taken on other powers, but rather that it has stepped in to fill the vacuum that others have left. This intervention appears legitimate to broad sectors of society who may feel there is at least one institution that acts progressively and with some ability.

Besides, Colombia has a historical tradition of weak social movements, compared to other Latin American countries. Not only are these movements not strong, in recent years, violence has considerably raised the personal risks and costs of their taking high profile action. Many leaders and activists have been murdered. These two factors – historical weakness and growing risks – tend to strengthen the judicial role, especially that of the court. Hence it is natural that many social groups are tempted to make use of legal arguments rather than recurring to social and political mobilization, given that access to constitutional justice is cheap and easy and constitutional judges tend to adopt progressive positions,

All of the above may explain the court's activism but an obvious question remains: why did this court take on a progressive role, when it could have engaged in activism of a non-progressive kind? The events of the constitutional and political transition shed light on this matter.

As we have seen, the 1991 Constitution is a forward looking document that tries to overcome some of the problems of the past. This explains the strict regulation of the emergency powers in this constitution, which also is generous in the protection of human rights. The court's active intervention in developing the progressive components of this constitution would not have been necessary if the political forces themselves had taken on this task. However, many of the social and political actors that dominated the 1991 Constituent Assembly were considerably and rapidly weakened in the following years. The forces that have come to dominate Congress and the electoral scene since 1992 have not shown much commitment to furthering the constitution's aims even though they are not obviously hostile to the 1991 Constitution. Over the years, the court has therefore, gradually, come to present itself as the one body that implements the freedoms and social justice values set out in the constitution. This affords it with significant degree of legitimacy, among certain social sectors including some that are very critical of other state institutions.

To sum up, some of the first justices in the court decided to take advantage of the political context to promote the constitution's progressive content. They succeeded in doing so, at least at the legal level, though not without considerable effort and difficulty. During these early years, the personality of some of these justices played a very significant role in shaping the progressive orientation of the court. In this way, step by step, a sort of alliance has grown between the Constitutional Court – or at least some justices – and certain social sectors in order to defend and develop the progressive values enshrined in the 1991 Constitution.[33] Later on, this progressive orientation became not only something like a hallmark for the court but also one of its main sources of legitimacy and support. A social understanding developed that the court's mission in the political system is to protect and expand the progressive content of the constitution. This institutionalist idea of the role of the court has been so noticeable – even for the justices themselves – that while in 2001 seven of the nine justices were replaced, because their eight year period was completed, the general orientation of the court's remained the same.[34]

Of course, this progressive orientation provoked strong opposition from other sectors. In particular, businessmen's groups and the government attack the court's jurisprudence, calling it populist and ingenuous, and arguing that Colombia is slipping into a sort of judge's government in which the court could become a sort of super-legislature. These actors have not limited themselves to reproaches, they have also, so far unsuccessfully, attempted to pass numerous reforms to eliminate the court or at least seriously to curtail its power. The court has been on the knife's edge; on some occasions, the government, some sectors of Congress and representatives of the business elite have tried to bring about constitutional reforms to limit the court's power while the representatives and leaders of popular social movements have showered it with praise and support.

However, it is quite conceivable that things could have been different. Arguably, some purely causal and timely incidents had a decisive influence on the developments so far. In accordance with chaos theory, a slight variation in certain decisions could have had enormous consequences for the unfolding of constitutional jurisprudence in Colombia. For example, some of the progressive decisions were taken by a narrow five to four margin. In 1992, the Senate elected some judges considered to be progressive only by the narrowest of margins over more conservative rivals.[35] Had only one of these progressive judges not been elected, it is very likely that some of the court's jurisprudence would never have come into existence. Also, at times various attempts to suppress the court's powers seemed on the verge of succeeding. To date the court has managed to keep to its progressive activism and held on to the power of material control, but the future prospects do not look too favourable. Unlike previous governments, which were weak in terms of legitimacy and popular support and so were ill-positioned to confront openly a well-accepted court, the present government is in a stronger position. For the time being, President Uribe is quite popular and public opinion favours harsh measures to stop the violence and challenge the guerrillas. It remains to be seen whether this will translate into political support sufficient to carry the President's proposal to amend the constitution to suppress the judiciary's material control over the declaration of a state of emergency.

The court's active intervention in the control of governmental emergency powers can be summarized as follows: the design of the Constitutional Court and the legal culture have made the activism by the court institutionally possible. The representation crisis and the weakness of the social movements are conducive to the use of legal mechanisms, by certain social actors. The 1991 Constitution also stimulates a progressive vision by the court, which because of the vacuum left by the weakening of the constituent forces tends to see itself as the one body left implementing values enshrined in the constitution. The court's progressivism is made possible, in turn, by the relative weakness until now of the forces that oppose it and the failure of the attempts at constitutional counter-reform.

Possible Effects of Material Control

The most important point in evaluating the influence of the Constitutional Court's decisions is to see if they have made a real difference to the length of time the country has been under an emergency regime – whether a total state of siege or a state of Internal Commotion, the two kinds of regime that have generated the most serious abuses and threats to civil liberties and the rule of law. Tables 2 and 3 illustrate there has been a substantial change. According to Table 2, in the 1970s and 1980s Colombians literally lived under a permanent emergency regime. This situation changed dramatically. Thus, whereas President Barco's government was a total state of siege regime throughout, there was no declaration of an Internal Commotion state during President Pastrana's government. The findings are summarised in Table 3, which presents the time spent under an emergency regime in the different decades. They show that the time Colombians lived under an emergency regime fell from 80 per cent in the 1980 to less than 20 per cent in the 1990s.

One conclusion seems clear. The material control of the declaration of a state of emergency has been instrumental in reducing constitutional

TABLE 2
STATES OF EMERGENCY DURING DIFFERENT PRESIDENTIAL PERIODS: TIME IN TOTAL STATES OF SIEGE OR INTERNAL COMMOTION

	President	Number of months in emergency	Percentage of the period in emergency
1	Lleras Camargo 1958–62	4	8.3
2	Valencia 1962-66	14.5	30.2
3	Lleras Restrepo 1966–70	30	62.5
4	Pastrana Misael 1970–74	39	81.3
5	Lopez 1974-78	34	70.8
6	Turbay 1978–82	47	97.9
7	Betancur 1982–86	27	56
9	Gaviria I-1990–91	11	100
10	Gaviria II 1991–94	14.6	39.5
11	Samper 1994–98	9	18.8
12	Pastrana Andrés 1998–2002	0	0

Note: Gaviria's Presidential period is divided in two, because of 1991 Constitution

Source: Based on an analysis of the decrees that declared states of emergency.

TABLE 3
STATES OF EMERGENCY DURING DIFFERENT DECADES

Decades	Number of months in emergency	Percentage of the decade in emergency
1958–1970	48.5	33.7
1970–1991	206.0	82.1
1991–2002	23.6	17.5

Source: Based on author's analysis of the decrees that declared states of emergency.

'anormality' in Colombia. This is important because the abuse of emergency powers has distorted Colombian democracy. However, this positive point has to be balanced against some negative impacts of this judicial intervention.

First, these decisions have implied high costs for the court itself. Several attempts to curtail court powers, or even suppress the institution, have been made. Second, some scholars, who are sympathetic to court efforts to make the government accountable have nevertheless strongly criticized the court's opinions on this matter. They say the court has not been able to develop a consistent doctrine or a clear judicial standard to exercise the material control on a declaration of a state of emergency.[36] The result is that it is not easy to predict on the basis of just legal arguments the results of the judicial review in this field. Can such doctrinal inconsistency be corrected, or is it a shortcoming that inevitably follows from the nature of the judicial review on emergency regimes?

Third, this intervention of the Constitutional Court is an expression of what might be called 'dramatic justice', that is, the intervention of the judicial system in events that transfix the media. Sometimes, a form of dramatic justice can be positive for the consolidation of democracy because of its symbolic effect. But the risk of dramatic justice is that it can hide the problems of the everyday or 'routine' justice, which can be more important for the lives of the citizens. In Colombia, the great political salience and visibility of the Constitutional Court contrasts sharply with the inability of the routine justice system to respond to the demands arising from social conflicts.[37] If the judicial system as a whole does not raise its performance and become actually accessible to most citizens, then the highly visible interventions of the Constitutional Court will prove insufficient for the effective protection of rights in Colombia.

Last but not least, during this decade of material control, the public order situation has worsened in Colombia and armed conflict has increased. Even if it is very difficult to establish a clear link between material control and the worsening of public order, some critics argue that Constitutional Court involvement in this field is in part responsible for the aggravation of the Colombian crises.

Some Provisional Conclusions

Empirically speaking, Colombia's experience offers an interesting case because the country's political evolution, including the role of the judiciary, has been so complex. More important, in normative terms, the case could teach some lessons about the possibilities, risks and limits of judicial review as an instrument to avoid the abuse of emergency powers in a democracy. First, it shows that some kind of judicial review is possible and can have real impact on the control of the government. It also shows that several particular and difficult conditions must be resolved for this kind of control to become possible. And finally, the Colombian case makes evident that judicial intervention in this field can involve high risks. The question that remains open is, if we take into account all the costs, is it still worth trying to establish some judicial control over emergency powers? The writer's answer, based on the Colombian experience, is yes, but at the same time he urges more comparative analysis in order to gain a better understanding of how to reduce the risks.

NOTES

1. On the history of the abuse of emergency powers in Colombia see Libardo Jose Ariza, Felipe Cammaert and Manuel Alejandro Iturralde, *Estados de Excepción y Razón de Estado en Colombia* (Bogotá: Universidad de los Andes; 1997); Antonio Barreto, *The Dynamics of Emergency Powers Within Constitutional Systems: The State and the Civil Society of Colombia – Besieged Between Violence and Emergency Powers* (unpublished JSD dissertation proposal, Yale University, 2002); Gustavo Gallón, *Quince Años de Estado de Sitio en Colombia 1958-1978* (Bogotá: Librería y Editorial América Latina, 1979); Mauricio García Villegas, 'Constitucionalismo perverso, normalidad y anormalidad constitucional en Colombia: 1957-1997', in Boaventura de Sousa Santos and Mauricio Garcia Villegas (eds), *El caleidoscopio de la justicia colombiana* (Bogotá: Uniandes, UN, Siglo del Hombre, 2001).
2. For some classical approaches to the concept of constitutional dictatorship, see Carl Friedrich, *Teoría y realidad de la organización constitucional democrática* (México: Fondo de Cultura Democrática, 1946), p.246 and Clinton Rossiter, *Constitutional Dictatorship. Crisis Government in the Modern Democracies* (New York: Habringer Edition, 1963), p.7. The essence of this institution is that it is a mechanism of concentration of power and restriction of liberties (and in that sense it is a dictatorship), but with the goal of defending the constitutional order and not of destroying it (in that sense it is still a constitutional regime).
3. This stance has been adopted by some Latin-American scholars and human rights activists due to the extensive abuse of emergency powers in the region. For instance, in a workshop in Montevideo in 1986, many participants expressed support for 'promoting a legal and political consensus to exclude from constitutional texts any norm that authorizes any kind of emergency powers'. See Coloquio de Montevideo, 'Declaración final' in Diego García Sayán, *Estado de emergencia en la región andina* (Lima: Comisión Andina de Juristas, 1987), p.58.
4. See for instance Article 4 of the International Covenant on Civil and Political Rights and Article 27 of the Interamerican Convention on Human Rights. See also the General Comment 5 adopted by the Human Rights Committees and the so-called 'Syracusa Principles', on the Limitation and Derogation Provisions in the International Covenant on Civil and Political Rights (E/CN.4/1985/Annex 4).
5. For a presentation of the different theses concerning judicial review in times of constitutional crises, see Barreto (note 1) pt II.
6. Robert Burt, 'Judicial Supremacy, Judicial Impotence and the Rule of Law in Times of Crisis', in <http://www.yale.edu/lawweb/lawfac/fiss/eburt.pdf>, VI-39.
7. Malcom Deas, 'Algunas notas sobre la historia del caciquismo en Colombia', *Revista de Occidente,* No.127 (1973), p.29.
8. See Alain Tourraine, *Les sociétés Dépendantes* (Paris: Duculot, 1976), p.85.
9. See Luis Jorge Garay, *Colombia, entre la exclusión y el* desarrollo (Bogotá: Contraloría General de la República, 2002), p.28.
10. Comisión Colombiana de Juristas, *Panorama de derechos humanos y derecho humanitario en Colombia* (Bogotá: Comisión Colombiana de Juristas, 2000), p.9.
11. See Ann Mason, 'La crisis de seguridad en Colombia: causas y consecuencias de un Estado en vía de fracaso', *Colombia Internacional*, No.49–50 (2001).
12. For a good analysis of these different approaches to the Colombian crises and their implications, see Ana María Bejarano and Eduardo Pizarro, 'De la "democracia restringida" a la "democracia asediada": Para entender la crisis colombiana', paper submitted to the Workshop 'Advances and Set-backs in the Third Wave of Democratization in Latin America', Notre Dame University, Illinois, USA, 2001.
13. See Gallón (note 1); Rodrigo Uprimny, '¿De la constitución inacabada a la constitución de excepción? El debate sobre la ley estatutaria de los estados de excepción', *Revista del Colegio de Abogados Penalistas del Valle*, No.31–32 (1999), p.25; and García Villegas (note 1) p.334.
14. See Gallón (note 1) p.139.

15. See ibid. pp.121–7; and García Villegas (note 1) p.359.
16. The AD-M19 was a political group that grew out of the peace process with the M-19 guerrilla group. The UP (Patriotic Union) was a left-leaning group that was severely targeted by paramilitary violence.
17. For information on the Constituent Assembly, see Jaime Buenahora, *El proceso constituyente* (Bogotá: Tercer Mundo, 1992).
18. See Ruti Teitel, 'Transitional Jurisprudence, The Role of Law in Political Transformation', *Yale Law Journal*, Vol.106, No.7 (1997), p.2014.
19. According to the 1991 Constitution, extraordinary powers are called 'states of exception' (*estados de excepción*) and are of three different types: (1) the 'external war state', in case of an international armed conflict; (2) the 'internal commotion state' in case of very serious perturbations of internal public order; and (3) the 'social and economical emergency state', in case of a very serious economical crises or a natural catastrophe. The term 'state of emergency' rather than a 'state of exception' is used in this account owing to its greater familiarity in the English language.
20. See Gallón (note 1); García Villegas (note 1); Ariza, Cammaert and Iturralde (note 1); Baretto (note 1).
21. According to García Villegas (note 1) p.336, 10 out of 237 decrees were declared unconstitutional because of the absence of a 'link' (*conexidad*) with the public order disturbance.
22. See García Villegas (note 1) p.370. The figures alone do not give a clear meaning because the orientation of the decisions in judicial review depends not only on the severity of the judicial control but also on the nature of the measures taken by the government. But it is nevertheless realistic to assume that the government during both periods took very similar and harsh measures. If that is correct, the quantitative data is a valid indicator to express differences in the strictness of judicial control.
23. Constitutional Court decisions are identified by a number that corresponds to the sequential order in a given year; and a second number that identifies the year itself. Thus, sentence C-004/92 is the fourth sentence that the court issued in 1992.
24. On the other hand, almost all commentators agree that the second social emergency was justified, because Colombia faced a very serious electricity crises throughout the country.
25. Libardo Ariza and Antonio Barretto, 'La Corte Constitutional frente a la excepcionalidad: diez años de control material laxo y discursivo', in *Observatorio de Justicia Constitucional. Derecho Constitucional. Perspectivas críticas,* No.2, (Bogotá: Universidad de los Andes, 2001), p.163.
26. Ibid., p.158.
27. On the preliminary attempts to restrict the powers of the court, see Juan Gabriel Gómez, 'Fueros y desafueros. justicia y contrarreforma en Colombia', *Análisis Político*, No.25 (1995).
28. For a general overview of the Court's work, see Manuel José Cepeda, 'Democracy, State and Society in the 1991 Constitution: The Role of the Constitutional Court', in Eduardo Posada Carbó (ed.), *Colombia: The Politics of Reforming the State* (London: Institute of Latin American Studies, University of London, 1998), p.91. According to Cepeda, 'almost all key issues of modern constitutional law have been dealt with by the court'. For an analysis of the progressive potential of the rulings of the Court, see Rodrigo Uprimny and Mauricio Garcia Villegas, 'Tribunal Constitucional e emancipaçã social na Colombia', in Boavertura de Sous Santos (ed.), *Democratizar a democracia. Os caminhos da democracia participativa* (Rio de Janeiro: Editora Cvilizacao Brasileira, 2002), pp.298–339 (available in English at <http://www.ces.fe.uc.pt/emancipa/research/en/texts.html>.
29. This point relies extensively on Uprimny and García Villegas (note 28)
30. See Herbert Jacob et al., *Courts, Law and Politics in Comparative Perspective* (New Haven, CT: Yale University Press, 1996), p.396.
31. See ibid., p.389.
32. See Santos and García Villegas (note 1) p.1996.
33. See Cepeda (note 28) p.76.
34. On the influence that the perceived mission of an institution has on the behaviour of its

members, see Howard Gillman, 'The Court as an Idea, not a Building (or a Game): Interpretive Institutionalism and the Analysis of Court Decision-Making', in Cornell W. Clayton and Howard Gillman (eds), *Supreme Court Decision-Making. New Institutionalist Approaches* (Chicago, IL: University of Chicago Press, 2001), p.83.

35. Nine justices form the Court and they are selected by the Senate, for a period of eight years, from lists of three candidates made by the president, the Council of State and the Supreme Court.
36. See García Villegas (note 1) p.358, Ariza and Barreto (note 25) p.171.
37. The distinction between dramatic and routine justice was proposed by Santos and García Villegas (note 1). It has been used also to study the Colombian judicial system. See César Rodríguez, Mauricio Garcia Villegas and Rodrigo Uprimny 'Justice and Society in Colombia: A Sociolegal Analysis of Colombian Courts', in Lawrence Friedman and Rogelio Perez-Perdomo (eds), *Legal Culture in the Age of Globalization: Latin Europe and Latin America* (Stanford, CA: Stanford University Press, forthcoming).

The Politics of Judicial Review in Chile in the Era of Democratic Transition, 1990–2002

JAVIER A. COUSO

In the last few decades, judicial control of the constitutionality of laws has come to be seen as an essential element of the rule of law and as a valuable instrument for democratic transition and consolidation. Without it, we are told, individual rights guaranteed by constitutional charters – a cornerstone of democracy – are worth less than the paper they are written on, because there would be no enforcement against abuses that even democratically elected governments often inflict on minorities and individuals. Accordingly, it has become natural to expect democratic regimes – old and new – to adopt constitutional courts or to give their regular judicial branches the power of controlling the constitutionality of laws and executive action. This trend has reached a global scope, with constitutional review introduced in states as different as Mongolia, Portugal and Chile.

Once such constitutional courts are in place, the question arises: What are their political consequences? Do they actually serve their purpose? Particularly in the case of emerging democracies: Do constitutional courts successfully enforce constitutional guarantees against government and legislative encroachment, thus contributing to democratic consolidation? If so, under what conditions?

This inquiry addresses these questions through an analysis of the politics of judicial review in Chile. The Chilean case is particularly relevant to the question of the development of constitutional review in non-consolidated democracies because, among comparable nations, Chile has achieved a relatively high degree of legality (or adherence to the rule of law), a context which is thought to constitute a propitious ground for the development of a sustainable practice of judicial review. Indeed, as recent comparative studies on the matter have demonstrated, Chile has one of the most solid rule-of-law regimes in the region, which expresses itself in levels of corruption comparable to that of Organisation for Economic Co-operation and Development countries, and a respect for legality that is legendary among Latin Americans.[1]

The Global Shift Towards Judicial Review and its Impact in Latin America

The power given to courts to enforce the constitutionality of legislation and administrative acts, including the ability to declare them void when they are deemed to violate the constitution, constitutes one of the most significant developments in the political structure of constitutional democracies in recent years. This trend, which in recent years reached global scope, is for this reason often referred to by specialists as the 'global expansion of judicial review'.[2]

The acceptance of judicial review has in fact become so widespread that scholars and the general public have begun to expect democratic regimes to include some form of constitutional judicial review. This is apparent in current scholarly rhetoric explicitly linking judicial review with the very idea of constitutionalism. One such case is Cass Sunstein's strong advocacy for judicial review in new democracies. He argues that:

> Constitutionalism is about the individual's right to challenge governmental acts in independent courts of law ... Without judicial review, constitutions tend to be worth little more than the paper on which they are written. They become mere words, or public relations documents, rather than instruments that confer genuine rights.[3]

Perhaps as a consequence of the growing acceptance of judicial review among advanced industrialised democracies, developing nations have also adopted constitutional courts or given review powers to their regular courts. Indeed, during the so-called 'third wave of democracy', which brought democratic rule to scores of nations across the world, there has been a similarly striking 'wave of judicial review' following democratic transitions in Asia, Latin America, and Eastern Europe.[4]

The linking of democratic transition and consolidation with judicial review is exemplified by a recent book on democracy and the judiciary in Latin America, in which the author starts his project stating that:

> Any effort to understand democratic consolidation in Latin America must pay particular attention to the process of institution building, particularly those institutions that sustain accountable government and nurture a strong democratic culture among the public and political elite. The role of the judicial branch in this regard is critical. At the most basic level, a strong judiciary is essential for checking potential executive and legislative breaches of the constitutional order, laying the foundations for sustainable economic development, and building popular support for the democratic regime.[5]

The importance of judicial review has also been acknowledged by economists, who have emphasised the role that secure property rights play in encouraging economic growth.[6] Cast in the language of enforcement of property rights against expropriation and over-taxation, scholars have developed sophisticated models explaining the contribution of constitutional constraints and judicial review in creating 'credible state commitments'.[7] This consensus among economists on the contribution of law and constitutionalism – protected by a strong, efficient, and independent judiciary – to economic growth, have also contributed to the academic acceptance of judicial review in Latin America.[8]

Finally, it is worth noting that judicial review has also been embraced by a globalized network of non-governmental institutions interested in the promotion of human rights and economic justice, which also expect their agendas to be furthered by activist courts.[9]

Whatever the reasons behind the current acceptance of judicial review as a normal feature of democratic states, the fact is that by the early 1990s most Latin American countries had adopted judicial review. One such case was Chile, the subject of the analysis here.

Chile's Mixed System of Judicial Review

The history of judicial review in Chile is relatively new, effectively dating from 1980. The new charter incorporated a complex system of judicial review of both legislation and administrative acts. This represented a significant change in the country's legal tradition, which had lacked a meaningful system of judicial review of the constitutionality of laws.

Although judicial review was introduced during the military regime, it was maintained afterwards, along with the rest of the constitution of 1980, because the opposition to President Pinochet's rule was forced to accept the charter as a condition of its entrance into government. A consequence of this political context was the weak legitimacy enjoyed by judicial review at the beginning of the democratic transition (a prominent Chilean political scientist actually included the new scheme of judicial review powers introduced by the 1980 Constitution within the 'authoritarian enclaves' inherited from the military regime).[10] Eventually, however, both politicians and the people at large came to accept the legitimacy of judicial review, partly due to the courts' behaviour during the transition era.

Chile's system of judicial review is peculiar. It consists of a number of mechanisms spread among different constitutional bodies, representing what Chilean legal scholars call a 'mixed' or 'disseminated' system of control of the constitutionality of laws and administrative acts.[11] The system is thus characterised by a division of labour between a Constitutional Court (*Tribunal Constitucional*) in charge of the 'preventive' control of the constitutionality of laws and executive decrees; the superior courts of the regular judiciary (the *Cortes de Apelaciones* and *Corte Suprema*), with jurisdiction over a newly devised constitutional injunction, the writ of protection (*recurso de protección*); a rarely used writ of non-applicability of laws (*recurso de inaplicabilidad*); and a special body endowed with the power to exercise control of the constitutionality of administrative acts (*Contraloría General de la República*).

According to this scheme, the Constitutional Court performs an 'abstract' (or *a priori*) review of the constitutionality of legislation, that is, the review of bills approved by Congress but not yet promulgated, while the regular judiciary performs the 'concrete' (or '*a posteriori*') review of already existing laws and executive decrees violating individual rights through the writs of protection and non-applicability.

Constitutional Court

According to the regulation provided for in the constitutional charter itself and the law regulating the Constitutional Court,[12] bills on subject-matters declared to be 'organic' or 'interpretative' of the constitution are automatically sent to it for review. In the case of ordinary legislation and executive decrees, the Constitutional Court can only be required to act if either the president, a portion of the Chamber of Deputies, or a portion of the Senate challenges their constitutionality. A declaration of unconstitutionality is final and effectively kills the bill in question.

The Constitutional Court has seven members. They are appointed by a complex method involving the executive, legislative and judicial powers. Its justices serve for a tenure of eight years and can be re-appointed. A quorum of five members is required to hear a case. In the years since the return of democratic rule to Chile, the Constitutional Court has handled an average of 25 cases per year, having issued about 340 decisions until December 2001.[13]

Writ of Protection

The 1980 charter introduced a new judicial procedure for the protection of constitutional rights called 'writ of protection'. This writ allows individuals to seek relief from a court of appeals when their constitutional rights are violated or put in danger by an act or omission of a governmental authority or another individual.[14]

The swift nature of the procedure, the priority it has over other matters in the courts of appeals' dockets, and the simplicity of the requirements for filing a writ of protection, have all contributed to make this mechanism an exceptionally useful judicial tool in a system which is slow and inefficient in dealing with ordinary procedures. Chilean legal practitioners do everything possible to use the fast-track route provided by it, and it has become a popular legal remedy for all sorts of suits that have little to do with constitutional litigation, such as contracts and torts.

Writ of Non-applicability

The 1980 charter also maintained the decades-old 'writ of non-applicability', which allows parties to a lawsuit to petition the Supreme Court to declare 'non-applicable' a particular statute deemed to be unconstitutional. According to the relevant clause (Article 80 of the constitution), the Supreme Court can declare the non-applicability of existing legislation only after hearing and deciding the case *en banc*. The same constitutional clause also allows the court to declare the non-applicability of legislation by its own initiative. In the event that the Supreme Court declares a given law 'non-applicable', however, such resolution only applies to the particular case at hand, not to others. Thus, such declaration does not void the law in question.

Contraloría General de la República

The main function of this entity is to control the legality of administrative action, which it does by declaring illegal any decree or regulation issued by the government which exceeds the legal basis authorising the president or an administrative agency to regulate the details of legislation.[15] This role has had great significance in the country's legal system, due to the lack of administrative courts in Chile during most of the twentieth century. In addition to its role in the control of the legality of administrative action, the *Contraloría* was eventually entrusted – in the constitution of 1980 – with the task of controlling the constitutionality of decrees and regulations issued by the government. In the case of the latter, however, the *Contraloría* has shown a remarkable passivity, rarely objecting to executive acts for violating the constitution. The gap between objections based on constitutional grounds as opposed to legality grounds reflects the uneasiness of the *Contraloría* with its new constitutional prerogatives.

Having described the main features of Chile's disseminated system of judicial review, the following sections analyse the political context and actual performance of Chile's system of judicial review.

The Political Context of Judicial Review During Transitional Times: 1990–2002

After experiencing a 17-year-long military regime led by General Augusto Pinochet, Chile eventually started a process of transition to democracy after the opposition defeated Pinochet in the plebiscite of 1988. This was followed by the accession to power of Patricio Aylwin, a former opposition leader. In his four-year term (1990–1994), President Aylwin had to carefully navigate critical moments of Chile's transition to democracy, in particular those involving General Pinochet's showdowns, which repeatedly came in response to events he deemed hostile to himself or the military.

The Regular Judiciary

During the Aylwin years, the judicial branch became the focus of intense public criticism, both from the government and opposition, but for different reasons. In the case of the government, the core criticism was the passivity exhibited by the courts vis-à-vis the widespread human rights violations during the Pinochet years.[16] In the case of the pro-military opposition, criticism of the judiciary stemmed from what they regarded as inefficient and corrupt behaviour, which was considered utterly unsuited for the needs of a modern economy.[17]

The Supreme Court reacted to the criticism from the Truth and Reconciliation Commission by issuing a complete condemnation of its report, stating that it was 'passionate, reckless, and biased',[18] and arguing that the commission had violated the separation of powers by intruding in adjudicative matters. President Aylwin rebuffed the judicial response by going on national television to declare that in his view the Chilean courts 'had shown a lack of moral courage in face of the vast human rights violations perpetrated by the military regime'.[19] The Supreme Court in turn accused the government of undermining the judiciary's independence and endangering the rule of law. It defended its trajectory during the military regime by declaring that the mission of the courts was just to obey the existing law, and not judge the justice or injustice of it. In regard to its action under the authoritarian regime, that meant the courts limited themselves to applying laws that made it impossible for the courts to defend human rights.[20]

On the other hand, the general sense that the Chilean courts had become more corrupt eventually led to a series of constitutional impeachment procedures filed by Congress against justices of the Supreme Court throughout the decade. The first was actually promoted by a coalition of senators from both the government and the opposition in December 1992, and resulted in the removal of one justice. This constituted one of the most important blows suffered by the Supreme Court in decades. Not since 1868 had Congress impeached a member of the court, and it had never actually succeeded in removing one.[21]

In this context, it is not surprising that the superior courts – whose personnel were gradually changing through new appointment[22] – eventually reversed their interpretation of the 1978 Amnesty Law,[23] and started to accept that the courts should actually investigate the deeds and identify the perpetrators. Some socio-legal scholars have mistakenly accorded this remarkable change in the courts' jurisprudence to a more liberal ethos among the new justices of the Supreme Court. The writer submits, however, that this dramatic shift in the courts' jurisprudence should be interpreted not as a sign of more democratic or liberal judicial personnel, but as a sign of accommodation by Chile's courts to a new correlation of political forces and a new social context – one where the drama of the disappeared was recognized by Chilean society at large, including groups who still supported the economic policies of the military regime.

The same conclusion applies to the handling by the Chilean courts of Chile's most famous human rights case, that involved General Pinochet. Indeed, it was only after the arrest of the former dictator in London, in 1998, and the subsequent promise of the Chilean government that he would by tried at home if released, that the Chilean judiciary ended its passivity with regard to lawsuits filed against Pinochet. Prior to 1998 Pinochet had managed not only to be free from prosecution for past human rights violations, but had also become senator for life.

Some scholars have interpreted the shift in the Chilean courts' treatment of criminal charges against Pinochet as yet another example of an emerging independent and more democratic judicial branch. Such a conclusion is, again, unwarranted. Indeed, just the opposite tendency was at work, that is, a judicial branch attempting to accommodate itself in a constantly moving scenario, trying to be attuned to the government's changing policies.

The Constitutional Court

The situation is similar with regard to the other important actor in Chile's judicial review politics, the Constitutional Court. When asked to assess whether the Constitutional Court's exercise of its review powers has been a significant element in the political life of the nation, most current observers agree that its role has been modest.[24] Interviews by the author with the top political actors during the first decade of democratic rule (1990–2000), including two of the last three presidents, confirmed that the Constitutional Court only imposed marginal constraints upon executive power, and that constitutional politics is still in its infancy in Chile. Asked whether the

Constitutional Court had been an obstacle to the policies of his administration, President Patricio Aylwin replied:

> I was at first concerned about the role that the Constitutional Court could play in my government, because most of the justices were from the opposition to our government and therefore I expected that this would mean that our government would lose in cases of constitutional conflict. This, however, did not turn out to be that way. Indeed, to be frank with you, although the membership of the Constitutional Court did not satisfy us I, as the President of the Republic, never experienced it as a significant obstacle to the core of our political programme.[25]

Aylwin's experience was echoed by his successor, President Eduardo Frei, who also expressed his satisfaction with the relatively easy way in which it handled the constitutional complaints presented against his government by the opposition:

> In general terms, our experience with the Constitutional Court was very positive. We did serious work in our responses to the complaints presented to the Constitutional Court, and I am happy to say that of the 10 or 12 really important cases decided by it during my administration, we prevailed in almost all of them. This great rate of success was possible, first because we were constitutionally right, and secondly, because we presented thorough, well-thought defences.[26]

The satisfaction expressed to the author by President Frei is also evident in a book he wrote containing a summary of the successful responses to constitutional cases that had been resolved by the Constitutional Court.[27]

Chile's Constitutional Jurisprudence: 1990–2000

In order to analyse the actual performance of Chile's constitutional review tribunals, it is worth distinguishing between the human rights and the property rights domains. The record of the Chilean constitutional court and judiciary's jurisprudence in the domain of human rights, which includes what is also referred to as civil and political rights, is examined first.

Civil and Political Rights

Analysis of the constitutional jurisprudence on civil and political rights in post-authoritarian Chile is informed by two of the most thorough works available, one by Jorge Correa and Gastón Gómez, the other by Lisa Hilbink. These authors have covered this particular area of Chilean law systematically and with great skill, and their methodologies – particularly in the case of the former two – are as reliable as is possible in the context of the poor record-keeping methods of the Chilean courts.[28]

Indeed, both the work of Correa and Gómez and that of Hilbink conclude that during the first decade of democratic rule, the Chilean courts largely failed to use their powerful instruments of judicial review in order to enforce constitutional rights against legal and administrative action. Such a critical conclusion coincides with that of the constitutional scholars and jurists interviewed by this author.

Starting with Hilbink's work, it is worth noting that her methodology was to analyse judicial decisions compiled in Chile's three main jurisprudential journals, which she searched using their indexes. A problem with this method of collecting data on judicial decisions, however, is that the cases actually published in those journals are selected by their editors (typically academic lawyers with no social science training) with no publicly stated criteria. Even more problematic is that the editors tend to publish decisions that are particularly innovative or otherwise useful to legal practitioners, the targeted audience of such journals. This methodology, which is perhaps most useful for legal practitioners, is, however, highly unsuited for social science, because to select decisions on the basis of their legal novelty or peculiarity does not guarantee that they are in fact representative of the complete universe of legal decisions they are extracted from. Having said that, the reason that Hilbink gave for using this data set was that it was one of the only ones she had access to, given that neither the courts nor anybody else publishes a comprehensive compilation of all the constitutional jurisprudence produced by the Chilean courts. The lack of more reliable judicial data was compensated for by Hilbink with an analysis of specialised Chilean legal literature, interviews of judges, and the like.

At any rate, Hilbink's data is nicely complemented by that utilized by Gómez and Correa, which consist of an exhaustive collection of writs of protections by Chile's most important court of appeals. Indeed, because they worked with over 5,000 decisions issued by the Court of Appeal of Santiago (which deals with over 60 per cent of all writs of protection annually filed) during the years 1990–98, Gómez and Correa's data provided a good complement to the more inclusive, but less reliable data used by Hilbink.

In spite of their radically different methodologies, both studies arrived at the same basic conclusion, namely, that the Chilean courts have shown a remarkable unwillingness to stand up against either the executive – and especially Congress – in order to protect constitutional rights. In Hilbink's words,

> Even in rights cases that post-dated the transition, judges showed little proclivity to defend and promote liberal principles and practices. Because the *recurso de protección* was by this time well established and more familiar to the public, citizens increasingly petitioned for judicial intervention when public or private parties infringed upon constitutionally protected rights. The vast majority of these petitions involved property rights, but these were far too numerous to review for this thesis. In the few cases involving other civil and political rights, however, the courts did not chart a new liberal course.[29]

Indeed, as Hilbink's work shows, the reluctance of the 1990s judiciary to engage in an active defence of individual rights through its writ of protection jurisdiction resembled the behaviour the courts exhibited during the initial years of this writ (in 1978–80), when they avoided confronting the military government. At this point it is worth noting that, unlike during the radically different political context of the military regime, in the 1990s violations of constitutional rights did not come from the government but from private individuals, legislators and even the judicial branch itself, which did not hesitate to use legislation passed under the military regime in order to limit core individual rights. According to Hilbink, the reason for the courts' poor constitutional jurisprudence was their weak commitment to the protection of individual rights and liberal democracy.

In the case of Correa and Gómez's study, the conclusions are similar, but they give a different explanation for the courts' passivity in exercising an active review of the constitution in this domain. They point to a functionalist account that emphasizes the institutional constraints of the writ of protection and the writ of non-applicability. Starting with the former, Correa and Gómez conclude that the courts of appeal have been unwilling to actually engage in a control of the constitutionality of laws and administrative acts. Instead they confined themselves to controlling legality, thus frustrating the direct application of the constitution to the cases they see. They argue that although there is sound doctrinal basis for maintaining that the writ of protection can be utilized both for the defence of constitutional guarantees against illegal and unconstitutional acts, over 98 per cent of the decisions they studied never reviewed the constitutionality of a governmental act, when the act was legal but not necessarily constitutional.[30] The unwillingness of the courts to engage in such control of the constitutionality of legislation is considered by these authors as a dereliction of duty. That dereliction is all the more unfortunate given that the abstract and a priori control of the constitutionality of law projects exercised by the Constitutional Court does not reach already existing laws that violate the very constitutional guarantees that the constitution prescribes can be remedied by the writ of protection.[31]

Property Rights Jurisprudence

We have seen how the courts in Chile have been reluctant to enforce the civil and political rights of individuals affected by either executive acts or by legislation passed in violation of those rights. Many scholars blame this lack of constitutional rights protection on the judges' lack of democratic values or the inherently conservative nature of the top members of the constitutional, supreme and appellate courts. The problem with this explanation, however, is that the Chilean courts have also been unwilling to use their judicial review powers in defence of property and other business rights.

Indeed, as we shall see below, even though the right to private property was the most explicitly protected in the constitution of 1980 – in fact the very reason that the framers had for introducing strong judicial review mechanisms – the jurisprudence of the Chilean courts regarding this domain was equally restrained. All this suggests that the presumably conservative nature of Chile's justices is an insufficient explanation for the courts' deference to the political branches.

In order to evaluate the constitutional jurisprudence of Chilean courts in this domain, the writer analysed all the property rights jurisprudence of the Constitutional Court, and over a thousand judicial decisions issued by the Court of Appeals of Santiago on writs of protection during 1990–1998. These suits were filed by individuals objecting to either legislative or administrative acts. In order to 'triangulate' the information provided by the judicial data, the author interviewed the justices of the Constitutional Panel of the Chilean Supreme Court and six of the seven members of the Constitutional Court, as well as three of the four members of the Subcommittee of the Constitutional Commission in charge of elaborating the property rights clauses of the 1980 charter.

It must be pointed out that the right to private property was considerably strengthened by the constitution of 1980. Indeed, the latter dedicates long paragraphs meticulously detailing the definition, nature and status of the right to private property in Chile's constitutional system, as well as a specific control of the limits imposed on Congress in its inevitable regulation of this right.

In the period between 1990 and 1998, Chile's most important Court of Appeals (of the city of Santiago) issued a total of 1,322 decisions on writs of protection filed by individuals against the government or its agencies for alleged violations of their constitutional rights. Of these, 781 decisions, or

59 per cent, were grounded on the property rights clause of the Constitution of 1980. In these cases, the court ruled in favour of the government in 597 decisions (or 76 per cent), while ruling in favour of the plaintiffs in 176 cases (or 22.5 per cent). These data, however, do not distinguish between the specific agencies of the state involved in those cases. This is an important caveat. Given that this writ is used for all sorts of legal conflicts – including the resolution of contractual matters – most of the writs of protection filed against local authorities and government agencies involved routine administrative conflicts with no or little policy or political implications. Indeed, most of the decisions in which a local or decentralized agency was the defendant in the sample concerned issues such as contractual disputes between an agency and its employees, or complaints against the Chilean tax agency over annual declarations.

In an effort to discriminate between the decisions (and based on the information that the reading of all the cases in the sample provided), the author decided to check if there was any significant difference in the rate of success of writs of protection directed against the local and decentralized governmental agencies, as opposed to the most central and politically crucial entities of the Chilean state – the president of the Republic, ministers, under-secretaries of state, and Congress. Once the two categories just mentioned were established, the cases falling in each of them were 652 cases (or 83.5 per cent) in which the defendant was de-centralized and politically minor, and 129 cases (or 16.5 per cent) in which the defendant was politically prominent and centrally based. The result of this separate analysis was revealing, because the rate of success for writs of protection in the former group was a hundred per cent higher than that of the more politically significant group. Indeed, in the case of the writs filed against local and de-centralized state agencies, the 'success rate' reached 26 per cent of the total number of writs filed. Yet in the case of writs filed against the president, cabinet members, or Congress, the 'success rate' was significantly smaller, reaching just 13 per cent of the cases.

The tendency of the courts to avoid ruling against the more politically significant state organs was confirmed when the cases declared 'inadmissible' were added into the equation. Here too, the rates varied significantly. Writs filed against local and decentralized state agencies were significantly less likely to be thrown out on 'admissibility' grounds (just five per cent) than those filed against the more politically salient defendants. The latter were 70 per cent more likely to be declared 'inadmissible' by the courts (because 8.5 per cent of the total writs filed were so declared). According to the interviews, the reasons behind the sharp differences in the willingness of the Chilean appellate courts to rule against the government when the defendant is a local or otherwise obscure administrative agency, as opposed to when it is a politically salient entity, are various. Some justices appear to be reluctant to rule against those powerful institutions (or even accept such cases) because they are afraid that the risk of being overruled by the Supreme Court rises significantly in such cases. Others recognise that to rule against the government in such cases is dangerous for the judiciary as a whole, particularly its independence, since it significantly raises the danger of what they call 'the politicization of the judiciary'. Finally, others point out that Chilean judges prefer to avoid the spotlight and media attention, and that such cases typically involve a great deal of public attention.

The 1,322 decisions issued by the Court of Appeals of Santiago on writs of protection cases in which individuals sued the government on property rights grounds during 1990–1998 also revealed that in more than 98 per cent of the decisions (that is in almost 1,300 cases) the court limited itself to a mere review of the legality of the challenged administrative act. Put differently, the court did not examine whether the law upon which the administrative act was based was itself unconstitutional. Indeed, in case after case, the court repeated the mantra: 'Since the objected act has been issued under the authority of the law ... we find for the defendant'. Furthermore, in the few cases where the government was found to have violated the constitutional rights of the plaintiff, the court did so using another expression: 'We rule for the plaintiff because the illegal act of the defendant violated her constitutional right to private property...'. As these expressions make clear, the reason alleged by the Court of Appeals of Santiago for deciding its writs of protection cases is the legality or illegality of the act or omission being objected, not its constitutionality. This feature of the property rights protection jurisprudence of the Court of Santiago is consistent with the findings of other specialists of Chilean public law.

These data show that that also in the area of property rights Chile's judges have not sought to defend constitutional rights. Instead, they have upheld the laws and administrative acts of the government, giving greater weight to current law and policy than to constitutional principles. For those disturbed by the embedding of a particular economic philosophy into the constitution itself, this may be good news. At the same time, however, it represents a weak commitment to constitutionalism in general, which may be troubling to those who would like to see Chile's judges take a stronger stand in defence of other fundamental rights.

Explaining the Deference of Chile's Courts to the Political Branches

Having reviewed the actual performance of Chile's different mechanisms for enforcing constitutional supremacy, we can now turn to the most common explanations offered for the lack of judicial control of the constitution in spite of the varied and potentially powerful constitutional mechanisms available to the organs already mentioned. Let us start with the regular judiciary, and then address the situation of the Constitutional Court.

Existing Theories Explaining Deference by the Regular Judiciary

When one reviews the explanations which have been given for the lack of a strong judicial review practice by the regular courts in Chile, it becomes immediately apparent that most of them are in one way or the other of a cultural nature. Indeed, among the most compelling accounts of the reason for judicial deference in the recent history of Chile, three are worth mentioning. First, those attributing such behaviour to the supposedly 'formalistic' (or 'positivist') legal culture of the judicial branch. Second, those that blame such behaviour on the supposedly non-democratic political culture of Chilean judges. Finally, those that attribute such behaviour to a corporatist and isolationist culture within the ranks of the Chilean courts. Of course, there are a few scholars who recognize that the fact that Chile has a unitary (that is, non-federal) political system does not help, but the emphasis is mostly on cultural, not institutional, explanations. The following sections briefly describe the main tenets of the 'cultural approaches' and then explain why they are unsatisfactory.

The first explanation of the seemingly paradoxical reluctance of the Chilean courts to exercise their potentially great powers of judicial review attributes it to the legal culture of the judges, specifically their supposedly formalistic (that is, literalist) attitude towards adjudication, with its traditional understanding of statutory law as the ultimate expression of sovereign power.[32] Accordingly, judicial reluctance to void legislation on constitutional grounds comes from the traditional sort of training received by Chilean judges, which is characterized by an approach that views constitutional law issues from the perspective of private law, thus distorting the individual-rights-oriented nature of the former.[33]

A different version of this cultural approach blames judicial passivity on the supposedly illiberal and anti-democratic ethos of its judges. Thus Hilbink argues that the failure of Chilean judges to defend fundamental individual rights is consistent with the historic-institutional characteristics of the Chilean judiciary:

> Forged in the 19th century, and maintained in its fundamentals for 150 years, the judiciary embodied and reproduced in its institutional structure and ideology the substantively conservative values of the early republic; that is, the courts upheld a 'rule of law' based in largely

> illiberal and predemocratic principles of political legitimacy: centralised, paternalistic authority, limited popular participation, and a premium on social order.[34]

From this perspective, an individual-rights-oriented constitutional jurisprudence would not develop in Chile until judicial personnel are fully converted to liberal-democratic values.

Yet another variant of the cultural approach ascribes judicial passivity to the supposedly 'corporatist' ethos characterizing the judicial branch. In this view, the problem is not the political philosophy of the judges, but their professional culture characterized by isolationism and indifference to the larger social and political conflicts of society. Thus, in Carlos Peña's opinion, Chile's political evolution throughout the twentieth century made the judiciary isolated:

> In order to understand the current plight of the judiciary in Chile it is useful to remember that during the 'State of Commitment' (circa 1925–73) social and political conflict was channelled mostly by the political elements of the State and the interests groups, not by the judiciary, thus leaving the courts at the margins of the political debate of the time, and giving them a certain degree of institutional stability and continuity ... This process in my view contributed to create within the judicial branch a certain distrust of politics and an ethos characterised by a strong corporate solidarity (coupled) with a certain legalistic positivism and a conception of the idea of separation of powers more proximate to corporative autonomy than to the reciprocal control of public functions (which in turn) led to a judicial culture disinclined to the control of political power.[35]

One could add to Peña's analysis that precisely because the courts achieved institutional stability and independence at that juncture, they instinctively return to the original 'recipe' of detachment from politics when confronted by uncertain times. Indeed, as Peña himself asserts, the judicial branch reacted to the onset of the military regime in 1973 by sticking to long-held habits of indifference to social and political conflict, in what was less a deliberate action than what Peña calls a 'blind spot'.

All these explanations are, however, either wrong or incomplete. With regard to the first one, it suffices to say that formalism (the tendency to engage in a literal interpretation of the law and the constitution) seems to be at odds with the refusal of Chile's courts to follow the explicit constitutional clauses giving them sweeping powers of judicial review. Such refusal reflects, instead of formalism, just its opposite, namely a retreat or abandonment of the court's constitutional duty.

The emphasis on the role played by the private law approach to constitutional adjudication and the de facto constitutional status given by the Chilean judges to the Civil Code seems to be more plausible. And it is possible that a whole new generation of judges trained in the public law paradigm will eventually abandon the deeply ingrained idea that the law is untouchable by judicial fiat because it represents the will of the sovereign. Such an outcome seems, however, unlikely, as we shall see below.

In regard to blaming judicial inaction on the supposedly illiberal nature of the Chilean judges, it is hard to see why the judges – learned people engaged in the constant resolution of disputes – would be so out of touch with the presumably more democratic and liberal strain in Chilean society. If, however, illiberal and anti-democratic leanings are truly representative of society, then it is hard to see how society will move to change the cultural outlook of its judges.

Finally, and regarding the 'corporatist' or isolationist account, the persistence of such a culture among Chilean judges itself begs explanation.

Advancing a New Explanation: Deference as a Survival Strategy

The cultural elements at work in the Chilean judiciary's reluctance to enforce the constitution against legislation or executive action are one thing. But there are also important institutional and strategic behavioural elements that reinforce those elements and merit attention, for they make an eventual transition from a subordinated body to an active political actor even more difficult. The following historical antecedent illustrates the point.

A couple of little-known but highly traumatic events suggest that the apparently paradoxical reluctance of the Chilean courts to exercise their enhanced powers of judicial review constitutes a perfectly rational form of behaviour in the face of a still precarious institutionalization of its political independence from the government. The first episode dates from the Civil War of 1891 (in which over 10,000 people were killed during a year-long confrontation between the president of the republic and Congress), and consisted in the extreme interference of the judiciary by the president, who expelled the members of the Supreme Court.[36]

A generation later, in February 1927, Chile's top judicial office was subjected to brutal intervention by the government yet again, in a series of events that ultimately led to the arrest and exile of the chief justice of the Supreme Court and the expulsion of half its members. The episode started when an ambitious minister of defence, Carlos Ibáñez, ordered the arrest of the minister of interior, Manuel Rivas, on charges of conspiracy. Upon his arrest, Rivas's lawyers filed a writ of habeas corpus challenging the arrest order. The case went all the way up to the Supreme Court, which ruled the arrest of Rivas illegal. Ibáñez reacted by ordering the arrest of the president of the Supreme Court, Javier Angel Figueroa, who happened to be the brother of President Emiliano Figueroa. After this extraordinary order was enforced by the military under Ibáñez' orders, President Figueroa resigned in protest.[37]

The effects of this second intervention by the executive in the judicial branch were long lasting, because it occurred just as the Chilean courts were beginning to enjoy a measure of political autonomy from the government. The fact that this crisis happened just after the introduction of the constitution of 1925, which gave the Supreme Court powers of judicial review of legislation – the writ of non-applicability' – doubtless encouraged the reluctance exhibited by the court in exercising such powers in the decades to come.[38] Indeed, this unhappy coincidence sent a clear message to the courts: 'do not mess with politics or you will be in great trouble'. Accordingly, over the next decades the Supreme Court made an exceptionally cautious use of the writ of non-applicability.

When, in 1973, another military coup took place the judiciary reacted in a way that would guarantee its corporate autonomy in an otherwise intrusive regime, which showed no hesitancy in intervening in Congress. The judicial branch was, then, left untouched by Pinochet's regime. But the unspoken agreement was clear: as long as the judiciary limited itself to do its 'normal business', and did not interfere with the 'political' issues of the time, the military would leave the courts alone. And so it was.

The historical background suggests that Chile's judiciary experienced throughout the twentieth century a process of institutional learning with regard to its relationship to the social and political actors of the nation. A chain of events beginning in 1925 have left a strong mark – an 'institutional trauma' – with long-lasting influence in the way the judiciary perceives its conditions of existence and the limits imposed by the political structure of the country.

Deference in Chile's Constitutional Court

Even though the Constitutional Court has shown deference to executive-sponsored legislation which resembles the regular judiciary's deference toward executive administrative acts, the different nature of the former warrants a separate examination. In this case, however, there is almost no legal or political commentary available, so the analysis comes exclusively from the author's interviews with justices of the Constitutional Court and with Chilean constitutional law scholars.

The interviews revealed that the lack of a writ or popular action allowing individuals to go directly to the Constitutional Court asking for the declaration of the unconstitutionality of law projects or administrative decrees may have played a role in the lack of public salience of this organ. This, however, cannot be the sole explanation for the court's relative political insignificance. For one of the models of the Chilean Constitutional Court, the French Constitutional Council, which too lacks the power to rule in cases brought by regular citizens, has nonetheless been able to be significant political player.[39]

A different factor which may explain the Constitutional Court's tendency to retreat from an activist use of its constitutional review powers is the presence in it of three justices from the Supreme Court – out of a total of seven. It is plausible that they bring to the Constitutional Court the deferential habits of the regular judiciary. The author's interviews with Supreme Court justices also serving in the Constitutional Court confirmed that, although they purport to distinguish between their normal function and the more 'political' role they are supposed to have in the Constitutional Court, in actuality they reproduce their professional habits.

Conclusion

The judicial review performance of Chile's Constitutional Court and tribunals during the transition to democracy era (1990–2002) is, on balance, disappointing. Although there were some exceptional cases in which the Constitutional Court and the judiciary did use their powers of judicial review in order to protect individual rights against government or legislative encroachment, they have generally failed to do so.

Furthermore, although some scholars have attributed this failure to the supposedly 'conservative' or 'anti-democratic' ethos of the justices that continue serving in the Chilean superior courts and half of the Constitutional Court, the fact that they have also been deferential in cases involving private property suggests the explanation lies not in political ideology but elsewhere.

Thus the question remains: why would courts explicitly endowed with the power to enforce the constitution against abuses by the executive and legislative powers largely refuse to do so? The argument offered here is that this apparently paradoxical behaviour becomes more intelligible when we look at the historical background of the relationships between the judiciary and other branches of government in Chile. The record reveals that the courts have managed to acquire high levels of institutional autonomy by deliberately avoiding challenges to the 'political branches' of government, even at the cost of retreating from their constitutional powers of review of administrative and legislative acts. Indeed, on the few occasions in which the judiciary inevitably found itself at the centre of political controversy, the results were catastrophic for its autonomy. This historical background has contributed to the persistent reluctance of the Chilean judiciary to actually use its powers of judicial review, particularly in politically controversial matters, thus explaining the seemingly paradoxical renunciation of its enhanced powers of review.

Given this record, Chile's experience with judicial review might be regarded by many as a 'negative model' of a judicial system that refuses to contribute to democracy and human rights. But such an interpretation would be simplistic. This because the courts' refusal to exercise their powers of judicial control of the constitution represents a reasonable response by a judicial system that gives priority to its survival as an independent branch of government. That in turn requires it to be extremely cautious in the use of powers that could easily place it at the centre of political controversy. So, the lack of interest in adopting an activist stance continues a long-held preference for maintaining the very autonomy that historically has allowed the Chilean judiciary to play a crucial role in the promotion and maintenance of the legality that characterises this country.

The deliberate passivity of the Chilean courts vis-à-vis their powers of judicial review constitutes a stark contrast with the activist use attempted by the judiciaries of other Latin American countries, where less institutionalized systems of courts went ahead with aggressive constitutional review. Their experience with activism was invariably followed by suspension of the Constitutional Courts or some other form of government intervention, thus not only depriving them of their control of the constitution, but also of the very existence of an autonomous judicial branch.[40]

The lesson of the Chilean judiciary's retreat from an activist use of its powers of constitutional review and the short-lived activism of other Latin American states is that a *premature introduction of judicial review of legislation in non-consolidated democracies could actually make things worse, by ending judicial independence, which is so vital to the rule of law.* This represents a danger seldom recognized in the democratization literature that so often claims judicial review of legislation would actually help democracy, assuming that judicial control of the constitution is an unqualified good. Yet this conclusion is in keeping with the long tradition of scholarship that identifies the dangers of transplanting legal institutions to radically different social and political contexts. The transplanting of judicial control of the constitutionality of legislation from well-established constitutional democracies to transitional regimes could be just such an example. Fashionable calls to introduce judicial review of legislation around the world overlook the fact that this institution has been successfully implemented mostly in countries that had already consolidated the rule of law and enjoyed government respect of judicial independence. Where these conditions do not apply, introducing judicial review would likely be either futile or, what is far worse, counterproductive. The former, because the courts, fearful of political intervention, will retreat from their new powers; the latter, by creating perverse incentives for the 'political' branches to intervene in the very courts that are supposed to control them. When democratization scholars turned to the role of law and constitutionalism in consolidating and deepening democracy, and embraced the importance of judicial review to democratic consolidation, they neglected a crucial finding of the comparative law and courts scholars: a consolidated democracy constitutes a necessary condition for the proper introduction of judicial review.

NOTES

1. See Robin Hodess (ed.), *The Global Corruption Report* (Berlin: Transparency International, 2003); and Freedom House Report: *Freedom in the World 2000–2002* (New York: Transaction Publishers, 2002).
2. For an account of this phenomena, see Charles Epp, *The Rights Revolution: Lawyers, Activists, and Supreme Courts in Comparative Perspective* (Chicago, IL: University of Chicago Press, 1998), and Neil Tate and Torbjorn Vallinder (eds), *The Global Expansion of Judicial Power* (New York: New York University Press, 1995).
3. Cass Sunstein, 'On Property and Constitutionalism', in Michael Rosenfeld (ed.), *Constitutionalism, Identity, Difference, and Legitimacy. Theoretical Perspectives* (Durham, NC: Duke University Press, 1994), p.384. See also Stephen Macedo, 'Liberal Virtues, Constitutional Community', *The Review of Politics*, Vol.50, No.2 (1988), pp.215–40, who says at p.225, 'If constitutionalism and the rule of law stand for anything, they stand for the idea that one system of law applies to government officials and citizens alike, and that citizens have a right to challenge governmental acts in independent courts of law.'
4. The list of many countries that have recently introduced judicial review include nations as diverse as Chile, Mongolia, Russia, Peru, Hungary, Bolivia, Taiwan and Romania.
5. William C. Prillaman, *The Judiciary and Democratic Decay in Latin America. Declining Confidence in the Rule of Law* (Westport, CT, & London: Praeger, 2000), p.1.
6. Robert Barro, 'Democracy and the Rule of Law', in Bruce Bueno de Mesquita and Hilton Root (eds), *Governing for Prosperity* (New Haven, CT: Yale University Press, 2000), pp. 209–31.
7. Pablo Spiller and Brian Levy, *Regulations, Institutions, and Commitment: Comparative Studies of Telecommunications* (Cambridge and New York: Cambridge University Press, 1996).
8. Maria Dakolias, 'A Strategy for Judicial Reform: The Experience in Latin America', *Virginia Journal of International Law*, Vol.36 (1995), pp.167–8.
9. Margaret Keck and Katherine Sikkink, *Activist Beyond Borders* (Ithaca, NY: Cornell University Press, 1998).
10. Manuel Antonio Garretón, *Hacia una Nueva Era Politica: Estudios Sobre las Democratizaciones* (Mexico: Fondo de Cultura Económica, 1995).
11. Gastón Gómez, 'Algunas Ideas Criticas Sobre la Jurisdicción Constitucional en Chile', in Gastón Gómez (ed.), *La Jurisdicción Constitucional Chilena Ante la Reforma* (Santiago, Chile: Universidad Diego Portales, 1999), Vol.41, p.93.

12. See the 'Organic Law of the Tribunal Constitucional', Law No.17.997 of 19 May 1981.
13. Patricio Zapata, *La Jurisprudencia del Tribunal Constitucional* (Santiago, Chile: Ediciones Corporación Tiempo 2000, 1994), p.250.
14. The writ, however, can only be utilized for the protection of some of the individual rights consecrated in the constitution. Thus, most 'social rights' are excluded.
15. For an account of the origins and evolution of this agency see Enrique Silva, *La Contraloría General de la República* (Santiago, Chile: Editorial Jurídica de Chile, 1945).
16.. Such was the conclusion of the so-called 'Truth and Reconciliation Report', which in one of its passages reads: 'The Judicial branch did not react with sufficient energy to the widespread human rights violations of the time (although) political conditions would have allowed the courts to take a more assertive behaviour in defending human rights ... Indeed, the attitude adopted by the judicial branch during the military regime resulted in a deepening of the process of systematic human rights violations both in the short term, because the courts did not protection to individuals detained, as well as in the long term, because gave repressive agents a growing sense of impunity for their criminal actions...'. Quoted in Jorge Correa, 'La Cenicienta se Queda en la Fiesta. El Poder Judicial Chileno en la Década de los 90', in Paul Drake and Iván Jaksic (eds), *El Modelo Chileno. Democracia y Desarrollo en los Noventa* (Santiago, Chile: LOM Ediciones, 1999), p.302.
17. Within the opposition, the most vocal critic of the judiciary's performance and outdated practices was the 'Centro de Estudios Públicos', a moderate right-wing think tank which, in 1991, published a book calling for the modernization of the Chilean judiciary. See Eugenio Valenzuela's *Proposiciones para la Reforma Judicial* (Santiago, Chile: Centro de Estudios Públicos, 1991).
18. Passage quoted from the text of the Supreme Court's response to the 'Rettig Commission Report,' issued on 17 May 1991, quoted in Alejandra Matus's *El Libro Negro de la Justicia Chilena* (Buenos Aires, Argentina: Editorial Planeta, 1999), p.59.
19. Ibid., p. 303.
20. See the document 'Respuesta de la Corte Suprema al Informe de la Comisión de Verdad y Reconciliación', in *Estudios Públicos* No.42 (1991), p.249.
21. Brian Loveman and Elizabeth Lira, 'Derechos Humanos en "La Transición Modelo": Chile 1988–1999', in Drake and Jaksic (note 16). Although formally the justices had been accused 'of having been negligent in defending human rights during the authoritarian regime', the right-wing members of Congress who voted against them did so because they considered some of them to be corrupt. Ibid., p.359.
22. Indeed, while in March of 1990 (when the new democratic government took office), 12 out of 17 justices of the Supreme Court had been nominated to it by General Pinochet, by 1998 the number of justices nominated during the military regime was only four. By then the number of justices of the Supreme Court had been increased to 21, so the proportion of justices coming from the military era was clearly significantly less towards the end of the 1990s. See Matus (note 18) p.183; and Correa (note 16) p.281.
23. The Amnesty law was promulgated as Decree Law No.2, 191, of 19 April 1978.
24. This assessment is general among most Chilean constitutional scholars. Among others, see Raul Bertelsen, interview with the author, 9 July 1999 and Zapata (note 13).
25. Interview by the author of former president of the Republic of Chile (1990–1994), Patricio Aylwin, 10 August 1999.
26. Interview by the author of former president of the Republic of Chile (1994–2000), Eduardo Frei, 21 August 2000.
27. Eduardo Frei, *Doctrina Constitucional del Presidente Eduardo Frei Ruiz-Tagle* (Santiago, Chile: División Jurídico-Legislativa, Ministerio Secretaría General de la Presidencia, 2000).
28. Indeed, the record-keeping practices of Chile's judiciary are so poor that not even the Supreme Court has an exhaustive compilation of all of its decisions. Professor Gastón Gómez, of the Universidad Diego Portales, explaining the difficulty in getting access to Chilean judicial decisions says: 'In Chile there are no rigorous registrar of judicial decisions issued at any of the levels of the court system ... And due to the fact that the formal records are filed manually, it is impossible to actually get access to them, because they do not have uniform codes for identifying them, or they are disposed after some time, or the books

where they are registered are lost etc. The hindrance that such poor record-keeping practices have to research is huge. And without precise information about how things actually work it is hard to elaborate feasible judicial policies.' Gastón Gómez, unpublished manuscript on file with the author (2001), p.6.

29. Lisa Hilbink, *Legalism Against Democracy: The Political Role of the Judiciary in Chile: 1964-1994*, unpublished dissertation, University of California at San Diego, 1999, p.442.
30. Gastón Gómez, unpublished manuscript on file with author (2001), p.9.
31. Furthermore, Gómez and Correa, (unpublished manuscript on file with the author) point out that the courts have persisted in this doctrine even though the vast majority of Chile's constitutional scholars persistently advocate a different, more activist approach.
32. Hugo Fruhling, *Law in Society: Social Transformation and the Crisis of Law in Chile, 1830–1970*, PhD dissertation, Harvard University School of Law, 1984.
33. José Luis Cea, *Tratado de la Constitución de 1980: Características Generales, Garantías Constitucionales* (Santiago, Chile: Editorial Jurídica de Chile, 1988), p.56.
34. Hilbink (note 29), p.466.
35. Carlos Peña, *Práctica Constitucional y Derechos Fundamentales* (Santiago, Chile: Corporación Nacional de Reparación y Reconciliación, 1996), p.147.
36. See Matus (note 18) , pp.198–9.
37. Gonzalo Vial, *Historia de Chile, 1891–1973. Arturo Alessandri y los Golpes Militares* (Santiago, Chile: Editorial Fundación, 1993), Vol.3.
38. Profesor Alejandro Silva Bascuñán, a noted constitutional scholar, now 93 years old, remembers the impact that Ibáñez's brutal intervention in Chile's Supreme Court had. He says: 'I was a young law student working part time in the Lawyers Guild ("Colegio de Abogados") when this incident happened. We were all shocked and concerned for our judicial system. I never forgot the incident'. Interview with the author, 18 August 1999.
39. See Alec Stone, *The Birth of Judicial Politics in France* (New York and Oxford: Oxford University Press, 1992).
40. During the 1990s the record of other Latin American nations with judicial review was nothing short of catastrophic, including the 'packing' of constitutional courts as in Argentina under Menem (1989), or the outright intervention by the executive in the judiciary, as in Peru under Fujimori (1992 and 1997) and Venezuela under Chávez (1999).

Legitimating Transformation: Political Resource Allocation in the South African Constitutional Court

THEUNIS ROUX

Introduction

Some degree of judicial intervention in politics is an inevitable consequence of the adoption of a supreme-law Bill of Rights. The political branches' power to allocate resources, however, is conventionally thought to be beyond 'the limits of adjudication'.[1] Judges, the standard argument runs, are neither mandated nor institutionally equipped to undertake the complex economic and interest-balancing inquiries that inform the allocation of public resources. It is therefore unwise to give them the power to review decisions taken by the political branches in this area, and foolish for judges to assume this power when they are not compelled to do so.

If these propositions are true for judges in mature democracies, one would expect that they would apply with even greater force in new democracies, where the judicial branch is by definition still in the process of building the legitimacy required to play a meaningful role in politics. It is therefore surprising that some of the most far-reaching decisions in this area have been handed down by courts in Hungary and South Africa – both countries that democratized within the last 15 years. It is even more surprising that, in the case of South Africa, judicial review of political resource allocation has not as yet triggered any significant protest from the executive.[2] Why has this happened? And what does the South African experience tell us about the capacity of courts to check the power of the political branches in new democracies?

This study attempts to throw some light on these questions by examining four recent decisions of the South African Constitutional Court in which it was required to review the allocation of resources by the political branches. The first case took the form of a socio-economic rights claim, that is a claim based on a right to a particular resource or distribution of public benefits. And, indeed, it is in this context that the judicial review of political resource allocation is most obviously implicated. But the issue has arisen in other contexts as well, most notably in relation to constitutional challenges to legislation or policies allocating resources *away* from the claimant. The other cases discussed here are all of this type.

The discussion of each case begins with a summary of the formal reasons given by the court for its decision. Thereafter, the purpose is to identify the discretionary gaps exploited by the court in its manipulation of the applicable legal rules. By 'discretionary gaps' is meant fissures in the normative structure governing the decision that enabled the court to fashion an outcome in accordance with its sense of the degree of intrusion into politics appropriate to the case concerned. The aim is thus not to engage in a full doctrinal analysis of each case, but to focus on the way the court has used the opportunities presented to it in these cases to define its institutional role in the South African political system.

This way of proceeding brings together two bodies of literature on the role of constitutional courts in new democracies that seem to depart from different premises. On the one hand, political science discussions of this issue tend to assume that courts have a fairly wide discretion to tailor the outcome of controversial cases to the exigencies of the political moment.[3] On the other hand, legal academics writing about such cases, certainly in South Africa,[4] are reluctant to admit that extraneous political factors exert any kind of influence at all on the way judges make their decisions. The approach taken here lies somewhere in between. Legal rules *do* constrain the exercise of judicial discretion in controversial cases. However, by exploiting ambiguities in the normative structure governing their decisions, courts are able to manage their relationship with the political branches to a considerable degree.

The South African Constitutional Court has shown itself to be particularly adept at this kind of strategic behaviour, using the space provided by the new constitutional order to good effect. In particular, the four cases discussed in this article suggest that the court is scripting a role for itself as *legitimator* of the post-apartheid social transformation project. The advantage of this role is that it has allowed the court to build its legitimacy by endorsing the political branches' social transformation efforts. At the same time, the court has been able to give meaningful effect to the Bill of Rights, whilst remaining respectful of the political branches' residual prerogative to determine public policy.

Before discussing the cases, it may be helpful to readers unfamiliar with the South African constitution, and who wish to compare South Africa to other democracies discussed in this collection, to make some introductory remarks about the composition, method of selection and workload of the Constitutional Court. Although the South African case is undoubtedly significant, it may not be completely generalizable to other new democracies because of these peculiar institutional factors.

The Composition, Method of Selection and Workload of the South African Constitutional Court

The Constitutional Court was established in 1994 under the so-called interim constitution,[5] an expressly transitional constitution that facilitated South Africa's passage from white minority rule to non-racial democracy. One of the more unusual aspects of the interim constitution was the role it gave to the court in certifying the final constitution[6] against a set of negotiated principles. This device, a clear pragmatic compromise between the desire for democracy and the need to keep the transition on track, necessarily thrust the court into the centre of politics. Its decision on this issue,[7] approving the bulk of the final constitution but remitting several important questions for reconsideration by the Constitutional Assembly, provided an early indication of the court's astute approach to controversial cases.

If one were to isolate a single non-contingent factor to explain the court's success in building its legitimacy, it would be that the court is composed of a remarkably talented group of people, all of whom possess impeccable human rights credentials.[8] Of the original eleven judges appointed, eight were still sitting at the beginning of 2003. When one considers that two of the vacancies were created by ill health, this statistic reflects a high degree of stability in the composition of the court. This has allowed it to build its relationship with the political branches through a series of cases in which it has largely spoken with one voice.[9]

The judges of the court are appointed by a Judicial Services Commission, which is effectively controlled by the majority party in the national government.[10] Given that South Africa is a one-party dominant state,[11] this might appear to be a reason for doubting the independence of the court. However, even in mature democracies, the national executive typically has the power to appoint a majority of the highest court on constitutional matters.[12] Few constitutional courts in the world are independent in the strict sense – composed of people with political views opposed to that of the governing political elite. Indeed, constitutional courts of this type, if they existed at all, would be at a distinct disadvantage when checking the power of the executive, since their decisions would be open to the charge of political bias. Conversely, as the South African case illustrates, the fact that a court's members have political views broadly sympathetic to those of the governing elite may be a necessary condition for them to assert their independence in the narrow sense: the capacity on occasion to say 'no' to the executive and 'make it stick'.

The other peculiar feature of the South African Constitutional Court worth mentioning is that it decides a comparatively small number of cases per year – never more than 30, and in some years as few as 20.[13] This is both an advantage and a disadvantage. The advantage of a low workload is that the court is able to pay close attention to the wording of its decisions, using them as the main means by which to manage its relationship to the political branches. The disadvantage, on the other hand, is that the court has concomitantly less control over its docket. This is compounded by the final constitution's very broadly framed jurisdictional provisions,[14] which have thus far precluded the development of a political question doctrine on the American model.[15] Deprived of this device, the court has very little option but to accept jurisdiction over controversial cases,[16] and then to use all its considerable rhetorical skills, both to *avoid* deciding issues that might bring it into conflict with the political branches,[17] and to *take on* politically useful issues that might not present themselves for decision again.

Discussion of the Cases

Government of the Republic of South Africa v. Grootboom

In the first major socio-economic rights case to come before the Constitutional Court – *Government of the Republic of South Africa and Others v. Grootboom and Others*[18] – a homeless community challenged their local municipality's refusal to provide them with temporary shelter. In a decision that has already attracted some international interest,[19] the court held that the state's failure to make proper provision for people in desperate need violated its obligation under section 26(1) and (2) of the final constitution to 'take reasonable and other measures within its available resources' to provide access to adequate housing. It accordingly declared the state's housing programme as applied in the municipal area in question unconstitutional to this extent.[20]

At first blush, this decision appears to be a remarkable slap in the face of a government that has made great strides in a short time to redress the apartheid housing-backlog. Closer examination of the reasons for the decision, however, reveals a diplomatically worded and respectful message to the political branches, generally endorsing their efforts, even as the court finds fault with aspects of the national housing programme.

The key discretionary gap exploited by the court in *Grootboom* was the ambiguity surrounding the application of international law, in particular, General Comment 3 of 1990 issued by the United Nations Committee on Economic, Social and Cultural Rights. Paragraph 10 of this Comment interprets articles 2.1 and 11.1 of the International Covenant on Economic, Social and Cultural Rights as meaning that States Parties have to devote *all* the resources at their disposal *first* to satisfy the 'minimum core content' of the right to adequate housing. Counsel for the *amici curiae* in *Grootboom* had argued strongly that this was the governing norm, and therefore that the court should order the state to redirect its spending so as to devote all available resources to meeting the needs of people in the position of the claimant community.

Clearly, the adoption of such an approach at the domestic level would have brought the Constitutional Court into direct confrontation with the political branches, since it would have required the court to substitute its own view of the needs that ought to be prioritized in the national housing programme for that of the legislature and the executive. Fortunately for the court, however, South Africa has not as yet ratified the International Covenant on Economic, Social and Cultural Rights.[21] And, although section 39(2) of the final constitution obliges the Court to 'consider international law', it clearly does not oblige it to apply non-incorporated legal norms.[22]

Taking full advantage of this discretionary gap, the court in *Grootboom* found that the textual differences between section 26(1) and (2) of the final constitution and Articles 2.1 and 11.1 of the International Covenant suggested that 'the real question ... is whether the measures taken by the State to realise the right afforded by s 26 are reasonable'.[23] The minimum core content of the right to have access to adequate housing, the court held, was only one indicator in respect of this larger inquiry.[24] In any event, there was insufficient evidence before the court to allow it to determine the minimum core content of the right, given regional variations in housing requirements and the rural/urban divide.[25]

Having opened out the normative structure governing its decision in this way, the court was able to develop the reasonableness review standard implied by the text of section 26(1) and (2) unconstrained by international law, or indeed by foreign law or past precedent. The court simply asserted, without relying on any authority, that the state's duty under section 26(2) to adopt 'reasonable and other legislative measures' implied that the national housing programme must be 'comprehensive',[26] 'balanced and flexible',[27] and targeted at those who were unable to access adequate housing through the market.[28] The precise holding in the *Grootboom* case, negatively expressed, was that it was unreasonable for the state to 'exclude' a 'significant segment of society' from the national housing programme,[29] especially where such a group was poor or otherwise vulnerable.[30]

The court must have been all too well aware, as it handed down this decision, that the standard of review set in this, its first major socio-economic rights case, would be a crucial determinant of the degree to which it would be required in future cases to involve itself in controversial policy issues, and in the allocation of resources in particular. It is therefore instructive to compare the standard of review adopted in *Grootboom* to the rational basis and proportionality standards in South African constitutional law, which mark respectively the low and high ends of the continuum of review standards from which the court might have chosen.

To lawyers familiar with the court's jurisprudence, the reasonableness review standard in *Grootboom* is clearly stricter than the rational basis standard applied under section 9(1) of the final constitution.[31] Although it insists on means-end rationality as a minimum,[32] the requirement that a social programme be comprehensive, balanced and flexible means that the court must do more than inquire into whether the legislation or policy at issue is rationally related to a legitimate government purpose. Rather, the court has to assess whether the social programme unreasonably excludes the segment of society to which the claimant group belongs. This assessment is closer to the one the court makes when applying the unfair discrimination standard it has developed under section 9(3) of the final constitution.[33] As such, it undoubtedly requires the court to substitute its view of what the constitution requires – the inclusion of the excluded group – for that of the political branches. It stops short, however, of a full-blown proportionality test.[34] The court's assessment is thus not directed at such issues as whether the state might have adopted less restrictive measures in pursuing the programme in question, but at whether the claimant group has *an equal or better claim* to inclusion relative to other groups that *have* been catered to.

It is now possible to see just how crucial the court's rejection of the direct application of General Comment 3 was. As noted above, the application of the standard set by the UN Committee on Economic, Social and Cultural Rights would have required the court to substitute its view of the needs that ought to be prioritized in the national housing programme for that of the political branches. By exploiting the discretionary gap in relation to the application of international law, the court was able to develop a subtly, but crucially different review standard, one that is less invasive of the political branches' resource-allocation powers in two respects.[35] First, the court was careful not to prescribe to the political branches the *temporal* order in which competing needs were to be met through the national housing programme. By rejecting the minimum core content argument, the court left the political branches free to meet a number of different needs in parallel, without prioritizing the needs of the most vulnerable over those who at least have somewhere to live where they are not in immediate danger of eviction or exposure to the elements.

The second important difference between the review standard developed in *Grootboom* and the standard set by the UN Committee on Economic, Social and Cultural Rights is that the former standard does not involve the court in prescribing to the political branches the precise amount of resources that have to be re-allocated in order to cure the constitutional defect it identifies. The court in *Grootboom* simply held that 'it is essential that a reasonable part of the national housing budget be devoted to [providing relief for those in desperate need], but the precise allocation is for national government to decide in the first instance'.[36] If the political branches were to attempt to give effect to this ruling, they would have to redistribute resources within the national housing programme, at the expense of people who might have benefited sooner from that programme but for the court-sanctioned diversion of resources to people in desperate need. But the political branches would not have to ensure that the shelter requirements of people in desperate need were met first, before going on to meet the needs of people whose situation was less desperate. Nor would they be required to allocate more resources to the housing programme, either by taking resources away from other programmes or by increasing the overall size of the national budget. To this extent, the *Grootboom* judgement remains respectful of the political branches' primary budget-setting and policy-making powers.

The impact of the reasonableness review standard developed in *Grootboom* on the political branches' power to allocate resources was directly addressed in the court's second major decision on socio-economic rights, *Minister of Health and Others v. Treatment Action Campaign and Others (No. 2)*.[37] In this decision, the court described the effect of its standard in the following terms: Determinations of reasonableness may in fact have budgetary implications, but are not in themselves directed at rearranging budgets. In this way the judicial, legislative and executive functions achieve appropriate constitutional balance.[38] The distinction the court draws in this passage between, on the one hand, the deliberate usurpation of the political branches' resource allocation powers and, on the other, the inevitable budgetary consequences of a determination of reasonableness, is very revealing about how it sees its institutional role. The former conception, the court implies, would amount to an unacceptable intrusion into politics, whereas the latter is just an inevitable consequence of the function given to the court by the constitution. Judicial motives, in other words, are important. If the motive for 'rearranging budgets' is to substitute the court's view on how resources should be allocated for that of the political branches, the intrusion into politics cannot be justified. However, if the primary motive is rights-enforcement, the political branches should (as a matter of constitutional law) and will (as a matter of practical politics) accept the resource-allocation effects of the court's decision as a necessary part of the constitutional compact.

Pretoria City Council v. Walker

Socio-economic rights claims, as illustrated by the *Grootboom* case, generally have to do with challenges to the way resources have been allocated in existing programmes, and a concomitant claim that resources be diverted to the claimant. The remaining cases discussed here all concerned challenges to legislative or executive action that had the effect of allocating resources *away* from the claimant. The first such case, *Pretoria City Council v. Walker*,[39] provides a good illustration of the role that the Constitutional Court is beginning to define for itself in relation to challenges of this type. The respondent had been sued in the Magistrate's Court for outstanding electricity and water charges owed to the applicant, the Pretoria City Council. In defence to this suit, the respondent argued that the council's policy of charging a consumption-based tariff in formerly white suburbs and a lower, flat rate in formerly black townships amounted to cross-subsidization of the latter group by the former. As such, the policy violated section 8 of the interim constitution (the right to equality).[40] The respondent further alleged that the council's practice of taking legal action to recover debt owed by residents of the formerly white suburbs whilst declining to sue residents of the formerly black suburbs similarly violated this section.

Section 8 of the interim constitution, which is substantially the same as section 9 of the final constitution, has been interpreted as entailing two separate, but related standards of review: a rational basis standard linked to section 8(1), and an unfair discrimination standard linked to section 8(2). The first standard amounts to the familiar, means-end rationality test applied in other jurisdictions. In terms of this test, the court's inquiry is limited to deciding whether the provision or conduct complained of serves a legitimate government purpose and, if so, whether the differentiation at issue is rationally connected to that purpose. In *Walker* the application of this standard took up just two sentences of what is otherwise a fairly lengthy judgement, the court finding that the measures complained of were temporary in nature, and were rationally connected to the legitimate purpose of achieving parity in municipal service provision.[41]

The second, unfair discrimination standard, applied under section 8(2) of the interim constitution and section 9(3) of the final constitution, is more complicated. It is most concisely expressed in the court's decision in *Harksen v. Lane N.O. and Others*,[42] where the two-stage enquiry into whether an impugned differentiation amounts to unfair discrimination is explained as follows:[43]

(i) Firstly, does the differentiation amount to 'discrimination'? If it is on a specified ground, then discrimination will have been established. If it is not on a specified ground, then whether or not there is discrimination will depend upon whether, objectively, the ground is based on attributes and characteristics which have the potential to impair the fundamental human dignity of persons as human beings or to affect them adversely in a comparably serious manner.

(ii) If the differentiation amounts to 'discrimination', does it amount to 'unfair discrimination'? If it has been found to have been on a specified ground, then unfairness will be presumed. If on an unspecified ground, unfairness will have to be established by the complainant. The test of unfairness focuses primarily on the impact of the discrimination on the complainant and others in his or her situation.

Applying this standard in *Walker*, the majority of the court held that the council's policy of charging different tariffs to residents of formerly white and formerly black areas, and of selectively suing residents of formerly white areas for the recovery of arrears, amounted to indirect discrimination on the basis of race.[44] Since race was one of the grounds expressly listed in section 8(2), this finding triggered the presumption in section 8(4) that the discrimination was unfair.[45] The major portion of the court's judgement is accordingly directed at assessing whether the council had successfully rebutted this presumption, namely whether it had proved that, even though its policy of charging differential tariffs and its practice of suing only residents of the formerly white suburbs indirectly discriminated on the basis of race, they were nevertheless fair.[46]

The unfair discrimination standard developed in its previous decisions required the court in *Walker* to focus on the *impact* of the discrimination on the complainant, taking into account three factors: (1) his or her position in society; (2) 'the nature of the provision or power and the purpose sought to be achieved by it'; and (3) 'the extent to which the discrimination has affected the [complainant's] rights or interests ... and whether it has led to an impairment of [his or her] fundamental human dignity or constitutes an impairment of a comparably serious nature'.[47] In *Walker*, the court added for the first time that the complainant need not prove that the state intended to discriminate,[48] although the absence of an intention to discriminate was relevant to the court's assessment of the second factor.[49]

Assessing these factors, the court found that the council's differential tariff policy did not amount to unfair discrimination. The issues that the court considered relevant were: (1) that the complainant was a member of a previously advantaged, though minority group;[50] (2) 'the adoption of a flat rate [in formerly black townships] as an interim arrangement while meters were being installed ... was the only practical solution to the problem';[51] (3) the inevitability of cross-subsidization;[52] and (4) the fact that the policy 'did not impact adversely on the respondent in any material way'.[53] The practice of selectively proceeding against residents of the formerly white suburbs, on the other hand, was not based on a 'rational and coherent plan',[54] but was rather a pragmatic way of dealing with the culture of non-payment in formerly black suburbs.[55] Official Council policy was in fact to enforce the payment of arrears by way of legal action against all ratepayers.[56] When coupled with the fact that, 'objectively', this practice affected the complainant and 'other persons similarly placed' in a manner 'comparably serious to the invasion of their dignity',[57] the presumption that this practice was unfairly discriminatory could not be said to have been rebutted.

What is significant about the majority judgement in *Walker* for our purposes is that the court was able to enter the politically charged terrain of municipal service provision and partially strike down a policy that favoured the previously disadvantaged majority over a still privileged minority. How did the court achieve this result without antagonizing the political branches?

First, it was perhaps not coincidental that *Walker* was the case in which the court chose to decide the question whether proof of an intention to discriminate on the part of the state is a necessary element of a successful unfair discrimination challenge. Although courts in the mature democracies cited by the court have taken different views on this question,[58] in a new democracy it is clearly preferable for judges not to have to rule on the motives underlying impugned executive conduct.

The second possible explanation for the apparent ease with which the court was able to hand down a judgement in *Walker* partially striking down a policy that favoured the previously disadvantaged majority, lies in the fortuitous fact that the case split into two parts. This allowed the court to uphold the differential tariff policy whilst sanctioning the practice of selective enforcement. In this way the court was able to balance its role as guardian of the constitution against the need to build its institutional legitimacy. It is also significant that the practice of selective enforcement did not enjoy the status of official policy, which meant that the court could attack it as irrational and incoherent without directly criticizing the political branches.

The third discretionary gap exploited by the court in *Walker* concerned the application of the unfair discrimination test. As noted above, where the ground of discrimination is listed in section 8(2) of the interim constitution, as it was in this case,[59] the formalistic enquiry prescribed by the *Harksen* case leaves very little room for manoeuvre until the final stage, in which the court assesses whether the state has rebutted the presumption of unfair discrimination thus arising.[60] At this point, however, the inquiry becomes quite open-ended. As the majority judgement in *Walker* shows, the third factor in the determination of fairness – the assessment of whether the impact of the conduct complained of is as serious as an invasion of the complainant's dignity – still leaves quite a bit of space for the court to exercise its political discretion.

To understand this point it is necessary to return to the facts of the case. On the court's own version, it is apparent that the constitutional claimant (Walker) was not indebted to the council because of his inability to pay. Rather he was part of a concerned taxpayers' association that was attempting to highlight the way in which the council charged for services by refusing to pay any more for services than the flat rate charged to black residents.[61] Indeed, it is fair to say that Walker deliberately exposed himself to the possibility of being sued so that he could draw attention to the alleged violation of his constitutional rights. Against this background, the majority's conclusion that the impact of the council's practice of selectively suing white residents must have 'affected them in a manner which [was] at least comparably serious to an invasion of their dignity'[62] seems a little strained. There was no principled basis for distinguishing the council's differential tariff policy from the practice of selective enforcement according to this factor. If anything, the impact of the tariff policy was outside Walker's control, whereas he might have avoided the impact of the selective enforcement practice by settling his arrears, something that he was financially capable of doing.

The real reason for the court's willingness to find for Walker on the latter issue, it is suggested, was its desire to sanction the haphazard way in which the council went about recovering arrear charges.[63] This comes closer to a finding of irrationality than one of unfair discrimination. Indeed, it is at first glance strange that the court did not use the opportunity provided by the section 8(1) rational basis challenge to strike down the practice of selective enforcement, and in that way avoid the more controversial finding of unfair (reverse) discrimination under section 8(2).[64] As the two cases discussed below illustrate, the court is far more comfortable in the role of enforcing good governance standards than it is in second-guessing the wisdom of policies self-evidently required to redress the legacy of apartheid.

The only plausible explanation for the court's becoming more embroiled in the politically fraught terrain of municipal service provision than was doctrinally necessary is that it deliberately *chose* to enter this terrain in order to endorse the political branches' social reform efforts. Had the court decided the case merely on the basis of section 8(1), it would have had far less scope to affirm the constitutionality of such crucial transformational strategies as cross-subsidization, and far less opportunity to show its appreciation for the difficulties faced by the council in trying to achieve parity in municipal service provision. On balance, the checking effect of the court's decision to strike down the practice of selective enforcement is outweighed by the ringing endorsement it gives to the post-apartheid social transformation project. In this way the court was able to legitimate that project even as it affirmed the minority-protection function of the Bill of Rights.

Premier, Mpumalanga v. Executive Committee, Association of State-aided Schools, Eastern Transvaal

Consequent on the inclusion of rights to administrative justice in both the interim and final constitutions, the Constitutional Court has on several occasions been required to review the constitutionality of administrative action in cases that in other jurisdictions would have been decided by the ordinary courts. The fact that a constitutional court should review administrative action does not, of course, render this widely accepted institution problematic. However, two further features of the South African situation warrant the inclusion of some of these cases in this analysis. The first feature involves the Constitutional Court's approach to the definition of administrative action, which, as in some other jurisdictions, has focused not on the 'arm of government to which the relevant actor belongs, but on the nature of the power he or she is exercising'.[65] As a result, the constitutional right to just administrative action has on several occasions been used to challenge decisions taken by ministers in the national and provincial governments, including decisions on the allocation of resources. The second feature of the South African situation is the enormity of the social transformation challenge facing the country, and the steadfastly legal framework within which the political branches have pursued the social transformation project. In combination, these two features mean that judicial review of political resource allocation under the right to just administrative action may pose as great a risk to the court's reputation and standing as that posed by judicial review in respect of socio-economic or equality rights. Even as apparently routine a review standard as procedural fairness may, if over-zealously applied, be perceived by the executive as undermining the achievement of the constitutional vision of a just and substantively equal society. By the same token, however, the judicious use of the court's power to review political resource allocation for procedural fairness may serve to legitimate the redistribution of resources by the political branches, which is a necessary part of the post-apartheid social transformation project.

The Constitutional Court indicated its awareness of this tension in the following extract from its decision in *Premier, Mpumalanga, and Another v. Executive Committee, Association of State-aided Schools, Eastern Transvaal.*[66]

> In determining what constitutes procedural fairness in a given case, a court should be slow to impose obligations upon government which will inhibit its ability to make and implement policy effectively (a principle well recognised in our common law and that of other countries.) As a young democracy facing immense challenges of

> transformation, we cannot deny the importance of the need to ensure the ability of the Executive to act efficiently and promptly.

The *Premier, Mpumalanga* case concerned a challenge to a decision by a provincial education minister terminating bursaries paid to needy students in state-aided schools. The policy change was motivated by a well-founded desire to eliminate racial discrimination in the system. However, in his budget speech for the year in question, the minister had failed to indicate that existing, racially-based bursaries would be withdrawn in that year.[67] Thereafter, at a public meeting, he announced the termination of all existing bursaries with retroactive effect.[68]

The respondent, an association of formerly white schools, some of whose pupils were adversely affected by this decision, challenged it as a violation of section 24(b) of the interim constitution (right to procedurally fair administrative action). The trial court set aside the decision and substituted it with a decision that existing bursaries should be paid until the end of the school year. On appeal to the Constitutional Court, the decision to terminate the bursaries was assumed to constitute administrative action, notwithstanding a clear acceptance later on in the judgement (in relation to an allegation of bias) that it was 'a political decision ... taken in the light of a range of considerations' by 'a duly elected politician'.[69] Finding that the respondent had a legitimate expectation that bursaries would be paid until the end of the school year, the court held that the decision to terminate the bursaries with retroactive effect without affording the respondent's members a hearing was unconstitutional against section 24(b).

The first part of the court's interpretation of the procedural fairness standard is contained in the passage quoted above. The emphasis in that passage falls squarely on the need to permit the executive to act 'efficiently and promptly'. The emphasis shifts as the court continues:

> On the other hand, to permit the implementation of retroactive decisions without, for example, affording parties an effective opportunity to make representations would flout another important principle, that of procedural fairness ... Citizens are entitled to expect that government policy will not ordinarily be altered in ways which would threaten or harm their rights or legitimate expectations without their being given reasonable notice of the proposed change or an opportunity to make representations to the decision-maker.[70]

The balance that the court strikes in these two extracts between the need to promote 'prompt', 'efficient' and 'effective' government, and the need to ensure respect for due process is a familiar refrain in many countries, including mature democracies. What is remarkable about this passage, however, is that the court assigns to itself both a passive and an active role in the striking of this balance. Note, for example, the subtle shift in the first extract from the need not to '*inhibit* [the executive's] ability to make and implement policy effectively' to 'the need to *ensure* the ability of the Executive to act efficiently and promptly' (emphasis added). Similarly, in the second extract, the court's reluctance 'to permit the implementation of retroactive decisions' is justified by the need to enforce procedural rights. As it did in the *Walker* decision, the court is here defining a role for itself as legitimator of the social transformation project. According to this conception of its role, the function performed by the court is neither that of passive watchdog nor that of active champion of citizens' rights against the state. Rather, the political context in which it is operating requires the court to work alongside the democratically elected government to consolidate the transition from apartheid to democracy.

Permanent Secretary, Department of Education and Welfare, Eastern Cape and Another v. Ed-U-College (PE) (Section 21) Inc.

The court's self-understanding as legitimator of the political branches' social transformation project is also evident in another case in which it was required to apply the procedural fairness standard to political resource allocation. The facts in *Permanent Secretary, Department of Education and Welfare, Eastern Cape and Another v. Ed-U-College (PE) (Section 21) Inc*[71] were almost identical to those in *Premier, Mpumalanga*. As in that case, the claimant challenged a provincial education department policy reducing the subsidies paid to schools, in this instance, independent schools.[72] The crucial difference between the *Premier, Mpumalanga* and *Ed-U-College* cases, however, was that the reduction in benefits in the latter instance had not been effected retroactively. Rather, it had followed by necessary implication from a reduced allocation to independent schools in the provincial education budget. This allocation had in turn been approved by the provincial legislature in its annual Appropriation Act. In all, three allocations were at issue in *Ed-U-College*: (1) the share of the provincial budget allocated to education; (2) the percentage allocation to independent schools; and (3) the allocation made to each independent school in terms of a subsidy formula determined by the minister.

The trial court had held that the first two allocations constituted legislative action, and were therefore not justiciable, at least in so far as the challenge had been brought under the right to just *administrative* action. However, the third allocation 'was a justiciable matter over which the ... Court had jurisdiction'.[73] On appeal to the Constitutional Court, the applicants – the permanent secretary for the provincial education department and the provincial education minister – argued that the allocation of resources to independent schools was in its entirety 'a matter of policy, taken [sic] by an elected person, after due deliberation'.[74] The court rejected this argument. The first two allocations, it held, were both clearly legislative in character – the first because the actual amount allocated to education was listed in a schedule to the Appropriation Bill,[75] and the second because the estimated expenditure on each educational sub-programme had been considered by the legislature when approving the Bill.[76] The third allocation was harder to classify. Although the minister's decision determining the subsidy formula purported to be a decision about how the budget allocated to independent schools should be distributed, it also conclusively determined the amount that each school should receive.[77] This fact, the court held, was decisive. It meant that the minister's conduct amounted to the implementation of legislation, rather than the formulation of policy. As such, it was subject to review as administrative action, notwithstanding the fact that the minister was a senior member of the provincial executive.[78]

This finding effectively concluded the Constitutional Court's role in the case, since the appeal had been taken to it before evidence had been led on the procedure that had been followed by the minister prior to determining the subsidy formula. Nevertheless, the court took the opportunity presented to it in *Ed-U-College* to comment on the procedural fairness standard articulated in *Premier, Mpumalanga*, as follows:

> Procedural fairness will not require that a right to a hearing be given to all affected persons simply because a decision is to be taken which has the effect of reducing the amount of the annual subsidy to be paid. Subsidies are paid annually and, given the precarious financial circumstances of education departments at present, schools and parents cannot assume, in the absence of any undertaking or promise by an education department, that subsidies will always continue to be paid at the rate previously established or that they should be afforded a hearing should subsidies have to be reduced because the legislature has reduced the amount allocated for distribution.[79]

As before, this passage reflects the court's striving for a balance between the need to enforce procedural rights and the need to promote efficient government. The primary distributional choice determining the amount to be allocated towards school subsidies in any particular year, the court makes clear, is within the preserve of the legislature. However, to the extent that the political branches, by their conduct, create a legitimate expectation that subsidies will not be reduced or withdrawn in any particular year without a prior hearing, the court will enforce citizens' rights to participate in any interstitial change in policy.

Once again, the court is here scripting a role for itself as legitimator of the social transformation project – endorsing the political branches' power to redistribute resources along more equitable lines, but indicating its preparedness to strike down poorly conceived policies that infringe on procedural rights.

Conclusion

The four cases discussed in this article indicate that, rather than abdicating responsibility for the transformation of South Africa from a racially divided and deeply unequal society to one in which resources are more rationally and fairly distributed, the Constitutional Court has chosen to put itself at the centre of that project. In *Grootboom*, the court developed a review standard that allowed it to engage the political branches in rational discussion over the fairness of the national housing programme, without, however, setting government's priorities for it. In *Walker*, the court appears to have deliberately elected to decide the constitutional challenge on a potentially controversial basis in order to give its stamp of approval to the restructuring of the municipal services sector. And in the *Premier, Mpumalanga* and *Ed-U-College* cases the court, without being required to do so, was at pains to express its appreciation for the balance that needed to be struck between the redistribution of resources in the education sector and respect for procedural rights.

All four of these cases involved constitutional challenges to the allocation of resources, an area of public policy that conventional wisdom dictates should be left to the political branches. Notwithstanding the possible threat to its legitimacy posed by involvement in these types of cases, and the considerable difficulties associated with reviewing the complex policy choices at issue, the court has entered this terrain with a remarkable degree of success. In so doing, it has scripted a role for itself as legitimator of the political branches' social transformation project, a role that simultaneously allows it to build its legitimacy even as it intrudes into one of the most sacrosanct areas of politics.

If that is an accurate assessment, the record of the Constitutional Court in these four cases confirms Ruti Teitel's insight that, 'during periods of political upheaval', the rule of law, 'rather than grounding legal order, ... serves to mediate the normative shift in justice that characterizes these extraordinary periods'.[80] Although this remark was made primarily in relation to countries in transition, it applies equally well to new democracies. Constitutional courts in this context, it would seem, cannot afford the luxury of the separation of powers doctrine. The consolidation of democracy after a long period of authoritarianism depends on the ability of the political branches to make law-governed social transformation work. If the social transformation project is to succeed, it must in turn be legitimated by law. Counter-intuitively, this means that judges in new democracies may have to intrude further into politics than their colleagues in mature democracies would deem necessary or prudent. In so doing, they run the risk that the political branches may become disaffected. However, if skilfully handled, intruding into politics may also become the means by which constitutional courts in new democracies build the institutional legitimacy required to survive, and eventually to assist in the consolidation of democracy.

ACKNOWLEDGEMENT

The author thanks Sandra Liebenberg, Siri Gloppen, David Bilchitz, Jonathan Klaaren, Stuart Wilson and Anne Chandler for comments on an earlier version.

NOTES

1. The term was coined by Lon L. Fuller in 'The Forms and Limits of Adjudication', *Harvard Law Review*, Vol.92, No.2 (1978), pp.394–404.
2. The only decision to have elicited a hostile response from the executive to date was that of the trial court in *Treatment Action Campaign and Others v. Minister of Health and Others* 2002 (4) BCLR 356 (T) (ordering the state to extend its programme for the prevention of mother-to-child transmission of HIV/AIDS). When asked on national television whether the government would implement the court's order if confirmed by the Constitutional Court, the Minister of Health unequivocally said 'no'. She was, however, quickly forced to retract this remark. And, when the Constitutional Court eventually did approve the trial court's order in substantially the same form (*Minister of Health and Others v. Treatment Action Campaign and Others (No.2)* 2002 (5) SA 721 (CC)), the executive did not publicly question it.
3. See, for example, Lee Epstein, Olga Shvetsova and Jack Knight, 'The Role of Constitutional Courts in the Establishment of Democratic Systems of Government', *Law and Society Review* Vol.35, No.1 (2001), pp.117–63 (attempting to model the strategic calculations made by the Russian Constitutional Court in relation to politically controversial decisions).
4. For a rare exception, see Thomas J. Bollyky, 'R if C>B: A Paradigm for Judicial Remedies of Socio-Economic Rights Violations', *South African Journal on Human Rights* Vol.18, No.2 (2002), p.165 (arguing that 'when remedying a violation of the Bill of Rights, courts intuitively weigh the degree to which they must make choices regarding policies and budgets against the extent of the constitutional violation').
5. Constitution of the Republic of South Africa Act 200 of 1993 ('the interim constitution').
6. Constitution of the Republic of South Africa Act 108 of 1996 ('the final Constitution').
7. *Ex parte Chairperson of the Constitutional Assembly: in re Certification of the Constitution of the Republic of South Africa, 1996* 1996 (4) SA 744 (CC).
8. Short biographies of the sitting and former judges are available at <http://www.concourt.gov.za>.
9. Complete statistics on the record of the South African Constitutional Court, including voting patterns, are published each year in the *South African Journal on Human Rights*.
10. Section 178(1) of the constitution provides for the appointment of 23 people to serve on the

Judicial Service Commission, including 12 whose appointment is directly controlled by the ruling party.

11. See Hermann Giliomee and Charles Simkins, 'The Dominant Party Regimes of South Africa, Mexico, Taiwan and Malaysia: A Comparative Assessment', in Hermann Giliomee and Charles Simkins (eds), *The Awkward Embrace: One-party Domination and Democracy* (Cape Town: Tafelberg, 1999), pp.1–45.
12. See Robert A. Dahl, 'Decision-making in a Democracy: The Supreme Court as a National Policy-maker', *Journal of Public Law*, Vol.6, No.2 (1957), pp.285–6 (demonstrating, through an examination of the interval between appointments to the United States Supreme Court, that presidents of the United States have generally been able to appoint a majority of judges who share their political views within their first term of office).
13. See note 8 above.
14. Section 2 of the final constitution provides that 'law *or conduct* inconsistent with it is invalid' (emphasis added), while section 167(7) provides that 'a constitutional matter includes any issue involving the interpretation, protection or enforcement of the Constitution', and section 167(1)(c) provides that the Constitutional Court 'makes the final decision whether a matter is a constitutional matter'. In theory, this gives the Court the power to review the constitutionality of all executive conduct, including conduct that would in other jurisdictions be regarded as purely political.
15. See Maurice Finkelstein, 'Judicial Self-Limitation', *Harvard Law Review*, Vol.37, No.3 (1924), pp.338–64 and Louis Henkin, 'Is There a "Political Question" Doctrine?', *Yale Law Journal*, Vol.85, No.5 (1976), pp.597–625.
16. The only exception to this rule concerns applications for direct access in terms of section 167(6)(a) of the final constitution, where the court has been more circumspect.
17. Cf. Iain Currie, 'Judicious Avoidance', *South African Journal on Human Rights*, Vol.15, No.2 (1999), pp.138–65. My approach in this article is both narrower and broader than that of Currie inasmuch as I am only interested in cases dealing with political resource allocation, whilst at the same time arguing that the court has sometimes deliberately taken on issues that it might have avoided.
18. 2001(1) SA 46 (CC) (hereafter '*Grootboom*'). The trial court decision is reported as *Grootboom and Others v. Oostenberg Municipality and Others* 2000(3) 277 BCLR (C).
19. See Cass R. Sunstein, 'Social and Economic Rights? Lessons from South Africa', *Constitutional Forum*, Vol.11, No.4 (2001), pp.123–32.
20. *Grootboom* par.99.
21. *Grootboom* par.27 n.29.
22. See sections 231-33 of the final constitution, providing for the incorporation of international agreements into domestic law through enactment 'by national legislation' (section 231(4)) and specifying that both international agreements and customary international law, in order to constitute 'law in the Republic', must be consistent with the constitution or an Act of Parliament (section 232).
23. *Grootboom* par.33.
24. Ibid.
25. Ibid. paras 32–3.
26. See ibid. par.40. Comprehensiveness has three different senses in *Grootboom*: geographic coverage (par.54); effective co-ordination of government action at all levels (par.55); and inclusion of all classes in the relevant programme (paras 63 and 64). The national housing programme was found to be lacking only in the third sense.
27. Ibid. par.43.
28. Ibid. par.36.
29. See *Grootboom* par.43: 'A programme that excludes a significant segment of society cannot be said to be reasonable'.
30. See *Grootboom* paras 36, 63–5, 69.
31. See *Bel Porto School Governing Body and Others v. Premier of the Province, Western Cape and Another* 2002(9) BCLR 891 (CC) par.46 (holding that the *Grootboom* reasonableness review standard was a 'higher standard' than the review standard applied under section 9(1) of the final constitution).

32. See *Grootboom* par.54 (finding that the national housing programme was 'not haphazard' but 'systematic').
33. This standard is discussed in detail in the analysis of the *Walker* case in the next section.
34. This test, which is applied under the general limitations clause in section 36 of the final constitution, empowers the court to strike down laws that are disproportional in the sense that the state might have achieved its legislative purpose by means less invasive of the right in question. This standard is a very strict standard since it permits the court to substitute its view of a less invasive policy for that of the political branches. The court in *Grootboom* clearly signalled that its reasonableness review standard was less strict than this when holding that 'a court considering reasonableness will not enquire whether other more desirable or favourable measures could have been adopted, or whether public money could have been better spent' (par.41).
35. This argument has been developed at greater length in Theunis Roux, 'Understanding *Grootboom* – A Response to Cass R. Sunstein', *Constitutional Forum*, Vol.12, No.2 (2002), pp.41–51.
36. *Grootboom* par. 66.
37. 2002(5) SA 721 (CC) (hereafter 'the *TAC* case').
38. Ibid. par.38.
39. 1998(2) SA 363 (CC) (hereafter '*Walker*').
40. Section 8 of the interim constitution provides: '(1) Every person shall have the right to equality before the law and to equal protection of the law. (2) No person shall be unfairly discriminated against, directly or indirectly, and, without derogating from the generality of this provision, on one or more of the following grounds in particular: race, gender, sex, ethnic or social origin, colour, sexual orientation, age, disability, religion, conscience, belief, culture or language....'
41. *Walker* par.27.
42. 1998(1) SA 300 (CC).
43. Ibid. par.54.
44. Ibid. par.32. Both section 8(2) of the interim constitution and section 9(3) of the final constitution prohibit the state from discriminating 'directly or indirectly'. Judge Sachs's dissenting judgement in *Walker* was premised on a finding that the differentiation at issue was based on 'objectively determinable characteristics of different geographical areas, and not on race' (Ibid. par.105.)
45. Cf. Section 9(5) of the final constitution.
46. *Walker* paras 37–81.
47. *Harksen* (note 42 above) para. 52 (cited in *Walker* para. 38).
48. *Walker* para. 43.
49. Ibid. par.44.
50. Ibid. paras 45–8.
51. Ibid. par.53.
52. Ibid. paras 57–63.
53. Ibid. par.68.
54. Ibid. par.79.
55. Ibid. par.72.
56. Ibid. par.74.
57. Ibid. par.81.
58. Ibid. paras 40–42.
59. Note that Judge Sachs's dissent was based on a finding that there was no evidence of *prima facie* discrimination on a listed ground (*Walker* par.107).
60. The presumption is contained in section 8(4) of the interim constitution (the provision applied in this case) and section 9(5) of the final constitution.
61. *Walker* par.22.
62. Ibid. par.81.
63. Ibid. par.79.
64. See Cathi Albertyn, 'Equality', in M.H. Cheadle, D.M. Davis and N.R.L. Haysom, *South African Constitutional Law: The Bill of Rights* (Durban: Butterworths, 2002), pp.51–121, at

p.70 (arguing that the *Walker* case 'provides one of the best examples of a failure to meet the rationality requirement ... although it was not decided as such').

65. *President of the Republic of South Africa and Others v. South African Rugby Football Union and Others* 2000(1) SA 1 (CC) par.141.
66. 1999(2) SA 83 (CC) (hereafter '*Premier, Mpumalanga*').
67. Ibid. paras 17–18.
68. Ibid. par.22(b).
69. Ibid. par.51.
70. *Premier, Mpumalanga* para. 41.
71. 2001(2) SA 1 (CC) (hereafter '*Ed-U-College*').
72. The challenge was brought under section 33(1) of the final constitution, which, like section 24 of the interim constitution, guarantees the right to procedurally fair administrative action.
73. *Ed-U-College* par.6.
74. Ibid. par.8 (citing the applicants' notice of appeal).
75. Ibid. par.12. The court made it clear that its finding that the first two allocations constituted legislative rather than administrative action was not necessarily a bar to judicial review under other provisions of the Bill of Rights. However, the respondent had based its case purely on 'administrative law principles' (ibid. par.11).
76. Ibid. par.14.
77. Ibid. par.21.
78. Ibid. par.18, citing *President of the Republic of South Africa v South African Rugby Football Union* (note 65 above) paras 141–3.
79. Ibid. par.22.
80. See Ruti Teitel, 'Transitional Jurisprudence: The Role of Law in Political Transformation', *Yale Law Journal*, Vol.106, No.7 (1997), p.2016.

The Accountability Function of the Courts in Tanzania and Zambia

SIRI GLOPPEN

Introduction

A judiciary with the ability to prevent political power-holders from abusing their powers is widely believed to be a precondition for good governance and consolidation of a democratic regime. The aim of this study is, first to assess to what extent judges in Tanzania and Zambia play a significant role in holding their governments accountable. Second, it seeks to understand why they perform as they do, and what explains the differences between the two countries. The focus is on the period since 1990, with moves to formal multiparty democracy, but viewed in the context of judicial developments in these countries since independence (Tanzania 1961, Zambia 1964).[1]

The courts' accountability function refers to their ability to prevent illegitimate use of political power. Judges contribute to accountable government by requiring power-holders to disclose and justify their actions and by *sanctioning* political authorities when they overstep the boundaries for their power as defined in the constitution, violate basic rights or compromise the democratic process.[2] Courts' accountability performance depend both on their willingness and ability to say 'no' when called for (manifest sanctioning), and the extent to which their decisions are respected (compliance) and actually influence political behaviour (latent authority).

To assess the judiciaries' accountability performance requires a broad contextual analysis of politically significant cases. Have the courts found against the government? If so, what has been the government's reaction? Is the court's authority respected? Focus is particularly on the higher courts and their relationship with the executive arm of government – the dominant political force in both countries as in most of Africa. Tension between the courts and Parliament is nevertheless relevant as it often involves the executive 'in disguise'.

In order to explain the judiciaries' performance, three sets of independent variables are identified: the legal culture, the institutional structure, and the courts' social legitimacy.

The legal culture, the professional self-understanding and 'norms of appropriateness' guiding judges in their work, influence their accountability performance. Of particular importance is the judges' understanding of what their role should be in a democratic system. There is no settled answer to this question in the literature – scholars offer attractive, competing, views on the proper function of courts in a democracy.[3] Some normative standards for judicial behaviour and independence are widely shared, but there is no clear 'benchmark' to aim for regarding the political role of the courts. How do judges in Tanzania and Zambia conceive their relationship with the other arms of government? Is a deferential attitude to political power prevalent, advising caution and judicial self-restraint in politically sensitive cases, or do they favour more assertiveness?

The institutional structure includes the legal framework, regulations and organization of the judiciary, as well as the financial and professional resources available – factors influencing the courts' capacity as well as independence. How do institutional and structural factors affect the ability of the Tanzanian and Zambian courts to perform their accountability function? Important indicators to consider are judicial appointment procedures, judges' security of tenure and terms of service, disciplinary mechanisms, budgetary autonomy and sufficiency of resources – infrastructure as well as jurisprudential resources (legal material, training, professional forums).

The social legitimacy of the judiciary – their support among important groups in society – is the third variable believed to impact on the courts' ability and willingness to stand up to other arms of government. Social legitimacy is partly a function of how the judges are perceived to fulfil their role – whether they are seen as relevant, competent, fair and independent, or corrupt, self-seeking, incompetent or irrelevant. Are Tanzanian and Zambian courts used by different sectors of society? Are they respected and trusted? Do they have the social support making it costly for the executive to contravene their decisions or encroach upon their independence?

Why Compare Tanzania and Zambia?

The two countries are similar in most respects relevant to this analysis: both are poor, aid-dependent, countries where resource constraints severely affect the administration of justice, and donors carry significant political influence. Their legal systems are marked by the deeply plural nature of these societies as well as the colonial past. British common law lies at the core of the formal legal systems while local customary law dominates in the lower courts and personal law. After independence both turned into one-party states with pressure on the judiciary to defer to the party's political priorities (just as pre-independence judiciaries were expected to conform to the priorities of the colonial government).

In Zambia, internal and external pressure brought multiparty elections in 1991. The victorious opposition – the Movement for Multi-party Democracy (MMD) – has held on to power ever since, partly by constitutionally controversial means. Tanzania moved to a multiparty system through a more gradual and government-controlled constitutional reform process culminating with multi-party elections in 1995, but with continued dominance by the Revolutionary Party of Tanzania (CCM). Despite formal multi-party democracy, both countries continue to see extreme concentration of political power in the ruling party and the executive president.

Given the very similar social and political situation – one where the accountability function of the courts is particularly crucial as well as exceedingly difficult – even minor differences in the judiciaries' accountability performance are interesting. To understand how they are related to variables in the judges' institutional and social predicament is relevant both from the perspective of judicial reform efforts, and for studies of democratic consolidation.

The Accountability Performance of the Tanzanian Judiciary

A Tanzanian legal scholar labelled the country's judiciary as *timorous souls,* fearing to tread onto politically contested terrain.[4] This broad picture does, however, contain significant deviations from the general pattern. While there are few spectacular rulings against the government in Tanzania, it is not unusual for the state to lose in cases where the political stakes are lower.

The direction of change over the past decade seems to be towards increased judicial independence and assertiveness, although not all shifts are in this direction. The judiciary's small size (the higher judiciary comprises less than 50 judges) and short institutional history, render individual personalities particularly salient. There are individual judges with a consistent path of politically bold judgements – most notably Judge Mwalusanya who made a string of assertive judgements on human rights issues in the 1980s and early 1990s, and whose retirement marked a sharp downturn in judgements challenging the government.[5]

Given the hierarchical structure of the judiciary, the personality of the chief justice is most significant. The first Tanzanian chief justice appointed after independence was weak and widely criticized for advising judges to consider party policies. He was replaced by Chief Justice Nyalali, who served almost three decades and three presidents, gradually developing an appreciation for judicial independence and a more secure position for the judiciary.[6] The current Chief Justice Barnabas Samatta is commended for placing an even stronger premium on judicial independence.

There are diverging assessments of the willingness of the Tanzanian courts to stand up to the government and say 'no' when called for, and regarding their authority vis-à-vis the government – or their ability to 'make it stick'.[7] In interviews, the judges generally expressed faith in the independence of the courts, holding that – at least since the introduction of the multiparty system – they were free to decide matters on purely professional grounds. But they acknowledged political influence as a problem in the lower judiciary, and that there are 'psychological constraints and fears, particularly among magistrates. The mental process of adjusting to the multiparty conditions is still ongoing'.[8] The scarcity of rulings against the government was also attributed to people's reluctance to bring cases against the government, and to the government's tendency to settle out of court in cases they are about to lose.

Academic observers of the courts, people in the media, and NGOs, however, expressed discontent with what was perceived as an unduly deferential attitude among the judges. This was attributed mainly to the legal culture. Few suspected direct political pressure or corruption in individual cases in the higher courts, unlike in the lower courts where corruption is considered rampant. And in contrast with mainland Tanzania, strong allegations of direct political influence were levied at the courts on Zanzibar. Zanzibar's Chief Justice has been seen to merge the political will of the executive with the disciplining force of the internal court hierarchy, dismissing and transferring pro-opposition personnel.[9] The Court of Appeal, which Zanzibar shares with the mainland is, however, seen as a safeguard: 'Almost all Zanzibar High Court judgements go on appeal – and about 80% are overturned.'[10]

Manifest Sanctioning

There are some significant cases in which the courts have sanctioned political power holders when they have acted outside of their constitutional powers. The most frequently cited is the so-called *5 million TSh judgement (2002)*,[11] characterized as 'the only important human-rights decision since 1994'.[12] In order to discourage frivolous litigation over elections – tying up resources and imposing costs on elected officers – Parliament passed a law requiring election petitioners to deposit 5 million TSh (approximately USD 5,500) as security for cost. Opposition parties argued that the law would effectively bar people from challenging flawed elections in court and an opposition candidate filed a case in the High Court arguing that the law was unconstitutional. A majority of the judges upheld the law, while Kimaro J, one of the few woman judges in Tanzania, wrote a dissenting judgement holding the provision unconstitutional. When the case came on appeal, the Supreme Court ruled that the increase from TSh 500 to TSh 5 million was arbitrary and in violation of the constitutional rights to equality and access to justice. By requiring uniform payment of this high amount the law discriminates on the basis of social status and effectively bars the right of poor people to challenge in court infringements of their right to vote. Parliament was found to have overstepped its constitutional powers in enacting the unconstitutional provision, which the court declared null and void.

Other significant examples include Judge Lugakingira's judgement in the *Mtikila* case, which found unconstitutional the ban on independent candidates and legislation regulating political rallies.[13] In *Peter Ng'omango* Judge Mwalusanya found unconstitutional the procedure for suing the government.[14] Previously, litigants were required to obtain permission from the government in order to sue them, which could take two to three years. The amended clause requires litigants wanting to challenge the government to give three months notice. The *Pumbun* case concerned the scope of the derogation clauses limiting the application of the basic rights in the constitution (Tanzanian Constitution, Article 30).[15] The Court of Appeal ruled that in order to be constitutional derogations or limitations of basic rights must be non-arbitrary and satisfy the principle of proportionality, meaning that the limitation imposed must not be more than is reasonably necessary to achieve the legitimate object.[16] Several of the Tanzanian judges interviewed pointed to this precedent, and similar cases internationally, as a way also to handle ouster clauses, shielding legislation (such as parts of the electoral act) from judicial review.

These politically significant cases, where the rulings of Tanzanian courts have been highly unpopular with the government, illustrate manifest judicial independence. Particularly the first example shows the Supreme Court laying down its authority in a way explicitly challenging the authority of Parliament (and by implication the executive, since the ruling party totally dominates in the National Assembly, the *Bunge*).

Compliance

Has the Courts' authority been respected? The judges found President Mkapa (1995–) more committed to constitutional government than his predecessor, and held that government officials, as a rule, respect the courts' authority and comply with adverse judgements. 'They may grumble and delay matters, exhausting all possibilities for appeals, but if they are ordered to pay, they eventually will.'[17] The increasing use of the courts by the government was also noted as a sign of recognition 'if the government wouldn't want to respect the rulings of the court – why use them?'[18] This is a valid point, although the possibility of delaying inconvenient matters for a decade through exhausting legal options may in itself be attractive.

Civil society representatives agreed that the government would normally respect adverse decisions, but noted that rulings had been overturned, most significantly in the Mtikila case referred to above (regarding independent candidates, and legislation regulating political rallies), where Parliament blatantly overruled the court and effectively reintroduced the clause. But this is seen as exceptional. While parliamentarians and government representatives occasionally use harsh words against the courts, this is normally followed by grudging compliance, as Parliament's reaction to the 5 million TSh judgement illustrates. When the courts ruled the clause unconstitutional, it caused commotion in Parliament. In a newspaper article the speaker more than hinted that the Appeal Court judges had failed to observe the proper separation of powers, and had overstepped their constitutional powers by taking on the role of legislator. A heated public debate followed. Prominent members of the legal community came out in defence of the court, and eventually the government signalled that the judgement would be accepted.[19]

Academic observers were more critical of the government's respect for the court's authority, arguing that there are many cases where Parliament has amended laws in ways effectively nullifying the courts' judgements and that what was different in the *5 million TSh* case is that there was a debate. Normally, politically uncomfortable rulings are met with immediate reaction and it is done in silence.[20] However, legal academics also note some improvement:

> The executive used to be hostile. In 1996 there was a judgement by the High Court in Moshi where an order was made for attachment of government property. The President went all out in the media, stating that the court would be overruled. Now it would surprise me a lot if it were to happen again. The government has come to realize that courts have their powers. There are still a few isolated incidents, but in general a very big improvement.'[21]

As for Parliament, 'There has been no direct frustration by parliament of court decisions since the Mtikila case – but on the other hand, how many cases have there been?'[22]

The scarcity of politically significant cases, where the courts have actually said 'no' to the executive or parliament when constitutional limitations are overstepped, indicates that Tanzanian courts do not perform a strong accountability function. Considering the adverse reactions by public officials against several significant judgements, the courts' authority seems weak. However, judicial authority may assess itself in alternative ways.

Latent Authority

Even when courts do not play their 'veto card' it may function as a *latent sanction,* keeping political actors and public officials from engaging in unlawful activities, or passing unconstitutional legislation and so forth. In established democracies this is arguably the most important part of the courts' accountability function. To assess the extent of this latent authority is complicated, but indications can be found in activities like the drafting process for laws and policies, the role of constitutional arguments and public debate.

The Attorney General who is drafting the laws in Tanzania, is supposed to advise on constitutionality, but generally speaking the interviewees doubted that constitutionality is a serious concern for the Tanzanian government. Some noted, however, that it is becoming more of an issue. 'In the media it is certainly an issue. Generally, people are more concerned with their rights, and also in Parliament it is used as a political argument.'[23]

While the picture of the Tanzanian judiciary's' *accountability performance* is more ambiguous when looked at in some detail, the general pattern indicated at the outset seems to hold: judges rarely put down their foot when government officials fail to comply with their mandate and the constitutional rules guiding their exercise of power. When the courts do come out with politically uncomfortable judgements, their authority is not always respected. And when it is, it is likely to be a grudging minimal compliance with the direct terms of the judgement. Court rulings seem to have limited effect on the political debate and the outcome of political processes. Despite notable recent developments, the overall assessment must be that the Tanzanian courts have not been able to significantly limit executive dominance or the 'hyper-presidential' nature of Tanzanian politics. Nevertheless, there are noteworthy examples of willingness – and ability – to stand up to the political branches when they overstep their constitutional mandate.

The Accountability Performance of the Zambian Judiciary

During 38 years of independence, Zambian courts have rarely delivered decisions that significantly inconvenience the sitting government by seeking to check its abuse of powers, failures to deliver on obligations, attempts to undermine the constitutional rules of the game or to overstep the mandate.

The independence constitution provided for an independent judiciary with significant review powers, but executive dominance, blurring of the party–state distinction, and close personal ties between the president and the chief justice, provided poor conditions for judicial independence in the one-party state (1973–90). The 1991 democratic elections raised hopes of change.

Soon after Frederick Chiluba (MMD) took over as president, Matthew Ngulube was appointed chief justice.[24] He wrote some outstanding judgements, highly commended by lawyers and human rights activists, most notably when in April 1995 he handed down a judgement finding unconstitutional certain provisions of the Public Order Act, a rare case of judicial review of legislation that was highly unpopular with the government (se below). By this time it was becoming clear that multiparty elections and constitutional changes had failed to diminish the dominance of the executive president. 'Parliament is totally useless in the governance of this country. It is just an extension of State House, and a very expensive one for that matter'.[25]

Subsequently the courts and the Chief Justice too came under criticism for moving towards a pro-government stance. Still it came as a total shock when Ngulube resigned in the last week of June 2002, after Zambia's main independent newspaper, *The Post*, revealed that he had secretly and irregularly received around K700,000,000 (or USD 184,000) from the government, beginning in 1997.[26] Despite criticism for being soft in cases involving the executive, his personal integrity had not been questioned. He was regarded as 'a legal giant' and shock, almost disbelief, was expressed by all parts of the legal fraternity, as well as by members of the political opposition and the NGO sector. That the most senior and trusted court official was caught red-handed has shaken the confidence of the courts in Zambian society, and strongly affects current perceptions of the judiciary.

Manifest Sanctioning

Despite the general pattern of political deference, judges of the Zambian High and Supreme Court have on occasion stood up to government officials in order to prevent unconstitutional laws and abuse of power. Most significant is the *Christine Mulundika* judgement.[27] In this case, the applicant and seven others, including former President Kaunda, were charged with unlawful assembly contrary to section 5 of the Public Order Act, requiring anyone who wished to hold a public meeting or demonstration to apply to the police for a permit. The constitutionality of the provision was challenged and the Supreme Court struck it down, finding that it infringed upon the freedoms of expression and assembly guaranteed by the constitution. It was not justifiable in a democratic society, due to the uncontrolled nature of the discretionary power vested in the police; the lack of safeguards against arbitrary decisions; and the failure to oblige the police to consider whether less invasive means could achieve the aim of averting public disorder.[28]

In a case before the 1996 elections, *The People v. Senior Chief Inyambo Yeta and 7 others,*[29] the High Court dismissed a treason charge against members of a main opposition party. The High Court also ruled in favour of three journalists from *The Post*, charged with receiving confidential documents, contrary to the State Security Act.[30]

Both in 1996 and 2001, allegations of electoral misconduct gave rise to large numbers of petitions, predominantly against the ruling party. Several of the parliamentary election petitions decided after the 2001 elections, have gone in favour of the opposition.[31] But, particularly with regard to presidential elections, the length of time it takes to decide petitions compromises this procedure.[32] Challenges against the presidential election cannot be brought until two weeks after the new president is sworn into office – and may take two years to decide – which severely complicates a ruling against the incumbent. In the case now pending, opposition parties approached the High Court immediately after the December 2001 elections, insisting that the Chief Justice not declare the winner and swear in the new president until there had been a re-count of the votes. The court dismissed the claim, holding that they had no discretion to delay the inauguration.[33] The result is that hearings in the *Second Presidential Petition,* brought against President Levy Mwanawasa, only commenced in mid-August 2002. A decision is not expected until late 2003.

The most frequently cited failure of the Zambian judiciary to hold the executive to account is the *First Presidential Petition,*[34] challenging President Chiluba's re-election. Here, the Supreme Court was widely presumed to have bowed to executive pressure. The background to the case was that the government in May 1996 forced a constitutional amendment through Parliament containing among other a controversial provision requiring that presidential candidates must be Zambian citizens born to parents who are Zambian by birth or descent, and must not be a tribal chief – requirements believed to be tailored to disqualify specific opposition leaders and damage the opposition's chances to effectively participate in the upcoming general election. The amendment was vigorously challenged by opposition parties and civil society.[35] Five opposition parties fielded a petition challenging Chiluba's election as president for failing to satisfy (his own) new criteria. Chiluba's father was alleged to come from Zaire, and the petitioners demanded that a DNA test be taken to ascertain this. This was rejected by the Supreme Court, a decision which was widely seen a politically motivated.[36] Poor electoral administration and questionable processes also formed part of the challenge. The court accepted that there were irregularities and instances of rigging, but not sufficiently grave and systematic to justify invalidation of the election.

Compliance

The Zambian government has normally complied with court orders: amended unconstitutional provisions (at least marginally, although not always to practical effect); released prisoners (sometimes re-arresting them soon after); and paid compensation when ordered to (although often with substantial delay). There are, however, times when it has reacted harshly toward adverse rulings or ignored court orders. For example the 1995 judgement on the Public Order Act (*Christine Mulundika)* attracted the wrath of the government and harsh rhetoric in Parliament. What was commonly seen as a smear campaign against the Chief Justice was initiated, including rape allegations. Lacking in credibility, this fizzled out but it is believed to have contributed to the Chief Justice's change of attitude towards the president. In another instance Judge Kabazo Chanda was suspended after ruling that awaiting-trial prisoners, who had not been charged within the set time limit, be released. The government was enraged by the decision, maintaining it to be outside the judge's jurisdiction, and appointed a committee to investigate misconduct. The protracted process effectively pressured the judge to resign.[37]

In 2001 the chief justice set up a tribunal to investigate allegations against three cabinet members, including the minister of finance, for diverting 2 billion Kwacha (US$ 500,000) from the treasury to pay for the MMD pre-election congress (allegedly on the instructions of the president). The minister of finance was cleared on a technical point, but the others were found guilty of the theft of public funds. The tribunal ordered that the two be relieved of their parliamentary seats and one minister prosecuted. However, the president refused to dismiss them and the director of public prosecutions refused to prosecute. Both were adopted as parliamentary candidates in the 2001 elections. During the 2001 election campaign, the minister of information instructed the National Broadcasting Corporation to cancel a televised election debate. The organizers obtained a High Court injunction to prevent this, but were turned away from the studios by armed police. Opposition parties also obtained an order to ban district administrators (civil servants) from taking part in MMD campaigns, but this was ignored by the government.[38]

Latent Authority

As discussed earlier, judicial authority may also function indirectly, keeping political actors and public officials from engaging in unlawful or unconstitutional activities.

Few of the Zambians interviewed believed that the government is restrained by the possibility of having unconstitutional laws, or unlawful actions or policies, struck down. Still, compared to Tanzania, there is much more engagement around constitutional issues in Zambian civil society and to some extent in the political opposition. Both the opposition and the government seem more ready to fight out their battles in court. This gives the Zambian courts more opportunities to hold the executive to account, but as we have seen, they have at times been reluctant to fulfil this function – and when they have said 'no' this has not always been respected.

On the basis of the evidence presented here we can conclude that there have been significant attempts from judges in both Zambia and Tanzania to hold their governments to account, but neither judiciary has developed a strong accountability function vis-à-vis the government. Why is this so? The introduction suggested that three sets of variables are relevant to understand why the judges perform as they do: the legal culture; the institutional structure; and the courts' legitimacy.

Legal Culture

A central premise in institutional theory is that actors are motivated by the 'norms of appropriateness' prevalent in the institution within which they operate.[39] Judges' behaviour is influenced by the collective conceptions within their communicative community of what a good judge should do. It is therefore useful to start by looking at the understanding among Tanzanian and Zambian judges of their proper role vis-à-vis the executive.

In both countries, the majority of the judges, while insisting on the importance of judicial independence, are quick to point out that there are strict limits to their ability to check the actions of the other arms of government ('our function is to merely to apply the law as it is, not to make it'). They identify themselves as part of the British common law tradition, and this identity is central in defining their 'norms of appropriateness'. They emphasize that, in the common law tradition, courts are reactive, rather than proactive, and can only decide matters brought before them. Some explicitly distance themselves from activist colleagues, who fail to comply with the proper judicial role: 'it's imprudent and brings problems to the bench – what if the politicians got to know?'[40]

The importance of observing the separation of powers is emphasized. A Tanzanian judge, commenting on the *Mtikila* case, where the Court of

Appeal was overruled by Parliament, noted that 'there is nothing wrong with that. It is the role of the courts to interpret the laws and the role of Parliament to enact laws.'[41] Some of the Zambian judges complained over the extent to which political battles were taken to court, holding that matters of politics should be fought out in other arenas, and that the separation of powers requires judges not to meddle in the business of Parliament and the executive. But there were also other views. Some Zambian judges expressed considerable ambition to hold political actors accountable, underscoring that after the resignation of Chief Justice Ngulube, the entire judiciary is 'on trial' and must demonstrate political independence. The most self-critical felt the judiciary has failed the Zambian people by not succeeding in holding the MMD government to the terms of the country's constitution.

In Tanzania, several senior judges, including the Chief Justice, communicated an assertive conception of the judicial role. This view, also demonstrated in recent judgements,[42] emphasizes the importance of the courts' accountability function in safeguarding democracy and human rights. It reflects international currents, strongly voiced also by very capable legal academics in Tanzania.

We may thus conclude that 'the un-political judge' is a central *norm of appropriateness* in both countries, explaining a reluctance to challenge the government if they can avoid it. But in both countries there are also more assertive positions among central judges, where the normative standard is to stand up to the executive where called for. So why does it happen so rarely? Are the institutional and structural conditions that surround Zambian and Tanzanian judges at all conducive to a strong accountability function for the courts vis-à-vis the executive?

The Institutional Structure

The term 'institutional structure' as used here embraces a range of structural and institutional factors believed to impact on the independence of the courts and their ability to set limits for government officials' exercise of power: the legal framework defining the courts' powers and jurisdiction, regulations and organization of the judiciary, as well as the financial and professional resources available.

Powers and Jurisdiction

Both the Tanzanian and Zambian constitutions provide for an independent, impartial and autonomous judiciary and each includes a Bill of Rights which – at least formally – grants the courts wide jurisdiction and power to review legislation as well as administrative action. Zambia enacted such provisions at independence, while the Tanzanian courts had a weaker constitutional position until recently. Judicial independence was only explicitly recognized in 2000. A Bill of Rights was adopted in Tanzania in 1984, but suspended until 1988. In the first years after it came into effect, the courts declared a lot of actions unconstitutional. But this changed after the 'Basic Rights and Duties Enforcement Act' (Act 33 of 1994) introduced a new procedure for dealing with constitutional, human rights and civil rights cases. Such cases now had to be heard by a panel of three High Court judges. This might appear unproblematic, but in Tanzania most High Court divisions only have one or two judges. The change caused delays and increased costs since in practical terms most constitutional cases had to go to Dar es Salaam. It also greatly increased the internal control of the chief justice and court administration over individual judges since they could avoid judges with a record for activism on such cases, or team them up with judges of a more conservative mindset. The result was a sharp decrease in constitutional cases. 'I used to collect 2–3 cases a week, but after 1994 there was a complete stop … now we have maybe 1–2 human rights cases a year.'[43]

Both Tanzania and Zambia have ouster clauses limiting the jurisdiction of the courts. Pieces of legislation are shielded from review, such as parts of the Tanzanian Election Act of 1984, which states that once a person is declared president this cannot be challenged in court. The declaration is 'final and conclusive' and the president is sworn in two days later. In Zambia, many of the basic rights acknowledged in the constitution are rendered unjusticiable. Constitutional changes and wide derogation clauses has undermined the constitutional protection of rights. While courts in various countries are now challenging the constitutionality of such clauses, this is not happening in Tanzania or Zambia. Leading Tanzanian judges hold that if such cases are placed before them they would not accept unreasonable ousting of the court's authority. Zambian judges seem less ready to challenge such limitations, for example by relying on arguments from international precedent and foreign case law.

Appointment Procedures

The question of who appoints the judges and the procedure and criteria for selecting them are widely regarded as important for their independence and for the public's perception of the courts.

Both in Tanzania and Zambia the president appoints the Chief Justice. But while in Zambia every new president has appointed a new chief justice upon taking office, Tanzanian chief justices have generally served their terms undisturbed by changes in the political leadership. In Tanzania,

Judges of the Appeal Court are appointed by the president on advice of the Chief Justice. This used to be the procedure also for High Court judges, but these are now appointed by the President on advice of the Judicial Services Commission (JSC). The president normally follows this advice, but is not committed to do so, and has on occasion appointed judges from outside the list of nominees.

In Zambia, the process is similar, but appointments as chief justice, Supreme and High Court judges must be approved by a Parliamentary majority.[44] As in Tanzania, the Judicial Services Commission nominates the High Court judges, and while the president generally follows the recommendation, this is no formal obligation. With a weak opposition in the 1990s the parliamentary approval process has been a mere formality. In the 2001 elections the ruling party lost its parliamentary majority, and this could favour a more active involvement of the legislature in the appointment process (although floor-crossing and by-elections have again tilted the house in favour of the MMD). On the other hand, President Mwanawasa was a senior advocate and knows the Zambian legal community. That he is in a position to personally scrutinize and handpick the candidates could mean a stronger executive influence over appointments.

Appointment procedures are criticized in both countries, particularly the strong involvement of the President. In Zambia, political appointments are seen to be a manifest problem, with the deputy Chief Justice cited as the main case in point. In Tanzania, the involvement of the President is primarily seen as a problem for public confidence in the judges' independence. With regard to the actual judicial appointments, there are few complaints. The internal judicial hierarchy is seen as much more important for who are appointed to the bench and assigned to various positions. The criteria for being eligible for appointment as a judge in Tanzania are a minimum of five years of practice after admission to the bar, or working through the ranks of the magistracy. The majority of the judges currently on the bench are appointed from the magistracy, but several recent appointments are from private practice. Neither country has a public selection process or formal procedure for nominating candidates and few, even within the judiciary, seem to have a clear understanding of the selection criteria and the practice followed or how seniority and merit are balanced against other factors such as gender, region – or loyalty.

Terms and Security of Tenure

Non-renewable terms of service and security of tenure are seen as crucial to insulate judges so that they can make rulings that are unpopular with the executive without fearing a direct political backlash. Both in Tanzania and in Zambia judges are appointed for life. The retirement age is 65 years after which they can be asked to stay on as contract judges. Due to lack of qualified local candidates, Tanzania used to have a number of foreign judges working on contract – Zanzibar still does. For contract judges tenure is not secure.

The process for dismissing judges is the same in the two countries: a commission of inquiry is appointed consisting of three judges of which one has to be from another Commonwealth jurisdiction. The committee recommends to the president, who may dismiss the judge if the committee has concluded that there is a case of gross misconduct or gross incompetence. In both countries this has happened, but rarely.

Interestingly, Tanzanians generally view judges' security of tenure as adequate (but not for judicial officers in the lower courts), while in Zambia there is more criticism of the procedure, and particularly of the president's role in the dismissals. A noted problem is transferrals: 'a judge who falls foul of the executive could easily find himself appointed to head an obscure Public Commission…'.[45]

Tenure is not only about protection from removal, but also whether judges' salaries and conditions of service are adequate and reasonably secure. If judges lose out economically from being troublesome, they are unlikely to try. Zambians interviewed noted the executive's influence on the judges' service conditions as a problem. The president approves pay rises and adjustments and both Chiluba and now President Mwanawasa approved large salary increases at times when the government had very important cases before the court. During the hearings on the first presidential petition (against Chiluba's eligibility as a candidate) the judges' salaries were adjusted twice. Similarly, it was adjusted while the petition against Mwanawasa's election remained pending. Observers of the courts recognize the need to improve the judges' salaries, but see the timing as a signal of an unhealthy attitude and an attempt by the president to influence the judges. The judges, seeing the rise as overdue and the timing coincidental, still hold that it would have been better – particularly for their public image – if they did not have to rely on negotiations with the executive for their salary.

Judges' remuneration should be sufficient to attract good candidates for office, secure a modicum of social respect and protect against petty bribery. Judges' salaries have improved in later years in both countries, placing them among the best-paid civil servants and with generous benefits (furnished house, car, driver, petrol, guards, domestic servants, retirement benefits – the Zambian judges' non-practice allowance almost matches their nominal salary). The judges appreciate that these are generous, but still regard the package as inadequate, claiming to be poorly paid compared to judges in other southern African countries and lawyers in private practice. That lawyers decline judgeship is a particularly acute problem in Zambia where a donor-sponsored NGO lawyer takes home more than a high court judge, and a reasonably successful private advocate could earn 'a hundred times more'.[46] It is suggested that in order to be attractive for the best lawyers, judges' salaries would need to be two to three times higher.

Budgetary Autonomy and Adequacy of Resources

In both countries and at all levels of the judiciary, lack of funds is identified as *the* major factor limiting their ability to function as well as they could. It is particularly acute in the lower judiciary (dilapidating buildings, lack of basic facilities, transport, even pens and paper to write judgements.) Also the higher courts complain of a notorious lack of resources (telephone, fax, copying machines, computer facilities, recording equipment, library resources) and trained support staff (secretaries, court reporters).[47] The situation causes frustration, disillusionment and long delays, affecting all aspects of their work, their standing in society, staff morale – and their accountability performance.

The situation has improved at the High Court level in both countries, particularly in the capital, mainly through donor-funded projects. There are plans to reform the lower court too, but it seems that priority is given to the higher courts where reforms are more manageable and results can be seen more quickly; each country has fewer than 50 judges in the higher judiciary but more than a thousand judicial officers in the lower courts. Appalling conditions are thus likely to persist in the section of the court system that most people encounter, contributing to the serious problems undermining ordinary people's faith in the courts.

In addition to inadequate resources, the judiciary's lack of autonomy in the administration of its budget is also a concern. Both in Zambia and in Tanzania, the judiciary depends on the cabinet to take their budget to parliament. And of the approved budget, only a portion is normally released. If the budget for the judiciary was directly approved by the parliament and released at the year's start, it would allow for more rational planning of activities. Even more important from the perspective of the courts' accountability function is that as long as the executive controls the budget, judges may have reason to fear 'starvation' if those in power believe them to be unhelpful. Few suggest that the current under-funding is deliberate in this sense, but it nevertheless remains a serious concern.

The Zambian courts have an advantage compared to their Tanzanian counterparts in that they may use the court fees to pay for running expenses. In Tanzania, fees collected by the courts are paid into the treasury and the courts have no funds beyond those released by the government (with one exception: the Commercial Division of the High Court negotiated an arrangement where the court fees are retained, but have to cover all the costs. Ordinary courts would have difficulties surviving on fees alone, but in the Commercial Division court fees are high, and the arrangement leaves them with a more predictable economic situation).[48] The lack of adequate and secured funds seems to be a major factor limiting the ability and willingness of courts to hold the executive to account. Lack of resources and the related difficulty of recruiting qualified judges (particularly in Zambia), are major causes of the backlogs and delays marring these systems, undermining the public's confidence, and thus directly and indirectly hampering the performance of the courts. The way the budget is allocated may condition them to stay on good terms with the executive to keep what little they have. Financial scarcity may also affect the courts accountability function negatively through the effect it has on their *jurisprudential* resources.

Jurisprudential Resources

The ability of judges to say 'no' to the executive and 'make it stick' depends not only on their independence in the sense of a willingness to go about their work 'without fear or favour', but also on their ability to use the law to this effect in ways that commands authority. This requires tools to sustain sound legal reasoning, and develop a consistent jurisprudence. These 'jurisprudential tools' include training for judicial personnel, relevant legal material, and professional forums for exchange of experience with 'relevant others'.

In Tanzania adequate *jurisprudential resources* are lacking at all levels: even the library of the Supreme Court of Appeal lacks essential law journals, law books, and updated material on foreign case law. High Court centres have libraries, but they often lack even case material from the national courts. The problem is almost as great in Zambia, but is overshadowed by the shortage of qualified personnel. In October 2002 there were 24 High Court judges in Zambia; six seats were vacant. The Supreme Court of Appeal had seven judges instead of nine.[49] The recruitment problems have resulted in a situation where, as one interviewee explained, 'the best legal minds in the country, with one or two exceptions, are not found on the bench'. In the legal community, the professional quality of the judges was seen to be the main factor detracting from their ability to hold the executive to account.

In the lower judiciary, the situation is particularly disturbing. Magistrates handle the bulk of criminal cases including all corruption cases.

Corruption is a prominent problem in Zambian political life. That high-level economic crimes and corruption cases, often involving government officials, are tried by magistrates who lack specialized knowledge and relevant case material, detracts from the judiciary's accountability performance. Few magistrates are qualified university lawyers; most have only undergone a two-year training course. Making matters worse, since 2000 there has been no training programme for magistrates in Zambia. When people retire or die (and the HIV/AIDS pandemic is taking its toll in the judiciary) they are almost impossible to replace; university law graduates are rarely willing to join the magistracy, given the poor conditions of service. Magistrates earn a fraction of what the judges do (less than 1:10), and do not have the benefits, accommodation or transport. The common view is that a magistrate's wage is insufficient to support a family, and that this drives the rampant corruption in the lower courts. Magistrates also lack the security for tenure that provides judges' political insulation. In Tanzania conditions in the lower courts are almost identical, but the recruitment of qualified staff is less of a problem. Tanzania has an operative magistrates' training programme, and university candidates are also recruited into the magistracy. Recruitment of judges is not a problem: most are appointed from among senior magistrates, but, as noted earlier, judges are also recruited from private practice.

Access to case material is a problem at all levels and in both countries. In some lower courts even statute books are missing and magistrates rely on notes from the training they had years back. High Court judges complain of difficulties accessing colleagues' judgements. Supreme Court judges lack access to international legal literature, journals and foreign case law. The situation did improve substantially both in Tanzania and Zambia after the publication of their Law Reports was resumed, although these include only a small number of judgements for each year.

Reading significant judgements where the courts assert their position vis-à-vis the executive, there is a notable reliance on foreign case material. Judges confirm that the authority provided by backing in foreign case law is welcome. Most of the Tanzanian judges interviewed (fewer in Zambia) found legal material from other countries useful. Some noted that international precedent, used effectively, could be used to overcome limitations on jurisdiction. British and Indian cases are commonly used, and also those from other Commonwealth jurisdictions. African case law is seen as highly relevant, but is often difficult to get hold of. The Law Reports that are published regularly are usually not widely distributed. Some judgements are available on the net, but most Tanzanian and Zambian courts lack Internet access.

This discussion of the institutional structure that the Zambian and Tanzanian judges operate within shows that the various aspects interconnect and work together to strengthen or weaken the courts' accountability performance. But there is also another important element in this picture. A paramount condition if the courts are to play an active role vis-à-vis the government is that relevant cases are placed before them. This in turn depends on a high level of rights awareness in the population, access to legal assistance, and active civil society organizations. For people and organizations to spend their resources on court cases, there must, however, also be a minimum of trust in the institution.

Social Legitimacy

The courts' ability to stand up to the executive depends on whether they have a secure basis in society, on whether people trust and use them and come to their defence if their independence and authority is undermined. The legitimacy of the judiciary is in turn affected by how they are perceived to fulfil their role: meeting people's needs for dispute resolution; upholding law and order; and preventing abuse of power by government officials. To what extent do Tanzanian and Zambian judges have legitimacy in the different parts of their societies? Are the courts respected and considered socially relevant? Do they have the social support that would make it costly for the executive to contravene their decisions or encroach upon their independence?

According to surveys the vast majority (72 per cent) of Tanzanians express trust in the courts.[50] Still, there are complaints, particularly over delays and corruption. That 'ordinary people have to pay for justice' is seen to be a problem in the lower courts.[51] The president's role in appointing judges is seen to compromise the independence of the higher courts, but many seem to believe that they are now moving away from a pro-government position. Nevertheless, they are considered to be for the elite: 'Political cases are irrelevant for most people.' Even this may, however, be changing. The judiciary is in the public eye, cases are reported in the media, there is an increasing awareness of the constitution in Tanzanian society, and particularly of rights issues: human rights, civil rights, even political rights – to some extent also issues of separation of power.[52]

None of those interviewed believed there would be significant public protest if the president was to clamp down on the judiciary, pressuring the chief justice to resign or removing a troublesome judge. Few thought it likely, but were it to happen it would only spark discussions for a couple of days, then it would be over. This ambivalent and disengaged attitude towards the courts on the part of ordinary Tanzanians may be related to poor access to justice. Those charged with capital offences are provided with a defence lawyer by the state, but otherwise, there is no legal aid. Poor people can apply and be granted permission to go to court without paying fees, but have to argue their own case. The university's legal aid committee takes on some cases; the Tanganyika Law Society offers legal aid, as does a handful of organizations, but they give mainly legal advice, only rarely is a lawyer appointed and paid to argue the case. NGOs in Tanzania may be de-registered for political activities, which may be why they have not themselves initiated test cases.[53]

The legal NGOs seem to have a good working relationship with the courts. The judges recognize the importance of their work in legal aid and legal literacy. But the NGOs operating in this field have limited capacity and most are based in the capital. Outside urban centres ordinary people can rarely access professional legal advice. The situation is somewhat better in Zambia, where the NGO sector is much stronger, but the Zambian courts struggle with legitimacy problems of their own. Asking Zambians whether they have confidence in the courts attracts ambivalent replies. The Afrobarometer surveys found that a majority of Zambians (56 per cent) trusted the courts, a much higher percentage than for the political branches. Interestingly, the order is reversed in Tanzania, where the 91 percent of the sample express trust in the president (compared to 38 per cent of Zambians).[54] Interviewees' perceptions of the judiciary were marked by the corruption scandal that led to the chief justice's resignation in June 2002. They displayed a profound ambivalence, indicating that judges are fair in most cases but that they rule for the government in politicized cases, and take bribes if big money is involved. Despite complaints over widespread corruption and judges bowing to political pressure, Zambians continue to use the courts in large numbers, as do politicians from opposition parties. The lodging of petitions after the December 2001 elections is illustrative. Out of a total of 150 constituencies for the parliamentary elections, losing candidates (predominantly from the opposition) lodged petitions in 47 cases. After petitioners were ordered to pay K1million[55] as security for costs, 15 cases were dropped. This might not be a large amount of money for the contenders, but combined with fees and lawyer's charges it is far from insignificant, and would hardly be invested if there were no expectations of a fair ruling.

Another problem that Zambia shares with Tanzania is that the courts are irrelevant for a large part of the population, partly due to poor access. Many rural Zambians have considerable distances to travel to reach the nearest court; *traditional courts* continue to flourish outside the formal legal system, with chiefs and headmen adjudicating without legal jurisdiction. Punishment meted out is often severe, including corporal punishment, which is unconstitutional.[56] But being outside the legal system, there is no possibility of appeal. This disadvantages women in particular, as customary law is generally harsh on women. A development of customary law is taking place in the local courts, particularly in urban areas, according women a stronger standing, but this rarely reaches the traditional courts.[57] Despite these problems, the Zambian courts seem to have a stronger social base than their Tanzanian counterparts, mostly due to a better-resourced and more vibrant civil society which regards the legal arena as a useful channel in which to fight for their causes.[58] Some good organizations are willing to litigate important cases. There is also a private press, which focuses on legal issues, providing a forum for critical voices.

Concluding Remarks

This analysis has shown that the Zambian and Tanzanian judiciaries do not have a strong accountability function vis-à-vis their governments. In both countries executive dominance remains the dominating feature of political life. Yet the courts are not insignificant. In both countries judges have made politically important decisions and, with parliament dominated by the ruling party, courts emerge as perhaps the most significant accountability institution in the polity.

A pattern distinguishing the accountability performance of the two judiciaries have emerged: Tanzanian courts have few 'spectacular' political cases, but have on occasion explicitly undertaken the task of ensuring that political power-holders do not overstep their constitutional powers. In Zambia the courts receive more politically significant cases and the judges are conscious of and concerned by the possible dangers related to excessive politicization, favouring an 'apolitical' role where possible.

The analysis has investigated how these differences are related to a range of factors constituting the judges' predicament. These are grouped into three categories: The legal culture, which defines what judges believe they *ought to* do; the institutional structure, consisting of the institutional and practical conditions that enable and constrain judges in their work; and the court's social legitimacy, looking at whether the courts can draw input and support from groups in society.

In both countries, the 'un-political' judge who 'merely interprets the law' is the dominant professional norm, which does not favour a strong accountability function. Several Zambian judges felt there was a strong need for the judiciary to demonstrate political independence after the corruption scandal involving the chief justice. The Supreme Court was in the process of hearing the petition against the election of President Mwanawasa in December 2001, and this judgement was expected to send important signals regarding how the Zambian judiciary will redefine its role vis-à-vis the executive.

The 'apolitical' view is most clearly challenged from within the judiciary in Tanzania. Central judges, including the chief justice, portray the judge as active defender of constitutional rights and the operation of the democratic process, which equates to a strong accountability function. That this more assertive conception of the judicial role (in line with strong international currents) is more pronounced in Tanzania seems to coincide with larger share of academically-oriented judges. This in turn seems to be related both to their engagement with a stronger academic legal community in Dar-es-Salaam, and to the fact that the judiciary seems a more attractive option for ambitious lawyers in Tanzania than in Zambia, where the many foreign funded NGOs and the private sector offer much more lucrative options for bright legal scholars.

The institutional structure, which defines (and is defined through) the relationship between the judiciary and the political branches, differ in important respects between the countries. In Tanzania, the main response from political branches against judges asserting their powers has been to build restrictions into the legal framework, effectively limiting the scope of decisions and the flow of cases reaching the courts. This represents continuity with the first decades after independence, when the government marginalized the courts by resisting the enactment of a strong body of law (bill of rights, legislation to underpin policies). The case flow is also limited by the much weaker civil society in Tanzania, which in turn is also related to the legal restrictions on NGOs.

In Zambia judges have more generous formal powers. The executive seems to rely more on individualized and informal pressure to avoid strong judicial accountability: the driving forces of *social ambition* (the carrot of promotion, pay increases, or payments on the side) and *fear* (the stick of punishment through smear campaigns, loss of position, public disgrace). Consequently, self-censorship is notable.[59] As a consequence the Zambian judiciary is generally perceived as more politicized than in Tanzania, in spite of stricter formal procedures for appointment, tenure and so on designed to insulate against political influence. An effect of the differences in legal–political relations between the two countries appears to be that the Zambian courts while more politicized, are less affected in their ability to carry out *routine justice*.

Significant in explaining the higher level of politicization of the judiciary in Zambia is the historical fact that chief justices, although formally serving for life or until retirement age, have in practice changed with every new president, whereas Tanzania has not changed the chief justice with the political administration. This can be explained by the political continuity in Tanzania (where all changes of government have been 'within the CCM family'). Nevertheless, this de-linking of the processes of political and judicial change may have prevented politicization of the courts. Neither the Zambian nor the Tanzanian judiciary seems to have strong social support that would render the political cost of undermining them prohibitive. Yet in both countries the courts have a form of diffuse support in the population, as well as certain 'constituencies' strengthening them in relation to the government. Important among these are the international donors, who increasingly emphasize the importance of the judiciary in securing good government, and on whose co-operation these governments depend. Closely linked to the donors are the domestic NGOs who, with other groups in civil society are perhaps the courts' most significant local constituency. Organized civil society is comparatively larger and more vibrant in Zambia. Its weakness in Tanzania contributes to the relatively small number of politically significant cases argued before the courts there.

How the Tanzanian and Zambian courts will develop their accountability function is difficult to predict. There is potential in both cases, but also major challenges. Much depends on whether these judiciaries are able to secure the resources needed to institutionalize 'downwards' in a way that make them socially relevant.

ACKNOWLEDGEMENT

The account has benefited from useful comments in the workshop on 'The Accountability Function of Courts in New Democracies' held in Bergen, November 2002, and from the political science group at the Chr. Michelsen Institute. Particular thanks to Sufian Bukurura, Arne Tostensen, Lise Rakner, Elin Skaar and Roberto Gargarella. I would also like to thank my Zambian and Tanzanian interlocutors who generously shared their time and knowledge.

NOTES

1. The analysis is based on interviews conducted in Tanzania in July/August 2002 and in Zambia in October 2002 with members of the judiciary and with users and observers of the legal system from the legal community, non-governmental organisations (NGOs), academia, the media, government, and 'ordinary people'. It also draws on existing studies: Sufian H. Bukurura, *The Judiciary and Good Government in Tanzania* (Bergen: Chr. Michelsen Institute, 1995); George Kunda, 'The Zambian Judiciary in the 21st Century', *Zambia Law Journal*, Vol.29 (1998), <http://zamlii.zamnet.zm/comment/zlj/artsfull/30z29.htm>; Chris Maina Peter, *Human Rights Case Book* (Konstanz: Hartung-Gorre Verlag, 1997), Lise Rakner *et al.*, *Analysing Political Processes in the Context of Multiparty Elections: Zambia 2001–2002* (Bergen: CMI/Inesor Project Reports, Chr. Michelsen Institute, 2002); John Ruhangisa, *Human Rights in Tanzania*, unpublished doctoral thesis, University of London, 1998; Jennifer Widner, *Building the Rule of Law in Africa* (New York: Norton Press, 2001).
2. See Guillermo O'Donnell, 'Horizontal Accountability in New Democracies', in Andreas Schedler *et al.* (eds) *The Self-Restraining State* (Boulder, CO: Lynne Rienner Publishers, 1999), pp 29–51.

3. See Roberto Gargarella, 'In Search of a Democratic Justice – What Courts Should Not Do: Argentina, 1983–2002', pp.181–97, this volume.
4. Professor Chris. M. Peter, interview, University of Dar-es-Salaam, July 2002.
5. See Peter, *Human Rights* (note 1), Widner (note 1), Bukurura (note 1) and Ruhangisa (note 1).
6. Widner (note 1).
7. On the term 'say "no" and make it stick', see C. Larkins, 'Judicial Independence and Democratization: A Theoretical and Conceptual Analysis', *American Journal of Comparative Law*, Vol.44, No.4 (1996), p.610.
8. Judge Munou, interview, Moshi, August 2002.
9. Interviews with several Zanzibar lawyers, August 2002. Permission to cite by name was not obtained.
10. Ibid. Chief Justice Samatta at the Court of Appeal could not confirm that they overturned significantly more cases from Zanzibar (interview, Dar-es-Salaam, August 2002).
11. *Julius Ishengoma Francis Ndyanabo vs. The Attorney General (C.A. no 64 of 2001, judgement on 14 February 2002).*
12. John Ruhangisa, Registrar of the East African Court, interview, Arusha, August 2002.
13. *Rev. Christopher Mtikila versus Attorney General* (High Court of Tanzania at Dodoma, 1993). reported in Volume I, *Commonwealth Human Rights Law Digest* (1996), p.11 and in Peter, *Human Rights* (note 1) p.674.
14. *Peter Ng'omango versus Gerson M.K. Mwarangwa and another.* High Court of Tanzania at Dodoma, (1992), reported in Peter, *Human Rights* (note 1) p.309.
15. Court of Appeal of Tanzania at Arusha, *Pumbun and Another versus Attorney-General and Another*, (1993) 2 LRC 317.
16. See Alfred Chanda, 'Constitutionality of the Public Order Amendment Act and its Application to Date', *The Human Rights Observer,* Vol.3 (October 2000), <http://www.oneworld.org/afronet/theobserver/Vol3_page6.htm>.
17. Munou interview (note 8).
18. Judge Nsekela, interview, Dar-es-Salaam, July 2002.
19. P. Mlebusi, Red Cross Society of Tanzania, interview, Dar-es-Salam, July 2002. For the public documents in the case see *Bunge News*, Vol.16 (July 2002), special issue on 'Separation of Powers between Legislature and Judiciary'.
20. Peter interview (note 4).
21. Ruhangisa interview (note 12).
22. Ibid.
23. Jenerali Ulimwengu, chairman of the Habari Corporation, member of Media Council, ,interview, Dar es Salaam, July, 2002.
24. Kabazo Chanda, interview, Bergen, January 2002.
25. Fred M'membe, Editor-in-Chief of *The Post,* 6 May 1996, quoted in Peter Burnell, 'Legislative-Executive Relations in Zambia: Parliamentary Reform on the Agenda', *Journal of Contemporary African Studies,* Vol.21, No.1 (2003), p.47.
26. Reported in *The Post* (Lusaka) 27 June and 2 July 2002, and remarked on by Sakwiba Sikota, United Party for National Development Member of Parliament, interview, Lusaka, October 2002.
27. Supreme Court of Zambia: *Christine Mulundika and 7 Others v. The People* (SCZ/25/1995).
28. See Chanda, 'Constitutionality' (note 16).
29. HCZ, 1996 (unreported), printed in *The Post* (Lusaka), 4–8 November 1996.
30. *The People v. Fred M'membe, Matsauso Phiri and Bright Mwape* (HP/38/1996, unreported), <http://www.post.co.zm/legal3.htm>.
31. See F M Ng'andu and K.C. Chanda 'The Role of the Judiciary in Promoting Transparency and Honesty in the Zambian Electoral Process', report presented at final workshop of the Norad/CMI/Inesor project on 'Political Processes in Zambia', Lusaka, October 2002.
32. Ibid.
33. *Godfrey Miyanda and Others v. Attorney General, the Electoral Commission and Returning Officer for Presidential Elections* (HP/1174/2001).

34. *A.M. Lewanika and others versus F.J.T. Chiluba.* SCZ/8/EP/4/96 ('The first presidential petition'). Judgement on 10 November 1998(9), at <http://www.oneworld.org/afronet/other/petition.htm>.
35. Human Rights Watch, *Zambia: Elections and Human Rights in The Third Republic*, Vol.8, No.4 (A) December 1996, <http://www.hrw.org/reports/1996/Zambia.htm>.
36. Ng'andu and Chanda (note 31).
37. Kabazo Chanda interview (note 24).
38. Ng'andu and Chanda (note 31).
39. John G. March and Johan P. Olsen, *Democratic Governance* (New York: Free Press 1995).
40. Nsekela interview (note 18).
41. Ibid.
42. See particularly the *5 million Tsh judgement.*
43. Peter interview (note 4).
44. Constitution of Zambia, 1995, Article 93 and 95.
45. Ng'andu and Chanda (note 31).
46. Geoffrey Mulenga, Legal Services Centre, interview, Lusaka, October 2002.
47. See also Widner (note 1).
48. Ruhangisa interview (note 12).
49. One is on long-term leave to the International Criminal Court, The Hague.
50. Amon Chaligha et al., 'Uncritical Citizens or Patient Trustees? Tanzanians' Views of Political and Economic Reform', *Afrobarometer Paper* No.18 (Cape Town: IDASA), p.43.
51. Almost half of the respondents believe judges are corrupt, which is about the same as for elected leaders and businessmen, and much better than for the police. Ibid., p. 44.
52. Clement Mashamba, Legal and Human Rights Centre, interview, Dar es Salaam, August 2002.
53. Ibid.
54. Chaligha et al. (note 50) p.43.
55. Exchange rate of one pound sterling = K7,600 or one US dollar = K4,800 at April 2003.
56. *J. Chanda vs. The People* (HCZ/1999, unreported).
57. Matrine Chulu, Wilsa, Lusaka, October 2002.
58. Ibid.
59. Ng'andu and Chanda (note 31).

Renegotiating 'Law and Order': Judicial Reform and Citizen Responses in Post-war Guatemala

RACHEL SIEDER

Introduction

In recent years political scientists have become increasingly concerned with issues of accountability and law in contemporary Latin America. It is over two decades since the return to elected civilian rule, yet the democratic rule of law remains extremely weak in the region and is generally agreed to be one of the major 'deficits' of existing democracies. Although the picture varies from country to country, in general levels of impunity are high and recourse to extra-judicial means of conflict resolution a commonplace, public security provision remains poor in the face of soaring crime levels, and the population's confidence in the judicial apparatus is low.

Domestic and international advocates of strengthening the rule of law in Latin America have, to date, tended to focus on institutional factors, advocating a familiar range of measures which aim to advance greater judicial independence, efficiency of the justice system and greater access to justice for the underprivileged.[1] These include the overhaul of court administration, updating legislation and codes, the creation of judicial councils to ensure less politicised appointments procedures for judges, better judicial training and the strengthening of legal aid and non-judicial conflict resolution procedures.[2] These measures have often been advanced within the broader context of post-transition and post-conflict reforms. Discussion focuses principally on how to achieve the 'correct' combination and sequencing of institutional change. Such procedural initiatives are generally uncontroversial in and of themselves: the need for more efficient and independent courts, better trained judges and lawyers and improved legal representation for the poor across the region is undisputed. However, although the institution-building approach is now undoubtedly the dominant donor strategy, all too often it pays too little attention to the broader socio-legal and political context in which reform takes place.[3] Prescriptions for strengthening the rule of law are invariably premised on an implicit model of law and legal institutions based on established western democracies or on an ideal Weberian-type state (after the German sociologist Max Weber). Too much emphasis tends to be placed on the design of judicial reform programmes and far too little on evaluating why such proposals are not successfully implemented. This perhaps goes some way to explaining why although over a billion dollars has been spent on judicial reform in Latin America during the last 15 years, the results have been singularly disappointing.

This analysis employs a path-dependent, long-run historical approach which pays due attention to national specificities in order to analyse the prospects for constructing or strengthening the 'rule of law' in any given country. Informed by recent debates and new methodological perspectives towards the study of law within the fields of social and cultural history and critical anthropology, such an approach seeks to locate examination of current legal reform efforts within a broader analysis of the historic interactions between individuals, different social groups and the law.[4] It understands law as an historical and social construct, rather than reducing it simply to a set of institutions. While it is certainly true that transitions from authoritarian rule or armed conflict offer important opportunities to reshape institutions and challenge existing practices and attitudes, such possibilities are constrained by the ways in which law has historically been configured, exercised, engaged with and understood. In this sense the investigation of historical patterns of legal ordering and of interactions of elite and popular perceptions of 'law', 'rights' and 'justice' in different local contexts is of critical importance. It should also be emphasized here that individual and group understandings of 'the law' are shaped not only by interaction with state law. Extra-national forms of law such as Spanish colonial law or international humanitarian law, and non-state forms of legal ordering such as indigenous customary law, have also had a major impact on the nature of the law in Latin America and popular attitudes towards it. As has often been observed, law is an arena of social, political, economic and cultural struggle and as such is shaped by multiple and overlapping contestations and negotiations. Due attention to specific regional and national histories illuminates the nature of state formation, interactions between the state and civil society, social attitudes towards acceptable or appropriate forms of punishment, and understandings of citizenship. All these are critical to shaping specific legal orders and legal cultures and, in turn, to conditioning the outcomes and effects of contemporary processes of legal reform.

The account focuses on Guatemala and considers the experience of legal reform linked to the peace process during the latter half of the 1990s. Space does not permit a comprehensive analysis of the historical development of law and legal cultures in that country – necessarily a much lengthier and more ambitious project. However, a number of key historical features of the

Guatemalan case relevant to analysis can be signalled here. They are, first, marked distance and separation between popular mechanisms for conflict resolution and the state's judicial apparatus; second, acute and persistent socio-economic inequality; third, military dominance of political and legal institutions of the state, fourth, racism and discrimination against the majority indigenous population, and; fifth, very high levels of state violence.

During the colonial period semi-autonomous and subordinate spaces existed for the majority indigenous population who were subject to the laws of the *República de Indios*, which provided for their segregation and limited protection at the same time as they guaranteed their continued exploitation. A dual legal system operated, with the non-indigenous population governed by the laws of the *República de Españoles*. The present day republic of Guatemala was a key centre of the Spanish colonial enterprise and legal interactions and mediation between Crown, *peninsulares*, criollo elites and the indigenous populace were central to the reproduction of colonial society. Traditions of legal engagement were as deeply rooted as the existence of separate legal spheres for Indians and non-Indians. In the early republican period attempts to raise taxes and introduce liberal reforms and legal institutions, such as trial by jury and a new penal code, contributed to a conservative-led indigenous revolt in 1837 that initiated three decades of conservative rule.[5] The conservatives restored the *Leyes de los Indios* and a paternalistic attitude of the state towards the indigenous population prevailed. After the victory of the liberals in 1871, state laws were used to aggressively promote the production of coffee for agro-export. Forced labour arrangements were intensified and the consolidation of a professional army allowed for their more rigorously policing by an increasingly centralized state. While communal land titles were not subject to the kind of wholesale assault that occurred in El Salvador during the 1880s and 1890s, state law actively promoted the privatization of so-called *tierras baldías* in favour of new coffee elites.[6] However, at the same time as the liberal legal order in Guatemala became highly centralized and militarized, subordinate semi-autonomous legal spheres for local conflict resolution continued to exist within indigenous municipalities, particularly in the western highlands. Whilst it declared an ideology of assimilation, in practice oligarchic liberalism in Guatemala continued to segregate the population along ethnic and class lines.[7] New vagrancy laws were introduced to ensure a supply of un-free labour for coffee production and road construction and the role of the military became ever more central in underpinning the economic order. Under the dictatorship of General Jorge Ubico (1931–44) the state's coercive and administrative apparatus was extended to more remote rural areas and increasingly also to the private sphere.[8]

Populist mobilizations of subaltern populations by the state were conspicuously absent in Guatemala. The ten-year experiment in social democracy known as the 'Guatemalan Spring' (1944–54) did sanction the mobilization of rural workers and peasants to advance a redistributive agrarian reform and created parallel legal institutions to implement this. However, this experiment was cut short by a United States-supported military coup in 1954 and the subsequent rollback of the agrarian reform involved both the legal restitution of expropriated lands and high levels of extra-judicial violence against peasant organizers and political activists. During the 1960s and 1970s the military consolidated their control over government, which was increasingly organized according to a national security, counterinsurgency logic. Levels of state violence rose steadily, culminating in the genocidal campaigns against the indigenous rural populations in the early 1980s carried out under the military regime headed by General Ríos Montt.[9] During the armed conflict the judiciary was entirely subordinated to the military and disputes were resolved by parallel, extra-judicial mechanisms with resort to extreme levels of violence.[10] According to the Commission for Historical Clarification (CEH), the United Nations-backed investigation into human rights violations that occurred during the armed conflict, the singular failure of the judicial system to act as a check on the de facto exercise of power and the systematic abuse of human rights by the state was a key factor that actively facilitated the violence. Some 200,000 people were killed, largely at the hands of military and paramilitary forces.[11] The military's control over government also sharpened the authoritarian character of law and its arbitrary application. Civilian elites tended to rely on the military to mediate disputes, further weakening the judicial apparatus. However, following the transition to elected civilian government in 1985, citizen demands for a more effective rule of law increased. This was partly an effect of international phenomena, in particular increased awareness of international human rights law and (latterly) international legislation on the rights of indigenous peoples, and of the focus of the donor community in the 1990s on institutional strengthening. It was also an effect of rising levels of crime and insecurity.

Since the signing of the peace accords in Guatemala in December 1996, ambitious initiatives supported by a range of international donors have been undertaken to reform the country's weak and ineffective judicial system and improve access to justice for the majority of the population. However, although widespread changes to the institutional architecture of the legal system have been effected, impunity and deep lack of citizen confidence continue to frustrate efforts to improve the rule of law. The main body of this study, then, examines judicial reform efforts in Guatemala since 1996 and considers their relationship with attempts by citizens to secure 'justice' 'from below', ranging from efforts to secure prosecutions of those accused of gross violations of human rights to summary executions of suspected petty criminals. Any analysis of attempts to promote the rule of law must examine what 'law', 'rights' and 'justice' mean for different actors in different places and to analyse the interplay between broader dynamics of internationally promoted judicial reform and national specificities. Such an analysis may help to explain why, despite unprecedented efforts to reform Guatemala's justice system during the last five years, that system remains weak and extra-legal forms of conflict resolution prevail.

The peace settlement, which brought an end to 36 years of armed conflict, aimed to lay the foundations for a democratic rule of law and transform an authoritarian, discriminatory and highly punitive legal tradition. It advocated the democratic modernization of the justice system, and particularly of the criminal justice system, through institutional reform. The stated aims were: first, to encourage the peaceful resolution of conflicts via the courts; second, to secure the accountability of state officials and institutions; third, to ensure respect for human rights and due process guarantees in the judicial process, and; fourth, to improve access to justice for the majority of the population. Such changes implied a fundamental overhaul of legal culture: rather than simply a means to punish, it was hoped that the courts would come to be seen as a means to secure accountability and restitution.

Following the transition to elected civilian rule in 1985, important attempts were made in the early 1990s to modernize the judiciary. Nonetheless, at the end of the armed conflict it remained bereft of legitimacy in the eyes of the majority of the population. Most Guatemalans rightly tended to see the law as something that operates to the benefit of powerful individuals and groups rather than as something to which they could make effective recourse to protect their fundamental rights. Opinion polls taken since the end of the armed conflict repeatedly indicated extremely low levels of citizen confidence in the justice system.[12] Most analysts listed a catalogue of problems: the justice system was under-resourced, inefficient, inaccessible – particularly to indigenous people, women, children and the poor, plagued by corruption, lacking independence from other branches of state, staffed by poorly trained, mediocre and under-motivated professionals, and subject to the *de facto* power of elite groups.

In addition to the historical legacy of citizen mistrust of the law, the justice system also faced the challenge of an unprecedented crime wave in the wake of the peace settlement. While violations of civil and political rights by the state declined relative to the 1980s and early 1990s,[13] new forms of insecurity became generalized towards the end of the decade. Armed robbery, car-theft, kidnapping,[14] child abduction for illegal adoption, drug trafficking, homicides and rape, gang-related violence and money laundering are now common occurrences.[15] Official figures are notoriously unreliable, but one recent study estimated that the total number of reported crimes increased by 50 per cent between 1996 and 1998.[16] Rising levels of crime constitute a central challenge for the post-war justice system, hampering judicial reform efforts and undermining citizen confidence in the legal system.

Justice Reform and the Peace Accords

The peace agreement which dealt most comprehensively with reform of the justice sector was the September 1996 *Agreement for the Strengthening of Civilian Power and the Function of the Army in a Democratic Society* (hereinafter *Agreement*) but in total five of the 13 accords made express reference to the justice sector. The proposed changes built upon ongoing reforms of the justice system promoted by domestic pro-reform constituencies and the different programmes supported by international donors. The donors include the World Bank, the Inter-American Development Bank (IDB), the United States Agency for International Development (USAID) and the United Nations Development Programme (UNDP), which focused on measures to increase judicial independence and strengthen due process guarantees.[17] However, as Pásara has observed, detailed proposals for change were principally drawn up by the UN; while key domestic sectors identified the weaknesses of the justice system, few concrete proposals were advanced through the peace negotiations.[18] The peace accords underlined the need to ensure access to justice for Guatemala's majority indigenous population. 'Multiculturalizing' the justice system was to involve such initiatives as increasing the numbers of state defenders, providing judicial interpreters and encouraging the use of indigenous customary law to resolve conflicts outside the courts. The accords also mandated a doubling of budget allocations to the justice sector between 1995 and 2000 and envisaged a massive extension of its institutional coverage throughout the country. In 1997 the multi-sector Commission for the Strengthening of Justice was set up according to the terms of the September 1996 *Agreement* and subsequently undertook a unique process of consultation on reform of the justice system with different civic and professional groups throughout the country. The Commission's comprehensive and broad-ranging recommendations, published in April 1998, included a series of measures to increase judicial independence and reduce corruption, professionalize the judiciary, guarantee basic rights, increase access to justice and make it more multicultural.[19] Many of these recommendations were subsequently incorporated into the judiciary's five year Plan for Modernization (*Plan de Modernización del Organismo Judicial*), supported by the World Bank and other donors and approved in mid-1997. Reform efforts advanced on a number of fronts.

Reform of Criminal Procedures

In common with other countries throughout Latin America, Guatemala reformed its Penal Procedures Code (*Código Procesal Penal* or CPP) during the 1990s. A new law entered into force in 1994 and a series of amendments were subsequently approved by Congress in 1996, introducing a framework for criminal justice based on ensuring due process and human rights guarantees for detainees, sometimes referred to as a *garantista* model. This emphasized the rights of the accused to due legal process, particularly the presumption of innocence, habeas corpus guarantees and the right to legal defence. To this end the code mandated the creation of an autonomous public defenders service (*Instituto de la Defensa Pública*) to protect the constitutional rights of all citizens to legal representation. It also separated the roles of investigation, prosecution and adjudication: the task of criminal investigation and preparing a case for prosecution was assigned exclusively to the public prosecutor's office or Public Ministry (*Ministerio Público*, MP). Court proceedings themselves were revolutionized. Previously trials had been secretive, written and formalistic affairs where the accused was often not aware of the charges laid against them until the sentencing stage: the CPP introduced public, oral proceedings. It also established the legal right to be heard in one's own language in a court of law, considered an important symbolic step in improving indigenous access to justice. Another significant change introduced by the CPP was that other civic actors were allowed to take part in criminal cases; for example relatives of victims and non-governmental organizations (NGOs), some of who subsequently became co-plaintiffs (*querellantes adhesivos*) in key human rights cases (see below). However, although it is a significant advance, the implementation of the CPP remains uneven: many judges, public prosecutors and defenders still lacking training in its usage, despite significant resources devoted by international donors to such ends; others are simply reluctant to implement the innovations mandated by the new legislation. The new code also had contradictory effects: in the face of the post-war crime wave the rights protection afforded to detainees by the *garantista* model became the subject of acute public criticism, with calls for more hard line measures and revisions to the code increasingly gaining ground.

Access to Justice

Since 1996 a marked improvement in access to justice has occurred, with a series of measures aimed particularly at the majority indigenous population. International institutions and donors, including USAID, the European Union and the UN's verification mission MINUGUA, have supported many of these initiatives. They include: (1) an increase in the coverage of the courts throughout the national territory; (2) the training of bilingual interpreters; (3) the creation of the public defenders service, and; (4) the greater use of mediation and alternative dispute resolution (ADR) at local community level.

In total, some 102 new courts were established after 1996, together with 35 posts for legal interpreters. Offices of Justices of the Peace (*juzgados de paz*), which covered only two thirds of the national territory at the end of the armed conflict, are now present in all 331 of Guatemala's municipalities, as recommended by the Commission for Strengthening Justice in 1998, and each departmental capital now has specialized criminal, civil, family and labour tribunals.[20] Reforms to the penal code in 2002 mean that justices of the peace can now try crimes punishable by prison terms of up to five years. MINUGUA and USAID have supported important initiatives to train bilingual interpreters for the courts, yet despite this the coverage of interpreters remain highly deficient, as does the coverage and performance of the public defenders' service.[21] A number of initiatives to promote non-judicial forms of conflict resolution were advanced. In September 1997 Congress passed a series of amendments to the CPP, which aimed to promote greater use of conciliation and mediation and by 2001 the Supreme Court had inaugurated 18 mediation centres throughout the country, with USAID's justice programme supporting the creation of a further 15 community mediation centres.[22] The original proposal recognized indigenous peoples' right to exercise their customary law, as mandated in the 1995 *Accord on the Rights and Identity of Indigenous Peoples* and the International Labour Organization's (ILO) Convention 169, ratified by Guatemala in 1995. Yet in the event congressional deputies vetoed this clause, viewing the granting of greater legal and political autonomy to indigenous peoples as a potentially dangerous concession. Instead a new form of 'community court' (*juzgado de paz comunitario* or *tribunal comunitario*) was introduced. Rather than recognizing existing community-level institutions and practices for dispute resolution, what this measure in effect did was to superimpose a new, officially sanctioned form of 'community court' in a handful of indigenous municipalities with little consultation with local inhabitants.[23] Nonetheless, despite their inauspicious beginnings these pilot courts had some success in providing greater access to more culturally accessible, bilingual conflict resolution, in some places co-ordinating their efforts with traditional and municipal local authorities providing different kinds of mediation services. However, the rejection of recognition of indigenous peoples' right to use customary law in the constitutional referendum of March 1999[24] effectively meant that local community conflict resolution procedures which fall outside of the limits set down in the CPP are not recognized by the courts.[25]

Failing Justice

Multiple donors were involved in justice reform, including the World Bank, the IDB, USAID, the UNDP, MINUGUA, the Organization of American States (OAS), the US Department of Justice, the European Union and numerous bilateral donors. A massive influx of aid to Guatemala occurred after 1996 and much of it was targeted at the justice sector, donations and loans between 1996 and 2001 totalling over US$188 million according to one assessment.[26] Yet while the coverage of the state justice system throughout the country undoubtedly improved after December 1996, the overall quality of justice did not. Every municipality in the country now boasts an Office of Justice of the Peace and a police station or sub-station, meaning the justice system is tangibly nearer to people than ever before. Such changes, together with the more generalized effects of the peace process, raised the expectations of ordinary citizens that the state would enforce the rule of law. In addition, the rise in crime and insecurity throughout the country led to ever-greater demands that the justice system provide an effective response. Yet these heightened expectations and demands far outstripped the ability and disposition of the judicial authorities to meet them, leading, in turn, to growing popular frustration and worryingly high levels of public tolerance for extra-judicial actions against suspected criminals (see below). Institutional weaknesses persist and impunity continues. Guatemalan judicial culture continues to be marked by inefficiency, bureaucracy, insufficient training of staff, routine violation of due process guarantees and a lack of commitment to the rule of law as a democratic resource for all citizens, irrespective of their gender, ethnicity or class. A number of factors should be noted.

Judicial Independence

The independence of the judiciary from the executive was greatly increased by the 1985 Constitution, article 215 of which established a process for selection of the Supreme Court which reduced the ability of the executive to pack the court. Nominations to the court and appellate courts are proposed by a 16 member commission, which includes five jurists selected by the Guatemalan Bar Association, five representatives from the appeals courts, five law professors and one university rector. Nominations are subsequently confirmed by Congress. Supreme Court justices are appointed for five-year terms which do not overlap with the presidential term of office, reducing the possibilities for presidents to appoint loyalists. Court justices also select the Chief Justice. The magistrates of the Constitutional Court, created by the 1985 Constitution, are selected by the Supreme Court, Congress, the executive, the national university, and the lawyers' association. The magistrates hold office for five years and the presidency of the court rotates between them on a yearly basis. The Constitutional Court played a vital role in halting President Jorge Serrano's attempts to dismiss Congress and the Supreme Court in May 1993, in an executive coup similar to that successfully executed by Peru's President Fujimori in 1992. The court has also twice blocked attempts by former dictator Ríos Montt to run for the presidency, upholding article 186 of the 1985 Constitution which prohibits former coup leaders and their relatives from running for presidential office. However, in a highly controversial move in July 2003 the Constitutional Court overturned this ruling. Following conflict between the court and the executive in 2000 and 2001,[27] the ruling *Frente Republicano Guatemalteco* (FRG) assiduously pursued a strategy of securing the appointment of party sympathizers to the Constitutional Court. Despite the fact that both the Supreme Electoral Tribunal and the Supreme Court voted in 2003 to uphold Article 186, four Constitutional Court magistrates voted against three to allow the former dictator to stand for presidential office, sparking a judicial and political crisis.

As a consequence of the peace process a number of initiatives were introduced to improve the independence of the lower ranks of the judiciary. In October 1999 a law was passed to regulate the training of judges (*Ley de Carrera Judicial*). Together with the creation of a Council of Judicial Training (*Consejo de Carrera Judicial*), a disciplinary body for judges (*Junta de Disciplina Judicial*), and the approval of a Code of Judicial Ethics, this aims to ensure that incompetent and corrupt judges no longer fill the ranks of the judiciary.[28] Yet despite these institutional advances, judicial training is poor, selection and appointment by merit is still not generalized practice and the tendency to make appointments on the basis of clientelism or nepotism persists. Neither periodic purges of incompetent or corrupt personnel nor improved training and institutional reform have proved sufficient to secure meaningful improvements in judicial performance and credibility. The vulnerability of judges, lawyers and public prosecutors to internal and external intimidation, interference and corruption explains much of the weakness of the judicial system. Powers to promote, discipline or dismiss judges and public prosecutors are concentrated in the Supreme Court. In one recent study some 25 per cent of judges interviewed and 87 per cent of public prosecutors acknowledged they had been the target of pressure either from their superiors or interested parties to alter the course of investigations and cases.[29] Low salaries and poor training also foment corruption. Disciplinary procedures remain inadequate and officials charged with malfeasance rarely face criminal prosecution. A section of the Public Ministry was created in April 2000 to deal with charges of official corruption. By August 2001 over 2,200 complaints had been received, but charges were filed in only 13 cases and a mere two convictions secured.[30] In addition to bribery, justice officials are also subject to intimidation; constant harassment and threats mean that many are scared to testify, investigate or judge impartially. A new office set up within the Public Ministry in 2001 to deal specifically with threats against justice sector workers (*Fiscalía de Amenazas*) had accumulated a case load of 55 within two months of its inauguration.[31] One NGO documented 158 cases of threats, intimidation and attacks against judges, prosecutors, lawyers and others linked to the justice system between September 1996 and June 1999.[32] Private insurance companies in Guatemala consider judges and magistrates to be such a high risk that they cannot obtain life insurance (and the Supreme Court declared in 2001 that it lacked the funds to pay for a scheme for its employees).

The Public Ministry

The public prosecutor's office, or Public Ministry (MP), is undoubtedly one of the weakest links in the judicial process. In 1999 one study for USAID found that, in Guatemala City alone, of approximately 90,000 criminal complaints filed in a year, success in prosecution in statistical terms approached zero.[33] In the face of the manifest failure to deliver results and the personal danger often involved in making a legal representation, most people do not file complaints with the MP and those that do tend to drop them after a short time. The shortcomings of the Public Ministry have been repeatedly pointed out by human rights organizations and institutions, including MINUGUA and the Human Rights Ombudsman (*Procurador de Derechos Humanos*, PDH), the latter observing in 2000 that 'the progress of criminal cases is slower and more delayed every day, bogged down in a web of corruption'.[34]

Delaying Tactics and Lack of Institutional Coordination

Another of the numerous factors that slows down the justice system is the excessive use of delaying tactics and appeals by defence lawyers, particularly the use of the constitutional right of *amparo* – an appeal to the

Constitutional Court against judicial decisions on the basis that they violate the fundamental rights of the accused. Recourse to such mechanisms is often formalistic or inaccurate and clearly designed to obstruct the course of justice. For example in the cases against civil patrollers for the 1982 massacres at Agua Fría, El Quiché and Río Negro, Baja Verapaz, defence lawyers lodged *amparo* writs, appealing to an amnesty law in a clear attempt to delay the process. As a consequence of such measures, it took nearly six years until three ex-patrollers were finally convicted of the Río Negro killings in April 2000.[35] The number of petitions of *amparo* presented to the Constitutional Court has risen steadily since 1986 and in 2001 the court received approximately five such petitions a day.[36] An additional and serious impediment to justice in Guatemala is the lack of coordination between the Public Ministry and the new civilian police force (*Policía Nacional Civil,* PNC). The PNC are also poorly trained in the tasks of evidence collection and analysis, often lacking adequate technical facilities such as forensic laboratories.

The Prison System

The Guatemalan prison system is in crisis. Abuse of due process guarantees is commonplace: a 1999 survey found that 67 per cent of the prison population was awaiting sentencing, with the length of pre-trial detention often exceeding the maximum sentence that would have been served in the event of a conviction.[37] The tendency to respond to increased crime with tougher sentencing is exacerbating poor prison conditions and the abuse of due process guarantees. Despite the creation of the public defence service in 1997 and of a section within the Human Rights Ombudsman's office to attend to the prison population in 1998, most detainees still have little or no access to defence lawyers. The CPP provides for a number of alternatives to incarceration, such as bail or house arrest, but these are under-utilized by judges. Prisons are invariably overcrowded with poor hygiene conditions; prisoners are subject to physical and sexual abuse and extortion by other prisoners and prison authorities. No attempt is made to rehabilitate them before their release and levels of recidivism are high. The corruption of prison officials also means that breakouts are frequent – between June 1996 and June 2001 some 203 prisoners escaped, amongst them some of the most dangerous convicted criminals in the country.[38]

Underwriting Impunity

In addition to the structural weaknesses of the justice system, a major reason why powerful individuals and groups who break the law continue to enjoy impunity in Guatemala is the continued influence of military intelligence and powerful elite groups within the judicial institutions. These forces operate to prevent thorough criminal investigations and bring pressure to bear in trials to protect the guilty, particularly though not exclusively in cases where military officers are implicated in human rights violations. Human rights activists have repeatedly signalled the existence of an extensive clandestine network operating throughout state institutions in the justice sector and the public security forces that works to systematically obstruct the course of justice. This network, often referred to as 'parallel powers' (*los poderes paralelos*), originates in military intelligence structures, is led by members of the armed forces and supported by members of the PNC, the Public Ministry and the courts. Its functions are multiple, including: carrying out parallel investigations;[39] manipulation of crime scenes; mislaying, altering or inventing evidence and testimonies; hiding crucial information; bribing police, prosecutors and judges; finding 'fall guys' to take the rap (usually a lower ranking military officer); and, when necessary, threatening or murdering witnesses and officials. These networks have entrenched interests in criminal gangs: a number of high profile cases, including the trial of three military officers for the murder of Catholic bishop and human rights advocate Juan Gerardi, have indicated the ways in which they use common criminals to gather information and threaten and attack their targets.[40] The political will to tackle these networks is lacking; despite promises to abolish the notorious presidential guard, the *Estado Mayor Presidencial* (EMP), as mandated by the peace accords; neither the administration of President Alvaro Arzú (1996–2000) nor of Alfonso Portillo (2000–2004) have reformed military intelligence structures.

Citizen Responses

The weaknesses of the domestic justice system and continued impunity have engendered a range of responses amongst the population. Those underlined here are: first, greater pro-activism by NGOs in the judicial sphere, including strategies to 'transnationalize' justice for high profile cases of gross human rights violations, second, the erosion of public confidence in the law and increasing disenchantment with state institutions in general, and, third, what is referred to here as the 'privatization' of justice, including the commission of highly authoritarian extra-judicial measures by a range of civic actors.

Challenging Impunity: NGO Strategies

Guatemalan NGOs have been at the forefront of efforts to fight impunity, secure improvements to the justice system and monitor the police and judiciary.[41] In recent years victims' groups, local NGOs, and broad transnational coalitions of human rights activists and supporters have attempted to secure restitution and accountability by bringing those responsible for these gross abuses to justice. Multiple tactics have been pursued, including domestic prosecutions before the Guatemalan courts; appeals before the Inter-American system; and petitions filed in third countries on the basis of universal jurisdiction for crimes against humanity and gross violations of human rights.[42] Attempts to prosecute in the domestic courts have been facilitated in part by the new CPP, which makes provision for third parties to assume the role of co-plaintiffs (*querellantes adhesivos*). In many cases individuals or civic groups have assumed quasi-judicial functions, carrying out forensic investigations or providing legal defence, which would normally be the remit of state authorities. Examples are the representation of survivors of the Río Negro massacre by the Centre for Human Rights Action (*Centro de Acción Legal para los Derechos Humanos,* CALDH), and of the survivors of the Dos Erres massacre by the organization of the families of the disappeared, FAMDEGUA.[43] However, in recent years such strategies have led to growing intimidation of individuals and organizations attempting to challenge impunity.[44]

In the wake of the 1999 report of the CEH into gross violations committed during the armed conflict, which found the Guatemalan state guilty of acts of genocide and other crimes against humanity, CALDH has assisted indigenous human rights activists in preparing two groundbreaking legal cases against former military heads of state. According to the terms of the amnesty signed in 1996 as part of the peace settlement, forced disappearances, torture and genocide are not eligible for exemption from criminal responsibility.[45] Lawyers for the prosecution maintain that acts committed against numerous indigenous communities during the early 1980s meet the Penal Code's definition of genocide.[46] On 3 May 2000 a charge of genocide against three former generals, including ex-head of state Romeo Lucas García, for ten massacres perpetrated between October 1981 and March 1982 was presented to the MP by the Association Reconciliation for Justice (*Asociación Reconciliación para Justicia*, ARJ), a group comprising massacre survivors. On 6 June 2001 the ARJ presented a second charge against five former generals, including former military rulers Efrain Ríos Montt and Oscar Humberto Mejía Víctores, for 11 massacres carried out between 1982 and 1983. Among the evidence amassed during four years of careful preparation are more than two hundred witness testimonies, formerly classified military documents gleaned from US sources and evidence gathered during ongoing exhumations of mass grave sites. At the time of writing the cases remain before the courts. In 2002 another legal rights NGO, the Myrna Mack Foundation, succeeded in bringing three high-ranking military officers to trial for planning and ordering the 1991 murder of anthropologist Myrna Mack. Mack's sister acted as *querellante adhesivo* in the landmark case, which was characterized by persistent death threats and attacks on witnesses and the prosecution team. In October 2002 two of the officers were acquitted and one convicted of the charges. However, such high profile attempts to challenge human rights abuses before the courts constitute the exception rather than the rule – the vast majority of past and present violations do not become the subject of legal proceedings.

A number of NGOs are also making recourse to the Inter-American system as a means to bring pressure on the Guatemalan government. CALDH have stated that if the genocide cases do not prosper before the national courts they will go to the Inter-American Court (IAHCR) to try and secure financial compensation for the 2,300 victims involved. In 2002 the Inter-American Commission admitted the case of the Rio Negro massacre to the IACHR. During the previous year the IACHR ordered the Guatemalan government to pay $500,000 in compensation to the families of five street children abducted, tortured and murdered by the police. Human rights organizations Casa Alianza and the Washington-based Center for Justice and International Law (CEJIL) took the case to the commission after two policemen were acquitted in the Guatemalan courts.[47] The Rigoberta Menchú Foundation has also appealed to the commission that military officers involved in the 1995 massacre of 11 returned refugees at Xamán be tried through the IACHR.[48] Attempts to secure prosecution of Ríos Montt, Lucas García and other former military officials on charges of genocide have also been presented before Spanish and Belgian courts, based on the principle of universal jurisdiction.[49] In December 1999, Nobel Laureate Rigoberta Menchú Tum brought charges of genocide and crimes against humanity before the Spanish High Court against former heads of state Lucas García, Ríos Montt, Mejía Víctores and other high-ranking former military officers.[50]

Disenchantment with Democratic Institutions

Citizen mistrust of the justice system and the resort to extra-judicial and violent means of conflict resolution has deep historical roots in Guatemala. Nonetheless, the failure to deliver more effective justice through the courts since the end of the armed conflict, combined with continued disregard for the law on the part of domestic elites has dangerously eroded confidence in state institutions. A survey by ASIES in 1997 found that 62 per cent of the population had little confidence in the courts and 18 per cent no confidence whatsoever.[51] A 1998 survey found that 94 per cent of the population thought that the justice system only favoured the rich and powerful, while another survey conducted by ASIES in 2000 concluded that only six per cent of the population felt their basic rights were fully protected by the legal system.[52]

In recent years, the credibility of the legal system has been greatly undermined by perceptions of widespread corruption and the ability of politicians to avoid accountability by securing favourable rulings through the courts. Since 1996 there has been a growing tendency towards the 'judicialization' of political conflicts, the inability of opposition politicians and groups to challenge the ruling party's congressional majority leading to increasing attempts to confront the ruling party in the courts.[53] Most of these efforts have ultimately been frustrated, reinforcing the message to the population that the justice system does not work, or at least that it works only to the benefit of those who wield most power. This perception in turn further encourages preferences for unofficial, punitive and authoritarian mechanisms to provide security and resolve conflicts.

The Privatization of Justice

Crime and the widespread sense of citizen insecurity currently constitute one of the greatest threats to democratic reform in Guatemala. Surveys conducted in 17 Latin American countries revealed that Guatemala had by far the highest rate (55 per cent) of those polled who declared that a member of their family had been a victim of crime at some time during the previous year.[54] The failure to implement coordinated policies to improve public security and the weakness of the courts as mechanisms to secure restitution and accountability has led people to turn to a range of private solutions. These include a growth in vigilante activities, the use of private security firms and an increase in private gun ownership, together with a rise in extra-judicial executions, so-called 'social cleansing' and lynchings. The rapid privatization of justice and security is not exclusive to Guatemala. Right across Central America the weakness of the rule of law and the rise in crime during the 1990s has made such responses a regional trend.

Private security firms have grown in number since the signing of the peace accords. In June 2001 the Association of Private Security Firms reported that some 85 private security firms were legally registered, comprising some 45,000 agents; in 1999 MINUGUA estimated that some 200 private security firms were in operation throughout the country.[55] This means that for every serving police officer in Guatemala there are now three private security guards.[56] These individuals often lack adequate training or supervision by state authorities and have sometimes been involved in acts of violence themselves. In addition, the fact that their services are only available to those who can pay for them makes access to security even more unequal, reinforcing existing socio-economic inequalities. Those who can afford such private services are less and less willing to contribute economically towards improving state security services.

The rate of reported homicides – which includes revenge killings and 'social cleansing' of suspected criminals – continues to rise. One comparative study estimated that the annual rate of violent deaths in Guatemala reached 77 per 100,000 inhabitants in 1998, second only in the region to El Salvador (82 per 100,000) and compared to approximately 10 per 100,000 for the US.[57] Only ten per cent of all homicide cases are sent to trial, and very few of these results in convictions.[58] All social classes use extra-judicial executions as a means of conflict resolution. However, as one recent study has pointed out, the homicide rate in Guatemala is much higher in the capital and coastal departments, where it predominates as a means of conflict resolution, and lower in the mainly indigenous highlands.[59] Yet collective mob executions of suspected criminals by indigenous communities have dominated the headlines. The incidence of such lynchings (often involving the accused being dragged from their homes or the local police station and beaten and burnt to death) has increased since the signing of the peace accords. According to MINUGUA's figures, the average rate of lynchings and attempted lynchings is now roughly two per week. Between 1996 and 2001 some 421 lynchings and attempted lynchings occurred, involving 817 victims and leaving 215 people dead.[60] The rate of incidence continued to increase throughout 2001. Lynchings have occurred in the capital and in the countryside, but tend to lead to fatalities more often in the countryside, the remoteness of many communities impeding swift intervention by the authorities. Not only suspected criminals have been the targets of such actions – in March 2001 a local judge was killed by a mob in Alta Verapaz and other justices of the peace also fear being the victim of attacks by the local population.[61]

Commonly cited reasons for lynchings in Guatemala include the breakdown of community structures and cohesion resulting from the armed conflict, lack of confidence in state institutions and lack of understanding by the population of existing due process guarantees. (Popular expectations of justice seem to demand the immediate incarceration of the accused or their public sanction and repentance, whereas recourse to the courts often involves the release of the accused for lack of evidence or on bail). During the armed conflict authoritarian and violent means, such as torture and summary execution, were used to resolve disputes in a highly public fashion and whole communities were obliged to bear witness to and participate in atrocities. In addition, an entire generation of Mayan men were militarized through the civil patrol structure and schooled in the immediate, violent and summary resolution of conflicts, a function that was effectively delegated to them by the armed forces.[62] Many instigators of lynchings have been identified as former paramilitary heads, who are now community leaders, and in some instances reports indicate that attacks were premeditated rather than spontaneous. The municipalities where lynchings have occurred most frequently are also amongst the poorest and most disadvantaged in the country, where the impact of robberies characterized as minor by the state legal system is keenly felt.[63] Lynchings are not peculiar to Guatemala; they are also reported in Brazil, Haiti, Mexico and Peru.[64] However, the spectacular and public use of disproportionate force, torture and summary execution by the armed forces and civil patrols during the counterinsurgency war has left a deep social and cultural legacy among a population historically denied effective access to the state justice system.

MINUGUA has criticised the government for failing to provide security, protect victims or sanction those responsible for such attacks. Although public condemnations and arrests are slowly becoming the norm, the conviction rate for such crimes is negligible: between June 1998 and June 2000 only 17 sentences were handed down by the courts in lynchings cases and two were later annulled.[65] In March 2001 a proposal was presented to Congress to make lynchings and the failure to prevent them by state authorities present at the scene a specific criminal offence. The Supreme Court, the Ministry of Education, MINUGUA and local NGOs have begun citizen education programmes in an attempt to reduce the incidence of such crimes, and in some areas programmes have been initiated to coordinate detentions of suspected criminals between communities and judicial authorities in order to save lives.[66] However, the results of such programmes will only be seen in the medium term and will depend on genuine improvements in citizen security.

Rights Guarantees Under Threat

Real advances in securing due process guarantees were made during the 1990s, but they are increasingly under threat, in part due to the corruption and inefficacy of the judiciary. Public pressure on the government to take more hard-line, repressive approaches to tackling crime is high and accusations that 'human rights' are to blame for the failure to punish criminals have become common currency. Tough stances on crime are popular with the electorate even though, as the current Portillo administration has demonstrated, they do not deliver effective results. In 1995 the government of Alvaro Arzú extended the death penalty to anyone convicted of kidnapping and in May 2000 Congress rescinded the law allowing the president to grant pardons in capital cases. This violated both the American Convention on Human Rights and the International Covenant on International and Civil Rights.[67] In June 2000 the execution of two convicted kidnappers was repeatedly broadcast on national television. Lawyers who have appealed against death sentences have received death threats, apparently from supporters of capital punishment,[68] and in 2002 the Constitutional Court upheld death sentences issued by the courts. Such developments bode ill for efforts to build a democratic rule of law.

Conclusions

Reforms of the Guatemalan justice system have advanced since the end of the armed conflict. There is widespread consensus on the weaknesses of the existing system, and civic groups and NGOs are more involved in developing proposals for justice reform and in monitoring official abuses than ever before. Nonetheless, despite the disbursement of massive sums of international aid and loans, the justice system remains weak, a consequence of inadequate or insufficient institutional reform, lack of coordination amongst donors, neglect and/or predatory colonization by the dominant political parties, entrenched impunity, corruption and the widespread influence of military and criminal networks. Thanks to the peace process and ongoing processes of legal globalization the majority of Guatemalans are more aware of their rights than a decade ago. Yet they continue to lack access to effective, culturally appropriate state justice. Popular dissatisfaction and the privatization of justice and security are increasing, undermining the gains made through the peace settlement in the 1990s. As the Guatemalan case illustrates, increased awareness of 'human rights' and evidence of 'rights claiming' does not necessarily translate into effective *respect* for the human and constitutional rights of all citizens: although it may at first glance appear paradoxical, in certain contexts claiming rights can mean advocating highly authoritarian measures. Social pressure from below for due process and the rule of law is weak in Guatemala. What is demanded instead is rapid and invariably highly punitive forms of justice.

Internationally promoted agendas for judicial reform generate very different outcomes depending on local context. Too much attention is currently paid to institutional design in discussions about how to strengthen the rule of law and too little to why implementation of such blueprints so often fails to yield better results. Different and often competing understandings and practices of 'law', 'order' and 'justice' depend ultimately on complex interplays of historical processes, cultural understandings and material interests. These, in turn, affect the development of new kinds of legal regulation, both formal and informal. Institutions do matter. But only by understanding the interaction of judicial structures and mechanisms and the subjective understandings of those actors who use (or do not use) them, and focusing on the role of law in long-run processes of state formation can we hope to understand the specificities of socio-legal change.

ACKNOWLEDGEMENTS

The author appreciates and has greatly benefited from comments made on earlier versions of this essay by Alan Angell, Pilar Domingo, Fiona Macaulay, Albane Prophette, Luis Ramirez, Jack Spence and Tracy Ulltveit-Möe. The usual disclaimers apply.

NOTES

1. For an overview see William C. Prillaman, *The Judiciary and Democratic Decay in Latin America: Declining Confidence in the Rule of Law* (New York and London: Praeger, 2000).
2. See ibid.; Linn. A Hammergren, *The Politics of Justice and Justice Reform in Latin America: The Peruvian Case in Comparative Perspective* (Boulder, CO and London: Westview Press, 1998); Mark Ungar, *Elusive Reform: Democracy and the Rule of Law in Latin America*, (Boulder and London: Lynne Reinner 2002); Maria Dakolias, *The Judicial Sector in Latin America and the Caribbean: Elements of Reform* (Washington DC: World Bank, 1996); Michael Dodson, 'Assessing Judicial Reform in Latin America', *Latin American Research Review*, Vol.37, No.2 (2002), pp.200–220.
3. Pilar Domingo and Rachel Sieder (eds), *Promoting the Rule of Law: Perspectives on Latin America*, (London: Institute of Latin American Studies, 2001).
4. Ricardo Salvatore, Carlos Aguirre and Gil Joseph, *Crime and Punishment in Latin America: Law and Society since Late Colonial Times* (Durham, NC and London: Duke University Press, 2001); Victoria Chenaut and María Teresa Sierra (eds), *Pueblos Indígenas ante el Derecho* (Mexico: CIESAS/CEMCA, 1995); June Starr and Jane Collier (eds), *History and Power in the Study of Law: New Directions in Legal Anthropology* (Ithaca, NY and London: Cornell University Press, 1989); Richard Wilson (ed.), *Human Rights, Culture and Context: Anthropological Perspectives on Human Rights* (London: Pluto Press, 1997).
5. Ralph Lee Woodward Jr, *Rafael Carrera and the Emergence of the Republic of Guatemala, 1821–1871* (Athens and London: University of Georgia Press, 1993).
6. David McCreery, *Rural Guatemala, 1760–1940* (Stanford, CA: Stanford University Press, 1994).
7. Arturo Taracena Arriola, *Etnicidad, estado y nación en Guatemala, 1808–1944* (Guatemala: CIRMA, 2002).
8. Rachel Sieder, 'Paz, progreso, justicia y honradez: law and citizenship in Alta Verapaz during the regime of Jorge Ubico', *Bulletin of Latin American Research*, Vol.19, No.3 (2000), pp.283–302.
9. Patrick Ball, Paul Kobrak, Herbert Spirer, *State Violence in Guatemala, 1960–1996: A Quantitative Reflection* (New York: American Association for the Advancement of Science, 1999); Oficina de Derechos Humanos del Arzobispado de Guatemala, Informe REMHI, *Guatemala: Nunca Mas* (Guatemala: ODHAG, 1998); United Nations, *Informe de la Comisión de Esclarecimiento Histórico* (Guatemala: UN, 1999). Online at <http://hrdata.aaas.org/ceh/report/english/default.html>.

10. A thorough analysis of the legal apparatus of the counterinsurgency state is set out in Alberto Binder et al., 'Informe sobre la participación del sistema judicial en la violación de los derechos fundamentales durante el enfrentamiento armado', draft document prepared for the UN Comisión de Esclarecimiento Histórico, on file with author.
11. See UN, *Informe de la Comisión de Esclarecimiento* (note 8).
12. A poll commissioned by the Supreme Court in 1997 revealed that 88 per cent of those surveyed considered the justice system to be 'inadequate'; four out of five admitted they had little or no confidence in the system; see Luis Pásara, 'Reforma judicial: el caso de Guatemala', draft paper on file with author (2002).
13. In April 1998 the UN Human Rights Commission excluded Guatemala from the list of countries singled out for systematic violations of human rights, signalling a marked improvement in this area.
14. One UNDP study indicated that in 1997 the rate of kidnappings in Guatemala was similar to that in Colombia; approximately 17 per 100,000 inhabitants per year; see PNUD, Proyecto Regional de Justicia, *Acceso a la justicia en Centroamérica: seguridad juridical e inversion*, 2nd edition, (San José Costa Rica: PNUD, 2001), p.45.
15. Manolo Vela, Alexander Sequén-Mónchez and Hugo Antonio Solares, *El lado oscuro de la eterna primavera: Violencia, criminalidad y delincuencia en la postguerra* (Guatemala: FLACSO, 2001).
16. Charles T. Call, *Sustainable Development in Central America: The Challenges of Violence, Injustice and Insecurity* (Hamburg: Central America 2020 Working Paper No.8, 2000), p.9.
17. Hugh Byrne, 'Trials and Tribulations of Justice Reform in Guatemala', paper prepared for the Latin American Studies Association conference, on file with author (2000), pp.7–9; WOLA, *La reforma judicial en Guatemala, 1997–1998: Una guía básica sobre los problemas, procesos y actores* (Guatemala: WOLA, 1998), pp.28–38.
18. Luis Pásara, 'Reforma' (note 12).
19. See Comisión de Fortalecimiento de la Justicia, *Una nueva justicia para la paz: Informe Final*, (Guatemala: Comisión de Fortalecimiento de la Justicia, 1998).
20. Between 1994 and 1999 the total number of judges and magistrates increased from 400 to 753. PNUD, *Guatemala: Informe del Desarrollo Humano 2000* (Guatemala: PNUD, 2001), p.109.
21. Between 1995 and 1998 MINUGUA developed a multicultural justice programme, which involved the setting up of pilot projects for linguistic pluralism and justice administration in various regional departments. USAID also supports a bilateral translator programme and the UNDP and the governments of Spain and Norway are also supporting the creation of *defensorías* indígenas – bilingual public defenders offices. See MINUGUA, *Ninth Report on Human Rights of the UN Verification Mission in Guatemala, 1 April 1998 to 31 December 1998* (Guatemala: UN, 1999), p.3; Steven E. Hendrix, 'Guatemalan "Justice Centers": The Centerpiece for Advancing Transparency, Efficiency, Due Process, and Access to Justice', *American University International Law Review*, Vol.15, No.4 (2000), p.848; ASIES, *Avances y dificultades en el proceso de reforma, modernización y fortalecimiento del sistema de justicia en Guatemala durante el año 2001* (Guatemala: ASIES 2002), p.24, <http://www.asies.org.gt/sistema-justicia/informe-final.htm>.
22. Ibid., p.5.
23. Five pilot community courts were established in 1998. Each had three 'justices of the peace' (*jueces de paz*); two people from the community and the local justice of the peace. See Luis Ramirez, Justo Solorzano and Mario Caxaj , *Informe: Tribunales Comunitarios*, draft document, INECIP, Guatemala, on file with author (1999); Jorge Murga Armas, *Análisis del funcionamiento de los Juzgados de Paz Comunitarios. Reformas al Código Procesal Penal*, draft document, PNUD, Guatemala, on file with author (1999).
24. The proposed reforms included a series of clauses related to judicial reform and the recognition of the state as multicultural and multiethnic. They were defeated on an 18 per cent turnout, following an effective campaign by opponents who appealed to racist sentiments, raising fears that such measures would balkanize the country and encourage reverse discrimination against non-indigenous people. See Cynthia Arnson (ed.), *The Popular Referendum (Consulta Popular) and the Future of the Peace Process in*

Guatemala, Working Paper No.241 (Washington DC: Woodrow Wilson Center Latin American Program, 1999); Susanne Jonas, *Of Centaurs and Doves: Guatemala's Peace Process* (Boulder, CO and London, Westview Press, 2000), ch.8); Victor Ferrigno, 'La nación a debate: constitución y derechos indígenas' in Jueces para la Democracia, *Libro blanco sobre la Independencia del Poder Judicial y la Eficacia de la Administración de Justicia en Centroamérica* (San José Costa Rica, 2000), pp.261–302.

25. Many of the new community courts and local authorities exceed their functions by dealing with a range of conflicts that are not currently within their competence, calling into doubt the legal validity of their judgements; MINUGUA, *Suplemento al décimo informe sobre derechos humanos de la Misión de Verificación de las Naciones Unidas en Guatemala: Funcionamiento del sistema de justicia* (Guatemala: UN, 2000).
26. Luis Pásara, 'Reforma', (note 12) p.13.
27. This was particularly evident during the 'Guate-gate' scandal, when the Supreme Court revoked the congressional immunity of FRG general secretary and president of Congress Ríos Montt and 23 other FRG deputies in order that they face charges of illegally altering a bill governing the duty levied on the distribution of alcoholic beverages after a previous version had been approved in Congress. The FRG unsuccessfully appealed to the Constitutional Court and subsequently approved changes to the law governing congressional procedures in an attempt to safeguard Ríos Montt's position, but these were declared unconstitutional by the Constitutional Court. Ultimately, however, Ríos Montt and the other deputies were exonerated of criminal charges by a lower court judge.
28. ASIES, 'Avances y dificultades' (note 21).
29. *Central America Report*, 17 August 2001.
30. Ibid.
31. Ibid.; Fundación Myrna Mack, *Hechos que afectan la independencia judicial y administración de justicia en Guatemala: amenazas, intimidaciones y atentados contra jueces, fiscales y abogados* (Guatemala: FMM, 1999).
32. Hendrix (note 21) p.837.
33. MINUGUA, *Suplemento al décimo informe*; ASIES, *Informe combinado sobre la situación de los derechos humanos en Guatemala durante 1999* (Guatemala: ASIES, 2000), <http://www.asies.org.gt/informe-combinado.htm>.
34. The patrollers were first convicted in November 1998, subsequently acquitted, retried and reconvicted in October 1999. A lengthy appeals process ensued and a definitive sentence was not reached until 25 April 2000.
35. See data contained in the *Gacetas Jurisprudenciales* of the Constitutional Court (Guatemala: Constitutional Court, various).
36. PNUD, *Acceso a la justicia* (note 13) p.87.
37. *El Periódico*, 19 June 2001.
38. The existence of investigative structures parallel to the official judicial process came to light when families of kidnap victims, frustrated with the inability of the police and criminal justice system to secure their release, turned to military intelligence, revealing a network run out of the presidency that co-ordinated operations between the Public Ministry and the Estado Mayor Presidencial (EMP). See *Prensa Libre*, 13 August 2000.
39. Francisco Goldman, 'Victory in Guatemala', *The New York Review of Books*, 23 May 2002.
40. In their efforts to lobby on such issues, human rights organizations, such as the Mack Foundation (*Fundación Myrna Mack*, FMM), the Center for Human Rights Legal Action (*Centro de Acción Legal para los Derechos Humanos*, CALDH), the Mutual Support Group (*Grupo de Apoyo Mutuo* GAM), the Widows' Confederation (*Confederación Nacional de Viudas de Guatemala* CONAVIGUA) and the Relatives of the Detained-Disappeared in Guatemala (*Familiares de los Detenidos-Desaparecidos de Guatemala*, FAMDEGUA) have made tactical alliances with elite civic groups such as Friends and Families against Delinquency and Kidnapping (*Familiares y Amigos contra la Delincuencia y el Secuestro,* FADS) and Madres Angustiadas, formed during the mid-1990s in response to escalating levels of crime and kidnapping. Specific proposals for criminal law reform have been advanced by the Institute for Comparative Penal Studies (*Instituto de Estudios Comparados en Ciencias Penales de Guatemala*, ICCPG), an advocacy and research NGO set up in 1990,

while the FMM has played a key role in studying reform of the intelligence services.

41. Amnesty International, *Guatemala: Breaking the Wall of Impunity – Prosecution for Crimes Against Humanity*, AI-index: AMR 34/020/2000 19/06/2000 (London: Amnesty International, 2000).
42. WOLA, *La reforma judicial en Guatemala, 1997–1998*, pp.7–8.
43. MINUGUA's 11th Report on Human Rights, covering the period December 1999–June 2000 noted an 'intensification of intimidation' against journalists and human rights groups; for a detailed recent account see Amnesty International, *Guatemala: Human Rights Community Under Siege,* AMR34/22/2001 (London: Amnesty International 2001). Intimidation of human rights organizations continued to worsen throughout 2002.
44. The UN's Comisión de Esclarecimiento Histórico (CEH) found that between 1981 and 1983 the state had carried out a deliberate policy of genocide against the Mayan population and recommended the prosecution, trial and punishment of those guilty of such non-amnestied crimes. According to the commission's report, over 83 per cent of the war's victims were indigenous and the army is responsible for over 85 per cent of human rights violations committed during the conflict.
45. Article 376 of the Penal Code classifies the crime of genocide as the intent to partially or totally destroy a national ethnic or religious group, or the act of undertaking efforts to bring about these groups' destruction.
46. *Central America Report*, 6 July 2001.
47. The trial of 25 soldiers took over four years and was condemned by international observers as a travesty of justice. Hearings were repeatedly delayed, the military withheld vital information and pressure was brought to bear on witnesses, including bribes and death threats. The Rigoberta Menchú Foundation withdrew as *querellantes adhesivos* in 1998, alleging judicial bias. The verdict reached in August 1999 returned convictions for manslaughter, not murder. The soldiers were sentenced to between four and five years in prison, but permitted to commute their sentences at a rate of Q5 (US$0.67) a day, enabling their freedom to be bought for around $1,000 each.
48. For a useful explanation of universal jurisdiction and recent developments see Geoffrey Robertson, *Crimes Against Humanity: The Struggle for Global Justice* (New York and London: New Press, 2000).
49. To date the Spanish courts have ruled the case inadmissible, arguing that attempts to resolve the cases through the domestic courts have not been exhausted.
50. ASIES, *La cultura democrática de los guatemaltecos* (Guatemala: ASIES, 1997). A similar study by the UNDP in 1997 found that 50 per cent of the population had no confidence in the judiciary and 60 per cent no confidence in the police – this reflected similar levels of lack of confidence in these institutions throughout Central America. See PNUD, *Acceso a la justicia* (note 14), p.44.
51. 1998 data cited in Pásara Luis Pásara, 'La justicia en Guatemala', *Diálogo*, FLACSO, No.3 (2) (1998), Guatemala, p.4; ASIES survey cited in PNUD, *Guatemala* (note 20) p.112.
52. The Constitutional Court received 1,186 petitions between January and August 2001; the number of *amparo* appeals to the CC has increased every year since the creation of the CC in 1986; *Prensa Libre*, 26 August 2001.
53. BID (Banco Interamericano de Desarrollo), *Desarrollo: Más Allá de la Economía: Progreso económico y social en América Latina: Informe 2000* (Washington DC: Interamerican Development Bank, 2001), pp.14–15. Only Panama and Uruguay had fewer than 30 per cent; El Salvador was second to Guatemala with 46 per cent.
54. *Prensa Libre*, 17 June 2001; MINUGUA, *Ninth Report on Human Rights of the UN Verification Mission in Guatemala, 1 April 1998 to 31 December 1998* (Guatemala: UN, 1999).
55. In June 2001 the PNC had 18,314 operatives (UN 2001). The private: public ratio is similar to that in the city of Sao Paulo, Brazil, where 1.5 million private security guards outnumber the police by three to one; *The Economist*, 18 August 2001, p.45.
56. The overall homicide rate (which includes intentional and unintentional killings) for Latin America in the 1990s was 30 per 100,000, making the region the most violent in the world. See Call (note 16) p.9.

57. Report of the UN Special Rapporteur on the Independence of Judges and Lawyers, Param Cumaraswamy, March 2000, cited in Human Rights Watch, *World Report 2001: Guatemala* (New York: HRW 2001), <http://www.hrw.org/wr2k1/americas/guatemala.html>.
58. This study includes a useful cross-regional statistical comparison of homicides; see Carlos Mendoza, 'Collective violence: an answer to the absence of justice and security in Guatemala', draft paper, Stanford University, on file with author (2001).
59. MINUGUA, *Los linchamientos: un flagelo que persiste* (Guatemala: UN, August 2002), <http://www.minugua.guate.net>.
60. *Prensa Libre*, 1 April 2001.
61. Marta Gutiérrez and Paul Kobrak, *Los linchamientos: post conflicto y violencia colectiva en Huehuetenango, Guatemala* (Huehuetenango: Centro de Estudios y Desarrollo de la Frontera Occidental de Guatemala (CEDFOG), 2001).
62. MINUGUA, 'Los linchamientos: un flagelo que persiste' (note 59).
63. Carlos Vilas, '(In)justicia por mano propia: linchamientos en el México contemporáneo', *Revista Mexicana de Sociología*, No.1 (63) (2001), pp.131–60.
64. *Prensa Libre*, 20 December 2000.
65. Such a scheme is currently operating in the department of El Quiché: judges and police negotiate the release of individuals detained by the community into police custody; if there is no proof of misdemeanour an effort is made to explain the subsequent release of the individual to the community and to establish acceptable conditions for their reintegration; Gutiérrez and Kobrak, *Linchamientos* (note 61) p.44.
66. Human Rights Watch, *World Report 2001: Guatemala* (New York: HRW 2001), p.4, at <http://www.hrw.org/wr2k1/americas/guatemala.html>.
67. Amnesty International, *Guatemala Annual Report 2001* (London: Amnesty International 2001), p.4.

Economic Reform and Judicial Governance in Brazil: Balancing Independence with Accountability

CARLOS SANTISO

Introduction: The Political Economy of Judicial Governance

The prevailing consensus on judicial governance posits that an independent judiciary is a prerequisite for the rule of law, which entails preventing the misuse of authority and bringing the government to account for its abuses of power. This study argues that it is not a sufficient condition and that it needs to be counterbalanced by the self-restraining mechanisms of accountability. It scrutinizes the role of the Brazilian judiciary in economic policy-making since the restoration of democracy in 1985 and unveils the central paradox of judicial governance in Brazil: while the judiciary constitutes a key institution of accountability, its effectiveness is hampered precisely by its lack of accountability.

Legal and judicial reform has become a core objective of reformers seeking to consolidate democracy and deepen market reforms. It is also a critical concern of those international organizations seeking to assist them.[1] Judicial reform is an essential dimension of the now much-lauded 'second-generation' economic reforms, which underscore the centrality of the institutions of governance for anchoring market-oriented reforms and consolidating democracy. The new paradigm of development economics identifies the strengthening of political institutions and reform of the state as determinant variables for effective economic governance.[2] There exists a substantive body of evidence correlating the rule of law with economic growth, foreign investment and the quality of governance.[3] Yet, effective judicial reform has been elusive in many transitional and developing countries.

International financial institutions and donor governments are funding a myriad of initiatives aimed at reforming judicial systems and strengthening the rule of law in transitional and developing countries. The fight against corruption, which now dominates the debates on development assistance and aid effectiveness, has created an added impetus for promoting judicial reform and enhancing the rule of law. The World Bank and regional development banks have been at the forefront of this agenda, which the International Monetary Fund (IMF) now also endorses.[4]

The judiciary fulfils two main functions in any democracy: a *political function* related to the republican system of checks and balances and a *legal function* aimed at applying the law and resolving disputes. The effectiveness of the rule of law hinges upon the existence of a judiciary imparting the law consistently and impartially. Accordingly, the credibility of the judiciary and the reliability of its decisions are largely dependent upon its independence from political power, and in particular the executive. Furthermore, an impartial judiciary, acting as an agent of restraint on political authorities, is the guarantor of the separation and balance of powers. As such, its is a central institution of 'horizontal accountability' complementing the mechanisms of 'vertical accountability' provided for by regular, free and fair elections.[5]

Judicial independence has been particularly damaged by the expeditious modes of government adopted by Latin America's newly restored democracies to swiftly implement radical market-oriented economic reforms. Government by decree beyond times of economic emergency has significantly eroded the quality of democratic institutions, as it entailed neutralizing the 'veto points' in the decision-making process. In particular, governments sought to circumvent and often succeeded in defusing the mechanisms of accountability that an independent judiciary would have provided. This trend has been particularly acute in economic policy making, as the radical market-oriented reforms in the late 1980s and early 1990s were implemented by recurring to expeditious modes of government. Wary of the obstruction potential of independent-minded courts, governments endeavoured to create politically pliant judiciaries by packing the courts with political allies. As a result, the credibility and reliability of the judiciary as a check on government power has been compromised, significantly undermining the quality of democracy and often leading to hybrid regimes, aptly labelled 'delegative democracies.[6]

However, Brazil appears to have been an exception. Endowed with a high level of independence by the Constitution of 1988, the Brazilian judiciary has provided an effective check on the executive, thereby fulfilling its accountability functions vis-à-vis the other two political powers. On repeated occasions, it has openly confronted political authorities over the misuse of executive decrees. The most dramatic instance of judicial independence and political accountability came in 1992 during the congressional impeachment of a sitting president, Fernando Collor. Similarly, in 1994, it suspended the mandate of a prominent senator for campaign financing irregularities. This was the first time in Brazil's history that the courts removed a legislator under democratic circumstances.

The Brazilian trajectory has largely been neglected in comparative analyses of judicial governance in Latin America. Unlike in the rest of the region, the main question in Brazil is not whether the judiciary is sufficiently independent, but rather whether it has become too independent. As such, the Brazilian case provides a useful contrast to the main thrust of this volume, which posits that independence is a central attribute of the judiciary's credibility. Judicial independence has proved excessive in many respects, creating an insulated, unresponsive, and, at times, irresponsible judiciary. The challenge of judicial reform in Brazil is thus radically different from that of the rest of Latin America. While strengthening judicial independence is a core objective of judicial reform in Spanish-speaking Latin America, in Brazil the challenge resides in strengthening the accountability of the judiciary vis-à-vis the society and the polity. In both cases, however, it has proved particularly difficult to reform judiciaries, no matter how dependent or independent the courts are.

Furthermore, the Brazilian experience is increasingly an illustration of things to come. It reflects, with a decade of anticipation, an emerging trend in Latin America, as the courts progressively re-assert themselves. It underscores the dangers of strengthening judicial independence without simultaneously enhancing the countervailing mechanisms of accountability within the judiciary itself.[7] In recent years, and for a variety of reasons, the judiciaries have regained strength. Often in the wake of crises of governance or regime transition, they have been able to create a new role for themselves. In Mexico, Colombia, Argentina, and more recently Peru, the courts are actively asserting their new-found authority in order to regain a semblance of popular legitimacy. The judiciary is one of the most discredited political institutions in Latin America.

This study assesses the governance of the judiciary in Brazil since the restoration of democracy in 1985. It focuses on the role of the judiciary in the process of economic reform and evaluates the judiciary's effectiveness in fulfilling its accountability functions. It argues that democratic governance in Brazil is hampered by excessive judicial independence, anchored in its strict interpretation of the separation of powers enshrined in the 1988 Constitution. It further posits that the challenge of judicial reform in Brazil resides in strengthening the countervailing mechanisms of accountability in order to enhance the judiciary's social responsiveness and political responsibility. After all, in formally democratic Latin America, the judiciary is the only non-elected branch of government. The paradox of judicial governance in Brazil is that while the judiciary contributes to the 'horizontal accountability' of the state, providing checks and balances on executive power, it lacks the restraints provided for by the mechanisms of 'vertical accountability' of democratic elections.

Moreover, the judiciary's entrenched independence renders judicial reform particularly difficult.

Judicial reform is likely to gain greater prominence following the historic victory of Luiz Inacio Lula da Silva in the presidential elections of October 2002. His campaign commitments included promises to tackle endemic corruption and overhauling the judicial system.[8] His *Partido dos Trabalhadores* (PT) has indeed been at the forefront of successive attempts at reforming the judiciary in the last decade. Judicial reform is one of the main priorities of the new Minister of Justice, Márcio Thomas Bastos, who assumed office in January 2003.[9]

The analysis is structured in four substantive sections. The first section focuses on the restoration of judicial independence during the democratic transition in the mid-1980s. The second section takes a closer look at the delicate interplay between economic reform and judicial governance. The third section underscores the need to strike a more adequate balance between independence and accountability for anchoring the judiciary's political credibility and social legitimacy, while the fourth section delves into the political economy of judicial reform. The article concludes with a series of remarks on the rule of law and judicial institutionalization.

Democratic Transition and Judicial Independence

By any standard, the Brazilian judiciary enjoys extraordinarily levels of independence. Judicial independence is both *nominal*, enshrined in extensive constitutional guarantees, and *substantive*, in terms of the powers granted to the courts and the willingness of judges to exercise them.

Restoring Judicial Independence

Reacting to decades of authoritarian rule (1964–1985), the Constituent Assembly of 1986–88 considered that the restoration of the judiciary's credibility and legitimacy necessarily entailed securing its political independence. It thus decided to insulate the judiciary from the other branches of government and granted it broad functional autonomy and a high level of nominal and structural autonomy.

The Brazilian Supreme Court, the *Supremo Tribunal Federal* (STF), had indeed confronted the abuses of the authoritarian regime on repeated occasions. For example, in 1968, it declared key portions of the military's National Security Law unconstitutional, prompting the latter to shelve the judiciary's independence by packing the Supreme Court in 1969. Indeed, the authoritarian regime sought to impose its authority through the legal system itself by issuing executive decrees with force of constitutional law, the so-called 'institutional acts.' Judicial assertiveness fluctuated thereafter as the military pursued its strategy of protracted decompression and gradual opening in an erratic manner in the mid-1970s.[10]

Furthermore, and even though the Supreme Court had largely been shaped by the military government, the new civilian authorities resisted purging the judiciary, as many civilian and authoritarian governments had done in the past. For example, following the military coup in 1964, the governing junta packed the court in order to neutralize legal challenges to its extensive use of emergency decree powers.

The constitutional drafting process significantly impacted on the design of judicial reforms. The constitution was drawn up by the Congress elected in October 1986, which decided to act simultaneously as a regular parliament enacting ordinary legislation and a constitutional assembly tasked with writing a new constitution. This choice rendered the constitutional drafting process particularly vulnerable to pork-barrel politics and political deal-making. Furthermore, it took place in the context of a fragmented political system composed of a myriad of political parties with few coherent proposals on what a judiciary ought to look like. Lacking technical expertise, the Congress delegated much of its law-drafting authority to judicial experts and the legal profession, such as the Brazilian Bar Association. Often oblivious of the broader institutional architecture of governance being designed by other parliamentary committees, these experts constructed an ideal type of judicial system based on the republican principles of the separation and balance of powers, which emphasized functional autonomy and political independence.

By any standard, the Brazilian judiciary was granted particularly high levels of independence. The 1988 Constitution restored most of the provisions of the republican Constitution of 1946, which was largely inspired by the United States Constitution. In an effort to strengthen the individual independence of judges, the terms and conditions of tenure were significantly enhanced. Judges were guaranteed life-tenure, with retirement at the age of 70 as well as generous and irreducible salaries. They were also shelved from undue political interference in the management of their careers as the judiciary was endowed with setting its own selection, nomination and promotion procedures. Furthermore, judges could not be transferred from one court to another.

An Atomized Legal System

Similarly, and in order to enhance the independence of lower courts vis-à-vis superior courts, the Congress constrained the powers of the Supreme Court by rejecting the binding nature of superior courts' decisions on lower courts, in particular in constitutional matters. It resisted the introduction of the precedent into the legal system, arguing that it would unfairly bound judges to a ruling of other courts, thereby constraining their individual independence. This system was chosen to ensure the effective protection of the myriad of economic, political and social rights enshrined in the constitution by allowing several means of recourse at different levels in the judicial system. However, while anchoring the independence of the judiciary as an institution of accountability, these arrangements have atomized the judiciary and created a diffuse judicial system, in particular in the field of constitutional judicial review.

The rejection of the legal principle of *stare decisis* ('stand by things decided') is the poisonous centre of the Brazilian judicial dilemma. There are many legal and political reasons why Brazil ignores the principle of precedent. It strengthens the independence of individual judges and the autonomy of individual courts vis-à-vis their hierarchies. Politically, it gives politicians more means of legal recourse against the government's decisions. This legal principle of determining points in litigation according to the precedent is the defining character of the United States' legal system and partly explains why the problems linked to the internal coherence of the justice system found in Brazil are largely absent in the United States. The precedent allows in particular for a coherent and vertically centralized legal system based on a set hierarchy of norms and judicial institutions

The constitution also strengthened the functional independence of the judiciary as a governance institution by insulating it from the broader political system. The courts were given total control over their administrative, personnel and disciplinary affairs. While the Senate can initiate impeachment proceedings against Supreme Court justices, only superior-level judges can remove lower-court judges. While this system contains pressure from political forces outside the judiciary, it nevertheless grants considerable disciplinary powers to the judicial hierarchy and exposes lower-rank judges to pressure by their superiors. Furthermore, in order to prevent any encroachment on its independence by the executive or the legislature through its finances, the judiciary has near total control over its budget. At the federal level, the STF prepares the annual budget for the federal court system and submits it directly to Congress, effectively circumventing the executive branch. The federal government has thus little control over the judiciary's budget, which can become problematic in times of economic austerity. Any infringement on these procedures is immediately considered a violation of the principle of the separation of powers.

The 1988 Constitution undeniably extended unprecedented power and independence to the judicial branch. Brazilian judges are particularly proud of their legal system. Supreme Court Justice José Neri da Silveira has praised the independence of the Brazilian judiciary, qualifying it as 'unique in Latin America'[11] and former Supreme Court President José Celso de Mello Filho has argued that the Brazilian judiciary is the 'most autonomous' in Latin America.[12] Indeed, the governance of the Brazilian judiciary exhibits characteristics radically different from their counterparts in the region. In a hearing of the parliamentary commission on the reform of the judiciary in April 1999, Supreme Tribunal of Justice Minister, Antonio de Padua Ribeiro, lauded the 'self-governance' and the 'sophistication' of the Brazilian judiciary.[13]

Economic Reform and Judicial Governance

The judiciary's leverage on the political process in presidential systems can best be assessed through the control of constitutionality of executive decrees. As Roberto Gargarella aptly underscores (see pp.181–96 below), the 'republican controls' provided by an impartial judiciary contribute to restrict 'the executive's tendencies to increase its own powers'. The effectiveness of this mechanism of accountability is thus a useful indicator of the performance of the judiciary in its political and constitutional role as a guarantor of the separation of powers and arbiter of the respective prerogatives of the executive and legislative branches of government.

Executive Decrees and Economic Policymaking

A central measure of judicial effectiveness resides in the judicial review of executive acts by constitutional courts. Judicial review powers are particularly important indicators of judicial performance in Latin America where most new and restored democracies have opted for presidential systems of government relying heavily on executive decrees to govern. This method of government has been resorted in response to economic crises, which have been recurrent in Latin America in the last two decades since the restoration of democracy in the early-mid 1980s, as it allowed for decisive policy making. In some cases, the legislature willingly delegated its law-making powers to the executive (delegated decree authority). In other cases, the constitution provided the executive with the right to rule by decree (constitutional decree authority), a prerogative often abused by impatient governments in centralized presidential systems.[14] In constitutional terms, executive decrees are often at the fringe of legality and have been compared to a de facto usurpation of legislative powers.

Judicial review has proved to be an effective means through which the Brazilian judiciary has exerted its influence in the policy-making process. The constitution grants extensive prerogatives to the courts in the review of the acts of the executive and the legislature and the judiciary has frequently displayed independence in its decisions. On repeated occasions, it has been able to block successive governments' attempts at reforming the economy and struck down numerous executive decrees, some of which were admittedly of questionable legality.[15] It often ruled against the executive and enforced some of the most ill-conceived welfare portions of the extensive economic and social rights enshrined in the 245-article constitution, sometimes to the detriment of economic rationality and the requirements of austerity. Indeed, judicial independence partly explains why Brazilian reformers have had to muddle through economic reform, in particular in the areas of labour and fiscal reform. To a certain extent, the constitution itself, rather than the judiciary, is to blame, as the courts must apply the law. However, in many instances, the courts have also interpreted the laws in particular ways, often to further their own corporate advantages.

The experience of President Fernando Collor's economic stabilization package of 1990 is illustrative in that regard. Collor introduced a heterodox shock programme aimed at taming Brazil's hyperinflation and, to do so, resorted to expeditious tactics. Although the decree law (*decreto-lei*) was considered a heritage of Brazil's authoritarian tradition, executive decree-powers were retained by the Constituent Assembly to enable presidents to govern even in a context of minority government, especially in times of acute crisis. Article 62 of the constitution allows the president to decree 'provisional measures with the force of law', 'in cases of urgency and relevance.' However, to deter abuses such as those of the military junta's 'institutional acts', the use of decree-laws was codified. If the legislature did not convert the executive decree, or *medidas provisórias* (MP), into law within 30 days, the decree would automatically become null and void.

Collor's presidential style soon led to increased tensions with an overwhelmed Congress over the constitutionality of such practices with the judiciary. Upon assuming office in March 1990, Collor introduced a radical stabilization package, the *Plano Brasil Novo*, issuing 22 executive decrees followed by a myriad of supplementary decrees. In particular, MP 168 included the introduction of a new currency and a freeze on bank accounts. Fearing potential legal challenges, Collor pre-emptively placed restrictions on judicial injunctions against the banking restrictions by issuing yet another executive decree. The Supreme Court stopped short of overturning the presidential decrees but nevertheless allowed citizens to recover their frozen assets, thus leading to the gradual unravelling of the ill-considered first stabilization plan.

Collor's decrees generated more controversies than those of his predecessor, José Sarney, as they were grounded on more fragile legal bases. While 'Sarney relied on executive decree power because he was weak, the early Collor relied on the MP because he was strong'.[16] Some of Collor's decrees were clearly intended to discourage or neutralize legal challenges to the stabilization package. They thus tended to undermine the separation of powers and strain executive–legislative relations as they often encroached on Congress' jurisdiction.

Collor's tactic was to inundate Congress with executive decrees and to re-issue any decree that Congress did not consider within the legal limit of 30 days. A shortcoming of constitutional provisions was their silence on the reintroduction of decree-laws not processed by Congress within the imparted period for doing so or rejected by it. In May 1990, Collor issued a decree that authorized the president of Brazil's highest labour court to suspend any wages increases won by trade unions in class-action suits that the government regarded as inflationary. The Chamber of Deputies ultimately rejected it but Collor immediately re-issued an almost identical decree. Acting on an injunction by the *Procurador-Geral da República,* the Attorney General, the Supreme Court struck down the second decree in June. It argued that the president had exceeded his constitutional powers and overstepped the bounds of presidential authority by re-issuing a measure that Congress had explicitly rejected. Collor complied with the ruling and, in his second year in office, refrained from over-stretching his decree powers.

This episode enhanced the authority of the judiciary and strengthened its position in the democratic institutional system then being shaped. It was particularly important because it took place at a time when the three branches of government were redefining their respective role in the new democratic context. By questioning the constitutionality of decree authority, the judiciary thus contributed to define the outer limits of presidential power and mediate executive–legislative relations. In March 1991, Congress adopted a bill that further regulated executive decree authority and constrained the president's use of decree powers.

Judicial Activism in Economic Policy

There are many other examples of judicial activism in economic policy making. Under the administration of Itamar Franco in 1993, the STF upheld the rulings of regional federal courts that generalized a pay rise that had been conceded to discontented military officers. It argued that, as the constitution mandates a national wage policy, any wage increase to one category of public sector employees must be granted to all state employees. Despite the government's protest that such a measure would further destabilize the country's shaky public finances and contribute to hyperinflation, the government was legally obliged to broaden the salary increase to any public servant who asked for it. The same year, in an attempt to narrow the fiscal deficit, the government attempted raising revenue by instituting a controversial new tax on financial transactions. It secured approval from the Congress and proceeded to implement the tax reform. However, lower courts overruled both the executive and the legislature arguing that the constitution stipulates that no tax can be levied the year it is created. The executive was thus forced to retract its measure and devise alternative to measures to control the fiscal deficit and tame inflation.

More recently, in 1999, the Supreme Court judged two critical fiscal reforms unconstitutional. In the pursuit of fiscal adjustment, Congress had adopted two reforms aimed at achieving a primary fiscal surplus equivalent to 3.25 per cent of gross domestic product, as part of the US$41.5 billion rescue package negotiated with the IMF. The reforms consisted of an increase in public sector workers' pensions contributions and a reduction of pension benefits. The Supreme Court judgement resulted in a US$1.2 billion shortfall in the federal budget at a particularly inauspicious moment. More fundamentally, it created an additional uncertainty about the credibility of the government's economic policy and austerity programme.

As William Prillaman aptly notes, these actions 'reinforced the notion that the Brazilian judiciary was able to ensure a fair degree of horizontal accountability among other branches and levels of government'.[17] In that respect, the Brazilian experience sharply contrast with that of its neighbours such as Argentina where the judiciary has been unable or unwilling to confront the executive's abuse of authority and indeed became one of its first victims.[18]

Independence and Accountability

Despite the above-mentioned activism of judicial authorities, the legitimacy of the Brazilian judiciary has reached abysmal levels. Popular frustration with the judiciary is pervasive across the political and social spectrum.

The Perverse Incentives of Excessive Independence

The unaccountable independence of the judiciary negatively affects its performance, as it distorts the incentives which shape judicial behaviour. Few incentives exist within the judiciary to discipline itself, reward good performance and sanction poor performance. The courts are slow, distant, inaccessible, and often corrupt. The weakness of the mechanisms for internal discipline and external control inhibits the effectiveness of performance-based management systems.

A decade of failed judicial reform has significantly increased backlogs and trial delays. The inadequacy of measures aimed at enhancing efficiency such as case management techniques and adequate human resources management have compounded the problems. Bureaucratic congestion of the courts is a major hindrance. Judges spend most of their time in routine administrative affairs rather than judicial decision-making. Not surprisingly, trial delays in the federal court system increased dramatically in the course of the 1990s. The crisis of efficiency of the courts is partly due to unreasonable caseloads. There is an acute shortage of judges (in 1995, about 6,000 judges for 158 million people, a ratio of one judge for every 25,000 citizens, compared to an average ratio of one judge for every 3,000 in the developed world) tasked with managing an increasing number of cases. However, the judiciary tends to resist any external interference in the way it manages its human resources, especially in the selection of new judges, as well as other efficiency enhancing reforms such as the creation of the system of justices of peace.

The number of cases entering the federal judicial system increased dramatically in the course of the last decade. This would appear to suggest that access to justice has improved and a growing confidence in the law and the courts as dispute-resolution mechanisms. However, this is not the case. The increase in the number of cases is principally due to the surge in the cases put forward to the superior courts, as constitutional provisions tend to turn even minor disputes into constitutional challenges. Indeed, efficiency-enhancing measures have focused on the federal court system and in particular the Supreme Court. A court of last appeals for non-constitutional issues, the *Superior Tribunal de Justiça* (STJ), was established to assist the STF, but proved insufficient. Second, access for average citizens regarding civil or criminal cases has continued to lag, further undermining popular trust in the justice system. Small-claims courts at the state level, which were foreseen by the constitution, were established under pressure from the federal government on unwilling and resource-constrained states.

As a result, recourse to the legal system is often considered a delaying tactic rather than a means to resolve disputes. Historically, the law has been often used as an instrument of political repression and social exclusion, reflected in the famous quote by Getúlio Vargas: 'for my friends, whatever they want; for my enemies the law'.[19] The lack of legitimacy of the judiciary is intrinsically linked to the lack of credibility of the law and the Brazilians' tendency to evade it. Paradoxically, although Brazilian citizens routinely evade the rules, they hope that the laws will eventually be respected and cure Brazil's ills.

The Dangers of Unaccountable Independence

The shortcomings of judicial governance in Brazil reveal the tensions, if not contradictions that exist between independence and accountability. While the prevailing consensus holds that independence is a critical dimension of the judiciary's credibility as an institution of 'horizontal accountability', reformers have often overlooked the corresponding need to enhance external accountability in the judiciary. This shortcoming is due, in part, to the fact that accountability is a difficult concept in the democratic framework of the separation of powers.[20]

The paradox of judicial governance in Brazil is that, as an institution of 'horizontal accountability', the judiciary is devoid of incentives for 'vertical accountability'. It is an unconstrained power in the sense that it is not subjected to the checks that periodic democratic elections would have provided. The question then becomes who guards the guardian?[21] Excessive independence tends to generate perverse incentives and insulate the judiciary from the broader economic and political context, converting it into an autarkic institution unresponsive to social demands. Hence, the puzzle is whether the courts 'have become too independent – whether the Brazilian judiciary in fact had become an entrenched bureaucratic oligarchy in need of restraint and devoid of all accountability to other branches of government and to the public'.[22]

Moreover, the judiciary has often misused its independence to protect its own corporate interests. Allegations of wasteful spending, nepotism and corruption are all too common, reflecting a bureaucratic disregard for financial accountability.[23] In 1994, for example, the federal court system had a budget of about half a billion dollars, but spent over 880 million dollars with little fear of sanction. The *Tribunal Superior do Trabalho* (TST) alone, which processed less than 5,000 of the nearly 80,000 cases brought before it in 1993, spent more than both chambers of Congress, an astonishing US$400 million. The luxurious buildings of the *Superior Tribunal de Justiça* (STJ), completed in 1995 for US$170 million, has more empty offices than full ones, yet it includes an indoor theatre, a ballroom and a swimming pool. As Prillaman argues, these examples are 'indicative of a bureaucratic class that has become oblivious to the austere conditions confronting the rest of the country'.[24]

The institutional abuse of functional autonomy is compounded by judges' individual abuses of their privileges. As the judiciary sets its own budget and spends as it sees fit, senior judges have granted themselves generous salaries and pensions as well as lavish institutional perks such as 60 days of paid vacation a year, a furnished apartment, and an impressive support staff. Indeed, Brazilian senior judges are amongst the best paid in the world: a Supreme Court justice earns over US$10,000 a month and a typical first instance judge around US$3,000. Retirement benefits tend to be similarly generous. Clearly, the judiciary has not shared the austerity reforms: between 1987 and 1999, personal costs in the judiciary rose by a staggering 760 per cent (compared with 220 percent for the executive branch), mainly in salary increases and new personnel.[25]

Constitutional Judicial Review

Structurally, the perverse nature of the Brazilian justice system and the dangers of excessive independence are reflected in the system of judicial review of the constitutionality of laws. While acting as a constitutional court, the STF does not possess the corresponding powers of enforcement, as it lacks exclusive authority to declare the constitutionality or otherwise of laws. The Acts of Unconstitutional Law (*Açãos diretas de inconstitucionalidade*, ADIs) allows groups affected by government decisions to petition against federal acts on constitutional grounds in front of almost any court. This measure represents an effort to enhance access to judicial recourse and protect against the government's violation of human rights and civil liberties. However, the shortcoming of the system of constitutional judicial review lies in the absence of a hierarchy of norms in constitutional matters, as lower-court judges are not necessarily bound by the decisions of the Supreme Court. The Brazilian system constitutes a 'hybrid system of constitutional judicial review of laws' reflecting the decentralization of the judicial system.[26] The resulting 'balkanization' of judicial review is particularly dysfunctional and prone to politicization.[27] Furthermore, the level of detail of constitutional provisions is such that almost any dispute can become constitutional, overloading the STF with minor disputes.

Recent reform proposals aim at rationalizing judicial review by making the STF's decisions binding on lower-level courts, thereby strengthening the role of the STF as a genuine constitutional court.[28] However, such proposals have been resisted by lower-court judges who have jealously defended their independence. For example, the 1993–94 constitutional revision adopted the declaration of constitutionality (*Ação declaratória de constitucionalidade,* ADC), an alternative mechanism for judicial review for which the binding principle was established. However, and although the main proponent of the ADC, Nelson Jobim, also defended the application of the binding principle to ADIs, the proposal was defeated by lower-level judges. Nevertheless, positions are gradually shifting. In a recent decision in November 2002, the STF appeared to support the binding nature of ADIs.[29]

Political parties, which can also challenge the constitutionality of laws, have also resisted the concentration of judicial decision making because the judicial system has proved to be an effective tool for doing politics by other means. It has enabled them to transpose political conflicts into constitutional ones. Between 1988 and 1993, opposition parties introduced over 100 ADIs to undo particular economic initiatives. They have manipulated the ADIs for partisan advantage to contest, delay and dilute government policies. The 'judicialization of politics' tends to transform 'judicial institutions into a locus for obstruction of the political majority by the political minority.'[30] More fundamentally, the debate over constitutional judicial review reflects the tensions between parliamentary prerogatives and judicial independence. As Rogério Bastos Arente notes, the most contentious issue concerns the 'very nature of superior tribunals of justice and their legitimacy to have the last word on specific types of cases'.[31] The main stumbling block is thus linked to the internal architecture of the judicial system and the hierarchy of judicial authorities.

The Elusive Quest for Judicial Reform

Judicial reform in Brazil is marked by an intractable paradox. Despite its importance in the public debate over the last decade, it has proven extremely difficult to craft a sufficient consensus on the shape of the reforms required, devise a credible reform project, and create a coherent pro-reform coalition.

The Governance of the Judiciary

Judicial independence makes it particularly difficult to reform an entrenched judiciary. The case of Brazil illustrates the degree to which excessive independence, lacking the balancing constraint of accountability, has enabled the judiciary to resist reform and avoid external oversight and control. The judiciary has been particularly effective at resisting reform and the creation of external controls, defending a strict interpretation of the principle of separation of powers enshrined in the constitution.

The most contentious aspects of the judicial reform agenda centre on the governance of the judiciary. Judicial reform has two principal dimensions. The first dimension concerns the internal structure and administrative efficiency of the judiciary and is part of the broader process of the modernization of the state. The second dimension concerns the role of the judiciary in the democratic system of institutional checks and balances and the respective powers of the three branches of government. While administrative reform has received broad support, the judiciary hierarchy has fiercely resisted any encroachment on its independence. This uncompromising stance has often derailed promising administrative and organizational reforms, further weakening the efficiency of and access to the justice system.

Working through the labyrinth of Brazilian politics is proving particularly damaging to the articulation of a comprehensive strategy for judicial reform. Judicial reform (or lack thereof) is shaped by the very nature of the political system and the inchoate party system that characterizes Brazil.[32] Successive ad hoc reform efforts 'do not reflect a harmonious and coherent project and end up creating new sources of instability in the judicial apparatus'.[33]

It is particularly telling that those on the left who advocated for maximizing judicial independence during the debates of the Constituent Assembly now lament the judiciary as the most unresponsive branch of government and the least fiscally disciplined. The judiciary is perceived as a power above the country and the laws themselves. José Dirceu, from the PT, has complained that 'there is nothing more arrogant than the Brazilian judiciary' and José Genoíno, a leading leftist intellectual, has repeatedly accused the judges of behaving as if they were 'untouchable.[34]

Although there has been no shortage of reform proposals, actual reform has been curiously absent. For example, during the 1993 constitutional review process, 12 of the 18 proposals for judicial reform called for introducing some form of external oversight of the judiciary. Judicial reform has hardly figured on the political agenda, nor was it pursued by President Cardoso's two consecutive administrations (1994–98, 1998–2002). More urgent reforms such as fiscal and labour reforms and the economic and financial crisis of 1998–99 have relegated judicial reform to the sidelines. Consequently, 'without more sustained pressure for judicial reform, the ability of the courts to resist reform efforts becomes much easier.'[35]

Nevertheless, and partly as a result of Carlos Magalhães's crusade against corruption in the late 1990s, in June 2000, the Chamber of Deputies finally adopted a much-diluted proposal for a constitutional amendment, which had been introduced in 1992 by PT's Hélio Bicudo. The proposal, which is currently being considered by the Federal Senate, is the result of long and protracted political negotiations. It delineates the three main axes for judicial reform: the creation of an institution of external control, with administrative and disciplinary functions; the rationalization of the judicial decision making; and the modernization of the administration of justice.

External Control and Oversight

A central thrust of the reform being considered resides in the need to establish some sort of external oversight, beyond the judiciary's own internal control mechanisms.[36] Indeed, the judiciary is the least supervised of the three branches of government. Proposals for enhancing external control by means of a judicial council go back to the Constitutional Assembly. The idea has gained renewed momentum with the accession of PT to power. It is a key objective of the new Minister of Justice, Márcio Thomas Bastos.

However, the motivations for establishing such a judicial council are radically different from those in the rest of Latin America. In many countries of Latin America the establishment of judicial councils responded to the need to strengthen the political independence of the judiciary by insulating the management of the court system from political interference.[37] In principle, the rationale for creating a judicial council resides in its ability to rationalize the administration of justice and anchor the independence of the judiciary. In Brazil, however, the prime objective is to increase transparency and strengthen accountability in the internal functioning of the judiciary.

The creation of a judicial council has been extremely controversial, being perceived as an attempt of the executive to interfere in judicial governance and a violation of the principle of the separation of powers. In 1977, President Ernesto Geisel enacted a controversial constitutional amendment by executive decree creating an external oversight body for disciplining and punishing recalcitrant judges. Since that time, the creation of a body for external oversight and control is a particularly controversial issue. This is an erroneous interpretation, however, as external control seeks to strengthen the judiciary's accountability in the administration of its internal affairs, especially its finances. It does not, and should not entail control over the independence of judicial decisions.

The debate has indeed shifted in the course of the last decade, as external oversight and control became to be increasingly perceived as an incentive mechanism for enhancing the judiciary's performance and responsiveness. A consensus progressively emerged concerning the mandate and attributions of a judicial council, grounded in the need to dramatically improve the internal administration of judicial resources. The composition of the judicial council proved to be a more contentious issue, as the judiciary resisted the inclusion of representatives of non-judicial professions, which was ultimately endorsed.

Why has then judicial reform proved so elusive in Brazil? The political economy of judicial reform has proven particularly intricate, embedded in the classical dilemma of collective action. Potential losers and hence opposition to reform are concentrated in the judicial hierarchy while potential winners are more diffuse and difficult to mobilize. Those more actively resisting reform are to be found in the legal profession itself and the judicial hierarchy in particular.[38] However, the judicial profession is not a homogeneous entity and its position has changed over time. While in the early 1990s most magistrates opposed the creation of a judicial council, by 2000 most of them supported it, although they favour an institution composed primarily of jurists. Moreover, while senior judges tend to resist reform, lower-level judges favour it. The private sector has also expressed increasing concern, if not frustration, with the lack of reliability of the judicial system and credibility of judicial decisions, especially in the field of commercial law and litigation.

Amongst political parties, the PT has been the most active proponent of judicial reform and the establishment of mechanisms for social control and political accountability. Its accession to power in 2002 may increase its chances of implementing such reforms. Both Dirceu and Genoíno are key members of the new government, the latter as the PT's secretary general and the former as the president's chief of staff.

Tentative Conclusions: How Much is Enough? How Much is Too Much?

The paradoxical conclusion of this essay is that, in Brazil, the social legitimacy of the judiciary as an institution of 'horizontal accountability' is undermined precisely by its lack of 'vertical accountability'. An often-held assumption of judicial reformers is that guaranteeing the independence of the judiciary is paramount to ensuring the effectiveness of the judicial system. The case of Brazil demonstrates that, without the restraining effect of accountability, independence in and of itself is not sufficient to anchor the rule of law.

Reformers clearly succeeded in restoring the political independence of the judiciary and isolating it from political pressures. The central question is whether reformers went too far and created a judiciary so autonomous that is has become devoid of all accountability, a 'power above the law'.[39] Unaccountable judicial independence has been widely criticized and both the executive and legislative branches of government have repeatedly stated their support for establishing mechanisms of external control on the judiciary. Public contempt for the judiciary has reached unprecedented levels but there is a high degree of public disinterest and resignation with increasing backlogs and trial delays. The unreliability and uncertainty of the judicial process also has a negative impact on economic growth and development, as it increases the 'Brazilian cost' of doing business.

Responsible independence rests on restraint and accountability. This requires

> the judiciary's recognition that independence is balanced by accountability, and that in the end it does provide a public service and is answerable to the public for the quality of its output. It also means that in certain areas such as budget management, compliance with rules on procurement or conflict of interest, it may well be subject to the same standards as any other public entity. Independence is most relevant to its role in deciding cases and applying the law, but not

necessarily to how it handles its finances, makes its purchases, or selects its support staff.[40]

Responsible judicial independence requires transparency and accountability in the management of judicial finances.

Finding the right balance between independence and accountability is the defining challenge of judicial reform in Brazil as elsewhere in Latin America.[41] Adequately balancing the four dimensions of judicial impartiality and credibility (independence, accountability, efficiency and access) is a permanent challenge. Most studies of judicial reform tend to presume the existence of a positive synergy or virtuous circle between these different dimensions. Few reformers have foreseen the existence of potential tensions and trade-offs amongst them. More fundamentally, variables such as judicial independence, accountability or efficiency are necessarily continuous rather than dichotomous variables. The central question is not whether or not the judiciary is independent, but rather how independent it should be considering a country's specific circumstances. How much is enough? How much is too much?

Ultimately, achieving 'the right degree of independence' is a challenging task for any democracy.[42] As Linn Hammergren convincingly demonstrates, a 'common feature throughout the region is the failure to admit that the underlying problem is inadequate judicial institutionalization, not too little independence'.[43] Indeed, 'accountability should not be understood as the diametric opposite of independence; the interaction of the two is more complex'.[44]

ACKNOWLEDGEMENTS

The author is particularly indebted to Linn Hammergren and Riordan Roett for their inexhaustible insights, inspiration and support throughout the years, and also gratefully acknowledges the comments on earlier drafts by Siri Gloppen, Elin Skaar, Roberto Gargarella, Carlos Pimenta and Oscar Schiappa-Pietra.

NOTES

1. Thomas Carothers, *Aiding Democracy Abroad: The Learning Curve* (Washington, DC: Carnegie Endowment for International Peace, 1999); Javier Ciurlizza, 'Judicial Reform and International Legal Assistance in Latin America', *Democratization*, Vol.7, No.2 (2000), pp.211–30; Pilar Domingo and Rachel Sieder (eds), *Rule of Law in Latin America: The International Promotion of Judicial Reform* (London: University of London, 2001); Michael Dodson, 'Assessing Judicial Reform in Latin America', *Latin American Research Review*, Vol.37, No.2 (2002), pp.200–220.
2. Douglass North, *Institutions, Institutional Change, and Economic Performance* (Cambridge: Cambridge University Press, 1990); Shahid Javed Burki and Guillermo Perry

(eds), *Beyond the Washington Consensus: Institutions Matter* (Washington, DC: World Bank, 1998.)

3. Robert Barro, *Determinants of Economic Growth: A Cross-country Empirical Study* (Cambridge, MA: MIT Press, 1997); World Bank, *World Development Report 2002: Building Institutions for the Market* (Washington, DC: World Bank, 2002); World Bank, *World Development Report 1997: The State in a Changing World* (Washington, DC: World Bank, 1997); Beatrice Weder 'Legal Systems and Economic Performance: The Empirical Evidence', in World Bank, *Judicial Reform in Latin America and the Caribbean*, Technical Paper 280 (Washington, DC: World Bank, 1995), pp.21–6.
4. Christina Biebessheimer and Mark Payne, *IADB Experience in Justice Reform: Lessons Leaned and Elements for Policy Formulation* (Washington, DC: IADB, 2001); IMF, *Good Governance: The IMF's Role* (Washington, DC: IMF, 1997); USAID, *Guidance for Promoting Judicial Independence and Impartiality* (Washington, DC: Office of Democracy and Governance, 2001); World Bank, *Reforming Public Institutions and Strengthening Governance* (Washington, DC: World Bank, 2000); World Bank, *World Bank Initiatives in Legal and Judicial Reform* (Washington, DC: World Bank, 2000); and Ibrahim Shihata, 'Legal Framework for Development: The World Bank's Role in Legal and Judicial Reform', in World Bank, *Judicial Reform* (note 3) pp.13–16.
5. Guillermo O'Donnell, 'Horizontal Accountability in New Democracies', *Journal of Democracy*, Vol.9, No.3 (1998), pp.112–26; Andreas Schedler, Larry Diamond and Marc Plattner (eds), *The Self-Restraining State: Power and Accountability in New Democracies* (Boulder, CO: Lynne Rienner, 1999).
6. Guillermo O'Donnell, 'Delegative Democracy', *Journal of Democracy,* Vol.5, No.1 (1994), pp.55–69.
7. 'Independencia y Responsabilidad Judicial,' Special Issue of *Sistemas Judiciales*, Vol.2, No.4 (2002).
8. Coligação Lula Presidente, *Combate à Corrupção: Compromiso com a Ética* (Brazil: 2002).
9. 'Bastos promote reforma radical do Judiciário', *O Globo*, 3 January 2003, p.10.
10. Javier Martinez-Lara, *Building Democracy in Brazil* (London: Macmillan, 1996).
11. José Neri da Silveira, 'Aspectos institucionais e estructurais do Poder Judiciário brasileiro,' in Salvio de Figueiredo (ed), *O Judiciário e a Constituição* (São Paulo: Saraiva, 1992), pp.1–22.
12. Quoted in: Maria Terza Sadek (ed.), *Reforma do judiciário* (São Paulo, Brazil: Fundação Konrad Adenauer, Série Pesquisas No.25, 2001), pp.129–33.
13. Ibid., pp.124–7.
14. John Carey and Matthew Soberg Shugart (eds), *Executive Decree Authority* (Cambridge: Cambridge University Press, 1999).
15. Timothy Power, 'The Pen is Mightier than the Congress: Presidential Decree Power in Brazil', in Carey and Shugart (eds) (note 14) pp.197–232.
16. Ibid., p.207.
17. William Prillaman, *The Judiciary and Democratic Decay in Latin America: Declining Confidence in the Rule of Law* (Westport, CT: Praeger, 2000), p.85.
18. Carlos Santiso, 'Política económica insular y consolidación democrática: La paradoja de las reformas de segunda generación en la Argentina de los 1990', *Contribuciones*, 4 (2001), pp.109–36.
19. Juan Méndez et al. (eds.), *The (Un)rule of Law & the Underprivileged in Latin America* (Notre Dame, IL: University of Notre Dame Press, 1999), p.303.
20. Joy Marie Moncrieffe, 'Reconceptualizing Political Accountability', *International Political Science Revue,* Vol.19, No.4 (1998), pp.387–406; and Scott Mainwaring and Christopher Welna, (eds), *Democratic Accountability in Latin America* (Oxford: Oxford University Press, 2003).
21. Carlos Acuña and Catalina Smulovitz, 'Guarding the Guardians in Argentina: Some Lessons About the Risks and Benefits of Empowering the Courts,' in James McAdams (ed.), *Transitional Justice and the Rule of Law in New Democracies* (Notre Dame, IL: University of Notre Dame Press, 1997), pp.93–122.
22. Prillaman (note 17) p.85.

23. These examples are drawn from ibid., pp.86-88.
24. Ibid, p.88.
25. Gerson Camarotti, 'Dossiê de ACM expõe gastos do judiciário,' *O Estado de São Paulo*, 23 March 1999.
26. Rogério Bastos Arantes, 'Jurisdição Política Constitucional', in Sadek (note 12) p.29.
27. Rogério Bastos Arantes, *Judiciário e política no Brasil* (São Paulo: Sumaré, 1997).
28. Carlos Mário Velloso, 'O Supremo Tribunal Federal, Corte Constitucional: Uma proposta que visa a tornar efetiva a sua missão precípua de guarda da Constituição', *Revista de Informação Legislativa*, Vol.30 (1993), pp.5–30.
29. <http://www.direitopublico.com.br> (accessed 12 December 2002).
30. Rogério Bastos Arantes, 'Jurisdição Política Constitucional' (note 26) p.38; Luis Werneck Vianna et al., *A judicialização da política e das relaçãos sociais no Brasil* (Rio de Janeiro: Revan, 1999).
31. Arantes, 'Jurisdição Política Constitucional' (note 26) p.43.
32. Scott Mainwaring, 'Brazil: Weak Parties, Feckless Democracy', in Scott Mainwaring and Timothy Scully (eds), *Building Democratic Institutions: Party Systems in Latin America* (Stanford, CA: Stanford University Press, 1995), pp.354–98; Scott Mainwaring, *Rethinking Party Systems in the Third Wave of Democratization: The Case of Brazil* (Stanford, CA: Stanford University Press, 1999).
33. Arantes, 'Jurisdição Política Constitucional' (note 26) p.38.
34. José Genoíno, 'O Contrôle do Judiciário', *O Globo*, 17 June 1995, p.7.
35. Prillaman (note 17) p.96.
36. Carlos Mário Velloso, 'O controle externo do poder judiciário', *Revista Brasileira de Estudos Políticos*, Vol.80 (1995), pp.53–76.
37. Linn Hammergren, *Do Judicial Councils Further Judicial Reform? Lessons from Latin America*, Working Paper 28 (Washington, DC: Carnegie Endowment, 2002).
38. María Tereza Sadek, 'Controle Externo do Poder Judiciário', in Sadek (note 12) pp.91–180.
39. Genoíno (note 34) p.7.
40. World Bank, *Peru Institutional and Governance Review* (Washington, DC: World Bank, 2002), p.112.
41. Maria Diakolias, 'A Strategy for Judicial Reform: The Experience in Latin America', *Virginia Journal of International Law,* Vol.36, No.1 (1995), pp.167–231; Pilar Domingo, 'Judicial Independence and Judicial Reform in Latin America', in Andreas Schedler *et al.* (note 5) pp.151–75.
42. Owen Fiss, 'The Right Degree of Independence', in Irwin Stotzky (ed.), *Transition to Democracy in Latin America: The Role of the Judiciary* (Boulder, CO: Westview Press, 1993), pp.55–72.
43. Linn Hammergren, *Do Judicial Councils* (note 37) p.35.
44. Linn Hammergren, 'Judicial Independence and Judicial Accountability: The Shifting Balance in Reform Goals,' in USAID (note 4) p.147.

In Search of a Democratic Justice – What Courts Should Not Do: Argentina, 1983–2002

ROBERTO GARGARELLA

Introduction

Many academics and international organizations have been using energy and resources to promote judicial reform in Latin America. Their efforts have produced valuable results. However, it is also true that after years of reflection and reform, the situation of the judicial system in the whole region continues to be very problematic: justices still produce questionable decisions, and large groups of people still find problems in acceding to and/or achieving justice.

The reasons for this frustrating situation are multiple, but at least part of them are connected to a previous misdirected analysis. Academics and leading reformers alike have placed too much emphasis on the politically dependent character of many Latin American judges, or the lack of basic resources both among judges and the people at large – such things as good salaries, administrative facilities, training, education, information. These are real and very important issues, but they are only one part of the story. Many Latin American courts[1] do not lack economic resources or bureaucratic facilities and nevertheless produce highly objectionable decisions. In addition, there are no good reasons for thinking that many of the most questionable judicial decisions produced by these courts would have been different if the judges had been more independent. Political dependence only explains some, however important, of these judicial decisions.

To reflect properly on possible judicial reforms, we should mainly concentrate our attention on the 'constitutional means' and the 'personal motives' allowed to the judges.[2] This suggestion is made within a broader investigation aimed at studying the behaviour of judges in Latin America during recent decades. The account consist of a normative part, which develops a 'regulative ideal' aimed at evaluating the role of judges, and a descriptive part, which applies that ideal to examine one particular Latin American example, Argentina since the last military dictatorship.

What Criteria Should Guide the Work of Judges in Latin America? In Search of a Democratic Justice

In the Anglo-American world, there are many attractive theories concerning the role of constitutions and particularly the constitutional role reserved to judges. Some say that judges should mainly concentrate their efforts on protecting the most disadvantaged groups of society.[3] Some others say that they should try to preserve the most significant popular expressions;[4] some say they should fundamentally protect democratic procedures;[5] and yet others say that, above all, they should guard certain basic moral values, implicit in the constitution.[6] Of course, the fact that these theories are attractive in the Anglo-American context does not necessarily make them attractive for Latin American countries. In fact, in Latin America, as in other regions, our main constitutional devices should primarily work, or be prepared to work, to protect us from the most threatening tendencies of our particular societies.[7] This does not mean that the constitutional structure should not be prepared for unexpected misbehaviour in politics, but simply that it should recognize certain priorities, taking into account the community's most traditional practices.

This point moves us to reflect upon what are the worst tendencies that Latin American societies are most inclined to develop. One of the main problems of Latin America's democracies has been their inability to gain stability. This problem seems especially serious because it is at the root of many others: it aggravates or makes more difficult the resolution of other significant difficulties. Thus it exacerbates social tensions, and helps to enlarge or reinforce existing inequalities. Surely, on many occasions the instability of Latin American democracies was mainly generated by external conditions such as dramatic changes in the international economic context. However, in many other cases political instability was originated from the inside, such as from military rebellions in the face of economic tensions. Now, among the different internal causes of political instability, some concern the institutional system itself. They could be tempered or aggravated by the different parts of that very institutional system, the judiciary included. Here the analysis will focus on the role that the judiciary could play in the context of fragile and still unstable democracies.

In the contemporary Latin American context a *democratic justice* should try to counteract two particularly dangerous tendencies in these new democracies. One is related to the gradual establishment of restrictions upon basic rights such as the right to freedom of expression or the existing and already limited political rights. The other is the executive's tendency to enlarge or strengthen its powers and overcome the structure of republican controls, that is, its tendency to dismiss or actually violate the division of powers and the structure of 'checks and balances'.[8]

These missions would first require the judiciary to provide a strong protection to basic civil liberties. Civil liberties deserve an additional protection given the essential role they play in guaranteeing an expansion of the whole system of liberties. Among the different but equally important civil liberties to which judges should give extra protection, the right to a fair trial deserves special mention, as does the right to privacy. In addition, the importance of defending the right to criticize the government, which has always been the first right to be curtailed by democratic regimes under stress, deserves attention. It must be noted in this respect that the right to criticize the government can be restricted in many different ways. These may include direct and visible actions, such as the creation of repressive laws against the press or the prosecution of journalists, as well as more indirect and invisible ones. The latter have been prevalent in Latin America's many authoritarian regimes, for example by allowing the press to become concentrated in a few hands, by making it very costly to make use of the media or, in general, by not ensuring adequate conditions for full public debate. Social and economic rights should also be guaranteed a privileged place within the structure of basic liberties, although this point requires a more extended discussion than is possible here.

In addition, judges should be especially attentive to limit the president's attempts to expand his or her own capacities at the expense of the other branches of power. It is worth noting that this claim differs significantly from the one that was most common among the 'founding fathers' in the United States, who believed that the main threat to the people's rights came from the ambitions and expansive tendencies of the legislature. In this respect, too, judges should be prepared to defend the controlling agencies from attacks. Latin America's history tells us the judicial branch has always been the main victim of these attacks. But, it has also been common to find executive's assaults against their own administrative agencies and even assaults against Congress, including in some extreme cases the closure of parliament.

Finally, judges should be exceptionally alert against manoeuvres aimed at discontinuing the democratic regime. On occasions such tendencies have derived from the attempts of military officers to expand their own powers and influence. In other cases, they may find expression in other developments like the suspension of elections or the declaration of a state of siege.

All these cases should be examined with what is sometimes called *strict scrutiny*, that is, the courts should subject them to the highest judicial scrutiny. In US constitutional law, to subject a certain public decision to the highest scrutiny is almost the same as saying that this norm will be invalidated.[9] In the writer's schema, this invalidation may or not be necessary, depending on how the whole constitutional structure is organized. However, what would certainly be true in the writer's view is that judges would scrutinize those decisions as *suspect*, and would not act in the face of them with the *deference* that most democratic decisions deserve. Confronting these suspect decisions, judges would have to be *active* rather than passive, and would have to reduce the *presumption of validity* that they should assume all democratic norms have.[10]

Some clarifications are now in order. First, the intention is not to enlarge the powers that the judicial branch enjoys but rather to refine and re-define them more strictly. In contemporary democracies, judges have these and many other capacities, whether they choose to use them or not. These capacities are too many and too significant (see below). In this respect, the proposed scheme attempts to narrow and re-direct the role played by judges and does not require them to become the 'last' institutional authority within democracy. Judges may help us to become a truly democratic community without themselves becoming the unguarded guards of that community. Second, by defining the judges' democratic mission no assumption is being made that they can or will develop that mission by themselves. It is obvious that without the help of other social forces, call them popular or social movements, a stronger network of civic organizations and so on, it will be difficult to expect much improvements in the present situations. It should be clear, on the one hand, that even if we had democratically committed and well-prepared judges, they would not be able to transform our democracies into stronger ones by themselves. They are not, and we should not expect them to become, super-heroes. On the other hand, we should not forget that the judicial system is fundamentally a *reactive* system, in the sense that judges do not tend to act of their own accord. The victims of an injustice are those who come to judges and activate the judicial machine. If nobody were able to initiate a case, the courts would be unable to adopt any decision at all. For this reason, it is of primary importance to examine whether the environment in which the courts act is favourable to people's legal activism. Also, we should not forget that sometimes this context is not favourable for popular activism precisely because of the very institutional mechanisms we have created, among them the judiciary, which may work against it. Finally, in order for this re-direction of judicial functions to happen, some more formal institutional changes are in order.

Can We Expect Judges to Act According to The Suggested Criteria? Constitutional Means, Theories of Interpretation and Civil Law Tradition

Assuming that we agree on the validity of the criteria outlined in the previous section, would it be reasonable, then, to expect judges to follow those patterns? To answer this question we first must examine the institutional capacities judges are granted in constitutional democracies, and the incentives they have for using those capacities in one way or another. This follows in the footsteps of James Madison who, in his now famous *Federalist Paper No. 51* (1787) examined the general structure of the system of 'checks and balances' and focused his attention on the 'constitutional means' and 'personal motives' granted to the members of the different branches of power.

Let us refer first to the constitutional means allotted to judges in our constitutional democracies. Most constitutions describe the attributions of the courts and particularly those of Supreme Court judges precisely. This is the purpose, for example, of Article 3 section 2 of the US Constitution, which reads '[the] judicial Power shall extend to all Cases, in Law and Equity, arising under this Constitution, the Laws of the United States, and Treaties made, or which shall be made, under their Authority; to all Cases affecting Ambassadors, other public Ministers and Consuls; to all Cases of admiralty and maritime Jurisdiction; to Controversies to which the United States shall be a Party; to Controversies between two or more States; between Citizens of different States; between Citizens of the same State claiming Lands under the Grants of different States, and between a State, or the Citizens thereof, and foreign States, Citizens or Subjects.' The constitutions of some other countries have simply copied this article (Argentina's 1853 Constitution, for example), and most others followed in some degree the model it established.

These powers are already very wide. Article 3 of the US Constitution implies that in that country, like in most Latin American countries, the judiciary decides all the important legal questions. It is worth mentioning that the same judges have been defining the scope of their mission through the decisions they have been adopting since the birth of our constitutional democracies. Among many others, two of the statements are worth mentioning. First, as the main guardians of the constitutions, judges have come to be the 'last' interpretative authorities within American nations. Second, the judges interpreted their constitutional powers to include invalidating the decisions of the political branches, when those decisions appeared to contradict the main legal texts of the country.

Undoubtedly, these capacities transformed courts into very powerful institutional actors. In the end, they have the final authority to determine whether the decisions of the political branches should be upheld or not. Now, it is not simply the case that judges have the 'last word' in all important constitutional questions and can prevail upon the political branches. The issue is of more concern than that because judges can decide all those cases with almost total discretion. Of course, they are obliged to follow and respect the constitutional text, but the problem is then a double one. First, those who finally decide what the constitution actually says are the judges themselves, since 'the Constitution is what the judges say it is'. Second, there is no general agreement about what *interpretative theory* the judges should use when interpreting the constitution.

By contrast, there is endless discussion about how to do it properly. Some authors believe that the constitution should be read as a 'living text' and develop a 'dynamic' approach to it;[11] others defend an 'originalist' approach, and look for its precise meaning sometimes in the intentions of its authors or in the ideas that were dominant at the time of its approval.[12] Still others defend a 'moral' reading of the constitution.[13] Clearly, each of these interpretative strategies may lead to completely different outcomes. It may well happen that one judge defends the death penalty through an originalist reading of the constitution; another rejects its constitutional validity through a moral reading; and finally another asserts that it all depends on the present context, taking into account a dynamic approach to the supreme law. Then, to assert that the only thing judges must do is to 'stick to the constitution' seems nonsense. As long as we lack a common agreement on an interpretative theory, and nothing indicates that we will achieve an agreement soon, the interpreters of the constitution will tend to have almost discretionary power within our constitutional structure.

The situation seems even more serious when we recognize that most Latin American countries follow a *civil law* rather than a *common law* tradition. In countries that participate in the latter practice, judges pay particular attention to previous decisions, which they are required to follow. They must strongly defend any deviation from that tradition, because any unjustified move away from it appears as a breach in their duties.[14] That is not the situation in civil law countries. There both judges and politicians tend to pay more attention to existing national codes (that is, the civil code, the criminal procedure code) than to previous judicial decisions.

Even worse, most Latin American countries have an unstable political history, which has deeply influenced the development of their legal history. So the norm is that politically unstable countries develop a *very unstable legal history.* The main laws and codes, and even the constitution, are subject to frequent changes. Many judges, and particularly Supreme Court judges, are removed after each new government comes to power, whether this government is democratic or not. As a consequence, judicial decisions also become very unstable. It is not only that courts at different levels develop different views, but also that the court itself does, even varying from one year to the next. This creates an obvious legal uncertainty that affects both citizens and legal practitioners. The fact is that even responsible and honest judges may find legal and judicial antecedents for asserting almost everything they want to assert. No matter what opinion they want to maintain, they may look at the past and quote a significant judicial opinion in their support – which most judges tend to do, trying to reinforce their own views.

In sum, the scope of the judicial powers, the lack of a shared interpretative theory, the absence of a common law tradition and the instability of the existing legal tradition all contribute to transforming Latin American judges into enormously powerful figures.

Motivating the Judges. What Means Could be Used to Channel Judges' Decisions in Specific Directions?

Given the ample margins of manoeuvre that judges have, and assuming that we want them to decide certain cases in certain specific directions, the important questions are as follows. Do we have institutional means for channelling their decisions in certain specific directions? What would these institutional means be? In reality we do not have adequate institutional means for ensuring that the judges would follow certain democratic patterns like the ones outlined in the previous sections.

Appointment Powers

This is probably the most important mechanism we have to ensure the prevalence of particular views within the courts. Through these powers, for example, liberal or conservative governments may try to ensure the nomination of liberal or conservative judges. But this seems to be a very weak instrument when we consider that judges have life tenure and we lack other additional means of controlling their decisions. Then, it may well be the case that, for example, conservative judges become liberal after some time. In those cases, a community that was committed to having conservative judges may not be able to ensure that view is represented in the court.

External Controls: Re-electing Judges

Usually, judges are given life tenure, and there are some good reasons for this. For example, Alexander Hamilton in *The Federalist Paper No. 78* (1787) reaffirmed that the permanent tenure of judicial offices was justifiable because 'nothing will contribute so much as this to that independent spirit in the judges which must be essential to the faithful performance of so arduous a duty'.[16] I am not sure that his argument was sound, but that is not important at this point. What matters is that we cannot punish or reward judges as a consequence of the decisions they have adopted during their mandate: they do not need to run for re-election, and we have no other tools for evaluating what they did during their years in office.

External Controls: Controlling Judges During their Tenure

We have neither the power to punish or reward judges at the end of their mandate, nor the institutional tools for approving, disapproving or re-directing their decisions during their mandate. As James Madison wrote in *The Federalist Paper No.49*, judges 'by the mode of their appointment, as well as, by the nature and permanency of it [would be] *too far removed from the people to share much in their prepossessions*'.[16] The fact that judges have been placed 'too far removed from the people' makes it very difficult for us to control their actions. Moreover, as committed citizens we have basically no capacities for establishing a dialogue with our judges. In the best case, we may write articles in newspapers or law journals but those means have no power to control the content of judges' decisions: they may choose to simply ignore our comments.

Internal Controls: The Right of Impeachment

It is possible to dismiss the importance of having external controls over our pubic officers given the importance of the internal controls created in our constitutions. Internal controls are those which belong to our system of 'checks and balances', namely, the capacities that each branch of power has for controlling the excesses of the others. Now, the main internal control we have to discipline our judges is the right of impeachment. However, this does not seem a very appropriate mechanism for the purposes we are pursuing here. First and most important, this power can be exercised only in very exceptional and extreme circumstances, such as when a judge commits a crime.[17] But these are not the cases we are thinking about. We do not want to be able to control our judges only in extreme cases, when they commit a serious offence. Rather, we may reasonably want to control them during the exercise of their daily activities.

Internal Controls: The Right to Correct a Judicial Decision

What capacities have the other branches of power for correcting judicial decisions they find wrong? Certainly not many. After rejecting a judicial decision they may try to insist on their invalidated projects, but this clearly seems to be a senseless choice. Being the 'last voice' of the institutional system, the courts will probably invalidate the statute again. The political branches may choose, instead, to correct their invalidated initiative, thus engaging in a dialogue with the courts.[18] This may be a plausible strategy, but adds very little to their powers to control the courts. In addition, the very idea of a 'dialogue' between political and judicial branches sounds strange in our institutional context. The attractiveness of the idea of a 'dialogue' comes from the notions of equality and fairness that seem implicit in it. The dialogic situation assumes that we are all equally well situated and open to change our views according to 'the force of the best argument'.[19] But this dialogic ideal seems to have very little in common with the institutional reality, where the judicial branch has reserved the power of the 'last word' for itself – something that allows it to change its view or not according to its own criteria.[20]

In any case, what seems to be true is that the powers judges are granted and the difficulties we have in subjecting them to any kind of control may help us understand why so many governments (or even interest groups) in America find it so important to get the main judges on their side. President Roosevelt tried to pack the courts and only desisted once the majority of the tribunal began to uphold his economic reforms. Many Latin American presidents have pursued such initiatives even further. Thus, they frequently pack the courts, or illegally remove some of their members or, in the case of the lower courts, improperly promote or change the functions of some of them, to gain support for their policies.

More generally, political and legal instability in Latin America, together with the absence of a common law tradition and an enforceable interpretative theory, help explain the ease with which the courts change their opinion. The homogeneous composition of courts in terms of gender, class, race and education, combined with their privileged institutional position and the absence of close ties with the ordinary citizens, also help explain the direction of their decisions.

What Do Courts Tend to Do, with the 'Means' and 'Motives' Granted to their Members? The Example of Argentina (1983–2002)

This section spells out the risks of creating an institutional structure like the one that characterizes the judiciary in most Latin American countries using the example of Argentina, 1983–2002. The Argentine case is particularly interesting because it illustrates what happens when wide discretion is allowed to the judiciary. In the course of a very few months the Supreme Court shifted from a very liberal position to a very conservative one. This came about because of the government's decision to enlarge the court, in 1990.[21] Two things must be noted here. First, the decision to augment the number of Supreme Court judges was undoubtedly dishonourable, but still legal: the constitution did not rule out such a move.[22] Second, what that event showed was that the citizens basically have no means of preventing the judges adopting certain decisions. Having said that, let us now analyze Argentina's judicial practice since the country's return to democracy in 1983.

The Protection of Civil Liberties, with a Particular Emphasis on the Right to Criticize the Government and the Right to a Fair Trial

Right after the end of the 1976–1983 dictatorship, Argentina's Supreme Court made significant efforts to ensure strong protection for fundamental individual liberties. For example, through the vote of some of its members the court began to defend the right to a wide, robust and uninhibited debate.[23] Also, in *Campillay, Julio, c/ La Razón y otros*, (CSJN, 15/5/85), the court defined the scope and limits of freedom of expression. With regard to the right to a fair trial, the court adopted other important decisions. For example, in *Fiorentino, Diego Enrique* (CSJN Fallos, 306–2: 1752), it judged the evidence found through an unauthorized home investigation to be invalid.

With its 1990s new composition, however, the court changed its views dramatically. In *Fiscal c/ Fernández, Víctor Hugo*,[24] for example, the court reversed its decision in *Fiorentino*, and admitted the validity of evidence found through an unauthorized police search in the house of a suspect. In addition, the new court began to qualify and restrict the protective doctrine it had been developing regarding the right to freedom of expression. For instance, in *Menem, Eduardo*,[25] a case involving the brother of Argentina's president and also a high public officer, the court distorted the protective requirements it has itself defined in *Campillay*. Thus, it asserted that the journalist who made an accusation against the brother of the president needed to carry out his own investigation, beside fulfilling the requirements of *Campillay*, if he wanted to publish his accusation. In this way, the court not only debased *Campillay* but also a long-standing international doctrine, originating in the case *New York Times v. Sullivan* (376 US 254 [1964]), aimed at giving extra protection to journalists who accuse public officers.[26]

Protection of the Right to Privacy

With regard to the right to privacy, Argentina's Supreme Court also dramatically changed its views. In its original composition, the court had begun to defend an expanded right to privacy, in cases such as *Sejean* (Fallos 308–2: 2287), where it recognized the validity of divorce; in *Portillo* (CSJN, 18/4/89, ED, 133–372), where it made ample space for the recognition of the right of conscientious objectors; and in a case involving the members of a religious sect, where it decided to protect the parents' rights to educate their children in their own religious beliefs (Fallos

303:151). Also, the court made an important decision in *Bazterrica's* (CS, 1986/08/29), a case where it affirmed that Argentina's constitution protected private consumption of drugs. Shortly afterwards, however, and with its new composition, this protective view was radically modified. In *Montalvo* (CS, December 11-990), by proceeding to neglect the importance of respecting its own previous decisions, the court considered the punishment applied to the indicted valid, although Montalvo was accused of the same crime as Bazterrica. In this way, and neglecting the need to protect individual's personal autonomy, the court diluted what it had previously considered a closed sphere of privacy. In another major case, *Comunidad Homosexual Argentina* (CS, 1991/11/22), the new court accepted a restriction on the right to association of Argentina's homosexual community. As Judge Boggiano claimed, the community could not be forced to tolerate all types of minorities, which would imply 'the erosion of society's cohesion' and thereby the disintegration of Argentina. Thus, the court ratified its decision to undermine each person's right to personal autonomy.

Restriction of the Executive's Tendencies to Increase its own Powers

In *Peralta c/ Nacion Argentina* (313 Fallos 1513 [1990]), the Court had the opportunity of analyzing the emergency powers of government, as well as the legislative capacities of the president. In *Peralta*, the court did the opposite of what we would have recommended here. In effect, in the previous sections we defended the importance of deliberating about public policies, and we affirmed the value of these deliberations, particularly, in cases of extreme crisis. We also maintained that a proper democratic deliberation ideally required consulting all those agents potentially affected by a decision. In contrast, the majority in *Peralta* asserted that 'given the problems at work, and the types of solutions that they are calling for, these questions cannot be efficiently and speedily treated and solved by pluri-personal bodies [such as the legislature]'. Through this decision, the court degraded the republican idea of division of powers, by stating that the tribunals should not deny the legislative functions of the executive, if they did not want to dissolve 'national unity' and avoid the 'fracture' of the state. A similar ruling situation appeared in *Cocchia v. Nacion Argentina* (316 Fallos 2624 [1993]), where the court had to examine an executive decree through which the president had exercised very ample legislative powers.[27] In that case, the court refused to exercise its controlling functions, asserting that it should avoid transforming itself into 'an obstacle to the resolutions adopted by the other branches that have electoral responsibility'.

Through these and other decisions the court refused to fulfil its constitutional role. It should have been more careful in its approach, given the fragility of Argentina's institutional organization. The court should have considered suspect, and thus subjected to close scrutiny, any attempts by the executive to expand its own powers.[28]

Preservation of Republican Controls

On 22 March 1990, the court had the opportunity of examining the situation of Judge Miguel Del Castillo, who was 'transferred' from his position to another, by an executive decision not supported by an explicit agreement of the Senate. The circumstances that surrounded the case made it evident that the executive wanted to replace Del Castillo by another, more amicable judge. Del Castillo's case was also very important because of its implications regarding the division of function between the different branches of power.[29] It is clear that when the Senate agrees with the executive to appoint a certain judge, it does so taking into account certain specific judicial functions that they want the judge to develop.[30] However, instead of bolstering the existing structure of controls, and subjecting the decision at stake to a strict scrutiny, the court simply enforced the executive's decision.

The court had another good opportunity to examine the executive's decisions in this area in *Molinas* (314 Fallos 1091 [1991]), a case where it had to review the removal of the attorney general of the nation. Molinas was in charge of investigating illegal decisions or behaviour by members of the executive branch, and had been very active, although not always successful, in his job. Worried about the work of the attorney general, President Menem decided to fire him without setting any impeachment process into motion. The above-mentioned facts should have moved the members of the court to drastically reduce the presumption of validity that all political decisions enjoy. By contrast, a majority of the tribunal affirmed that to prevent the president from removing Attorney General Molinas implied undue interference with the work of the executive.

Defence Against Attempts to Discontinue the Democratic Regime

Argentina's Supreme Court has a very bad record in terms of protecting democracy from authoritarian interventions. Actually, at the beginning of the twentieth century after the first military coup in the country's history, which took place in 1930, the court decided to make a decision by itself, that is, without any requirement from individuals or public officials. In that *Acordada* (Agreement), the court affirmed the validity of the military coup, and asserted that it was a legitimate exercise of force. In this way, the court inaugurated what was called the 'de facto doctrine,' through which it made a substantial contribution to the debasement of Argentina's fragile democracy. More recently, however, the court reacted against its previous decisions and began to dilute the force of its own pro-authoritarian tendencies. Thus, in *Aramayo* (306 Fallos 73) it made a sharp distinction between democratic and non-democratic legislation, and defended the higher value of the former decisions.

However, when the court majority changed in 1991, it went back to its previous position and re-validated the old 'de facto doctrine'. This change of attitude became explicit in *Godoy* (CS, 1990/12/27), when the court re-examined the distinction between democratic and non-democratic legislation that it had made in *Aramayo*. Actually, the case did not require the court to reflect upon the validity of non-democratic legislation, but the main tribunal decided to advance its opinion on the topic. According to the new court, there was no need to distinguish between the two types of norms because they both had the same constitutional status.

What do These Cases Suggest? What Should be Changed to Achieve Different Outcomes?

While the previous section examined the court's behaviour in Argentina after the end of the last dictatorship, some more general conclusions can be drawn from this particular case.

It is clear that what courts did in Argentina (and presumably in many other countries too) was to turn the writer's recommendations presented in the early parts of this account on their head. However, given the way the courts were organized, what they did should hardly be a cause for surprise.

In effect, given the power and incentives entrusted to judges, that is, given the 'means' and 'motives' that society has provided them with, everything seems to just let them act as they please. They have broad institutional powers and, given the absence of a common interpretative theory, and the civil law tradition, there is ample scope to exercise discretion in their decisions.[31] Also, they are detached from the people; they have life tenure, and in many cases excellent salaries that put them well above most citizens. They are protected by strong immunities that make it very difficult to remove or sanction them even in the case of crimes; and they are granted the 'last institutional say'. In sum, they have many precious things to offer, through their decisions, and at the same time there are few controls upon them. In addition, they are normally recruited from the same group in terms of race, gender and class; they are normally educated in the same environments; they have or develop fluid personal and institutional contacts with powerful political actors and interest groups; and they have no institutional obligation to take into account the suggestions or criticisms of people who disagree with them. Why be surprised, then, when we learn that they are placed under political pressure or that they 'sell' their decisions to powerful groups?

The previous comments, however, do not deny the possibility of having honourable judges, honourable decisions or honourable courts, like the Colombian Constitutional Court, for example. Such an outcome is neither more nor less possible than is its opposite, even though the latter tends to be more common in less consolidated or less stable legal communities.

The previous analysis leads us to another important point, namely, that many proposals for judicial reform and many studies on the judiciary tend to miss what is most crucial in terms of improving the work of the judiciary in Latin America. In effect, if judges have prosecuted homosexuals, rather than protected them; if they have dismissed the importance of fair trial, rather than reinforced it; if they have defended the '*de facto* doctrine', rather than attacked it; if they have misused the Human Rights Conventions, rather than implemented them; if they have favoured the interests of powerful economic groups, rather than limited them, then all this was not (or not simply) because they were politically dependent, or because they lacked administrative help or advanced technologies.

Of course, Argentina's case may be troublesome in this respect, because the most questionable decisions of the tribunal came right after the court was enlarged and its majority changed. However, it should be clear that crucial cases like *C.H.A.* or *Godoy*, among many others, were not the product of the political dependence of the judges but instead owed to their unfounded conservatism or lack of commitment to democracy. In other words, the ruling party had no particular reasons for being satisfied with decisions like *C.H.A.* or *Godoy*. At the same time, however, those decisions were totally compatible with the way in which the judiciary was organized. In effect, in Latin America, as in most other places, judges have no good incentives to do things like defend democracy or protect disadvantaged minorities.[32]

Now, the poverty of judges' bureaucratic tools (not a situation that applies everywhere with respect to the highest courts) may help us explain the slowness to make decisions. Their political dependency, which is real cause for concern, may explain their deference towards the government's initiatives. But none of these factors explains the bulk of their decisions – including some of the most important ones, all things considered.

Politically independent, well-educated and well-equipped judges could still write many of the questionable decisions that we examined above – particularly, but not only, in legally and politically unstable communities. That is to say, a certain degree of political independence[33] and the possession of bureaucratic facilities are necessary but not sufficient conditions for ensuring democratic justice. To ensure this goal we need to re-think whether we want judges to have the 'last institutional say'; whether we want courts to continue being fundamentally homogeneous bodies within fundamentally pluralist societies;[34] whether we want to preserve their detachment from society; whether we want to maintain them basically free from controls and free from any obligation to establish an egalitarian dialogue with the public. In sum, in order to achieve democratic justice we need first to take a fresh and thorough look at the 'means' and 'motives' we grant to our justices.

NOTES

1. Unless stated to the contrary, the following analysis refers in places to Supreme Courts and Supreme Court justices.
2. In stating this, I am basically following James Madison's opinion in *The Federalist Paper No. 51* (1787).
3. See, for example, Owen Fiss, 'Groups and the Equal Protection Clause', *Philosophy and Public Affairs*, Vol.5, No.2 (1976), pp.107–77.
4. For example, Bruce Ackerman, *We the People: Foundation* (Cambridge, MA: Harvard University Press, 1991).
5. John Ely, *Democracy and Distrust* (Cambridge, MA: Harvard University Press, 1980).
6. Ronald Dworkin, *Taking Rights Seriously* (London: Duckworth, 1977); idem, *Freedom's Law: The Moral Reading of the American Constitution* (Cambridge, MA: Harvard University Press, 1996).
7. Cass Sunstein, 'Against Positive Rights', in A. Sajo and K. Lauer (eds), *Western-Rights: Post-Communist Applications*, (Dordrecht: Kluwer Law International, 1996).
8. It is assumed there is general agreement on the importance of preserving the basics of our constitutions which are: the division of powers, the structure of 'checks and balances' and the defence of basic rights aimed at preserving our most valued liberties, although the writer's own personal view is that these 'basics' should also be discussed critically. What follows evaluates how the judges behaved during recent decades, given the role that we could reasonably expect them to assume and taking into account the constitutional structure that organizes their function.
9. G. Stone, L. Seidman, C. Sunstein and M. Tushnet, *Constitutional Law* (New York: Aspen, 2001).
10. Victor Ferreres Comella, *Justicia constitucional y democracia* (Madrid: Centro de Estudios Constitucionales, 1997).
11. William Eskrdige, 'Dynamic Statutory Interpretation', *University of Pennsylvania Law Review* Vol.135 (1987) pp.1479–1556
12. Robert Bork, *The Tempting of America* (New York: Simon & Schuster, 1990); Antonin Scalia, *A Matter of Interpretation* (Princeton, NJ: Princeton University Press, 1997).
13. Ronald Dworkin, *Law's Empire* (Cambridge, MA: Harvard University Press, 1986).
14. The problem can also exists in common law traditions. Precisely because of the

looseness of their interpretative capacities, a court may say that it is following precedent when it is actually not following it. The court may say, for example, that its view represents a 'natural' or reasonable reading of the existent body of decisions when it is actually following a different legal path.

15. *The Federalist Paper No.78*, in *The Federalist Papers* (New York: Mentor Books, 1961), p.469.
16. *The Federalist Papers* (note 15), p.316 (emphasis added).
17. Needless to say, the impeachment system seems too complicated. Probably, this fact explains why there have been so many problems surrounding its use.
18. Alexander Bickel, *The Least Dangerous Branch* (New Haven, CT: Yale University Press, 1962); also Bruce Ackerman, 'Discovering the Constitution. The Economy of Virtue', *The Yale Law Journal*, Vol.93 (1984), pp.1013–71.
19. Jürgen Habermas, 'Further Reflections on the Public Sphere', in C. Calhoun (ed), *Habermas and the Public Sphere* (Cambridge, MA: The MIT Press, 1992).
20. Probably, the framers of our constitutional democracies were not afraid of this situation because they assumed that given the way judges would be appointed, and given the stringent conditions required in order to become a member of the courts, these positions would actually be reserved to people like them, in terms of class, gender and race.
21. Through this decision the government created what was called an 'automatic majority', namely, a majority of five 'government-friendly' judges, who normally imposed their views over the remaining 'minority of four'. The minority did not always vote together, but did so in a large number of cases.
22. When President Menem's government improperly enlarged the court, it repeated the same mistake made by other constitutional and de facto governments in previous years. In effect, during the early 1940s President J.D. Perón had removed three out of five judges from the court. The military government that replaced him did the same with the whole court in 1955. President A. Frondizi (1958–1962) tried to enlarge the court from five to seven members, but before that a military coup put an end to his government. The same happened with A. Illia's government, which lasted less than three years. The military regime that came to power in 1966 simply removed all the members of the previous, democratic court. All of them resigned, however, with the arrival of a new democratic government in 1973. The bloody dictatorship that came to power in 1976 appointed a whole new court that year, and all its members resigned in 1983 when democratic President R. Alfonsín was elected. This remarkably unstable judicial history undoubtedly explains most of the differences we find between the rulings and respectability of the Argentinean Supreme Court and those that belong to politically more stable democracies.
23. See, for example, Judge Petracchi's opinion in *Ponzetti de Balbín, c/ Editorial Atlántida* (CSJN, 11/12/84).
24. CSJN Fallos, 400:22. See also *Ferrer*, CSJN, 10 July 1990.
25. Fallos 321:2848 (1998); see also *Espinosa*, Fallos 317:1448 (1994).
26. See also his decision in *Menem*, 2001, M. 368. XXXIV, where the court condemned *Editorial Perfil* for publishing some truthful information about the president having a child out of wedlock.
27. Jonathan Miler, 'Evaluating the Argentine Supreme Court under Presidents Alfonsín and Menem (1983–1999)', *Southwestern Journal of Law and Trade in the Americas*, Vol.7, No.2 (2000), pp.369–433.
28. It is possible to find similar problems in *Aerolíneas Argentinas* (313 Fallos 863, 1990), which indicates more careful scrutiny should also have been given to the substantial programme of privatization process that was then starting.
29. Carlos Nino, *Fundamentos de Derecho Constitucional* (Buenos Aires: Astrea, 1993), p.474.
30. This was also Judge Bacqué's opinion, in his dissent.

31. Although I want to emphasize this point, I do not think that the situation is or would be fundamentally different in a common law tradition.
32. Would things improve, however, if judges were more closely connected with the people at large? The answer to this question depends, among other things, on the way in which we re-build the relationship between judges and the people. There is certainly scope for many reasonable changes to be made, which can be easily justified. See, for example, Mark Tushnet, *Taking the Constitution Away from the Court* (Princeton, NJ: Princeton University Press, 1999) and Jeremy Waldron, *Law and Disagreement*, (Oxford: Oxford University Press, 2001).
33. I say 'a certain degree' of political independence because I disagree with the idea of having politically isolated judges. However, a prerequisite for a proper examination of the topic is some discussion of the meaning of 'political independence'.
34. John Rawls, *Political Liberalism* (New York: Columbia University Press, 1991).

Lessons Learned and the Way Forward

IRWIN P. STOTZKY

The tidal wave of democratization that has spread across the globe in the past three decades is remarkable for its underlying dependence on the rule of law and the role of the courts. It is also remarkable for the failure of scholars to engage in serious academic work in comparing the various nations and the role of their courts in this process of democratization. There is, of course, a simple explanation for this failure – the international democratic revolution is a 'work in progress'. Different nations are in different stages of democratic development. Some nations remain in the process of adjusting norms or institutions to the democratic rule of law. Political parties remain at different levels of competition and development. Independent, non-corrupt judiciaries that are able to interpret and enforce a bill of rights against a powerful executive branch are not yet functioning or are functioning poorly. In other nations, however, liberal democratic institutions such as an independent judiciary do exist in full force, but their stability is not yet completely secured.

These points make clear that authoritarianism and its remnants cannot be overcome merely because people favour democratic methods for resolving almost insoluble problems and developing a democratic nation. Powerful economic, social, and political forces block the passage from dictatorship to democracy. The underlying forces include an almost organic conception of society that leads to a dualistic vision of the social order, corporatism, anomie and unlawfulness, and extreme concentrations of institutional, economic and social power. A combination of these forces and the interplay between them are often directly related to massive human rights abuses committed by those who possess the power.

How can we compare various nations, their political, legal, social and economic conditions and the role of courts in the democratization process? Most of the previous scholarly work on the role of courts in democratic transitions focused on what to do about the human rights abuses committed by the former military dictatorships. There is a paucity of research on the role courts actually play or may play in different nations that are in various stages of democratic development. In particular, research is needed on when and how courts are able to check the executive when it takes anti-democratic actions, whether and how courts may play a positive role in promoting socio-economic development, and whether and how courts can provide access to marginalized groups. Research is also needed on how courts can perform these tasks while simultaneously creating and maintaining their independence and legitimacy.

The essays in this collection announce to the world that comparative work on these questions is not only possible but extremely important and fruitful. In one way or another, every author asks the question of what judges should aim for, given the constraints of their economic, political and social context. Every author has a somewhat different take on this question. This shows convincingly that there are different judicial visions of the role of courts based upon different histories, different methods of adjudication, different resources and different legal cultures in each nation. For example, as several of the authors make clear, judicial review makes sense in some nations on some issues and not in other nations or on other issues. See, for example, the contributions of Shapiro and Couso.

The studies suggest that one way of viewing questions of the judicial role is to argue that the function of a judge in a constitutional democracy is to give meaning and application to constitutional values, independent of political preferences. See, for instance, Gargarella on Argentina. Indeed, the right of the judge to speak and the obligation of others, like governmental agencies, to listen, depends not on the judge's personal attributes, nor even on the content of his message. Instead, it depends on his ability to be distant and detached from the immediate contestants and the body politic, yet fully attentive to grievances, and responsive in terms that transcend preferences and that are sufficient to support judgments deemed to be constitutional. Thus, the legitimacy of a judicial decision depends crucially on the quality of the process itself.

In addition, as some of the studies suggest, the political economy of many of these nations must be transformed, and courts also have a role to play in this transformation. This includes the ability to interpret and enforce a constitutional system. Comparing the accounts of Couso and Roux makes it clear, however, that to secure such a role for the courts may require different judicial strategies depending on the political context. In a country like Chile, the 'non-political' nature of the judiciary seems to be a factor explaining its relative strength and continuity. In other contexts courts can subtly influence political resource allocation, and use such a transformative role as a key to building judicial legitimacy, as indicated in the analysis of the South African case. In yet other situations, as Santiso argues on the basis of his analysis of Brazil, unrestricted judicial independence can harm economic development.

The stories each author tells of his or her particular country are diverse and wide ranging, – compare for example the approaches of Gloppen, Roux, Couso, and Sieder. Each author demonstrates a different method and approach. Some authors take more theoretical positions and others write more about case analysis. Each story is necessarily incomplete and subject to different interpretations and conclusions, but each provide a valid perspective and adds to our understanding. Moreover, some authors wisely refuse to make solid conclusions but simply list general factors to look at in the comparisons: Widner provides an exemplar.

This demonstrates that it matters importantly which viewpoint one adopts when studying the role of courts in new democracies. Each viewpoint – be it that of the executive, the legislature, the judiciary or the common citizen - selects different factors or looks at similar factors differently. There are also somewhat different sets of normative lenses depending on the factors and viewpoints selected. Some of these differences depend on the training and experience of the authors. Political scientists see the world differently from lawyers because of their background and training. Those with expertise in more than one area have an even more complex vision, as is illustrated here by Gargarella. Though each vision is necessarily incomplete, each discipline and the different methodological approaches within each discipline – as amply demonstrated in this volume – may combine to enhance our understanding of the role that courts should and do play in new democracies.

How do we proceed from here? How can we continue to push this project forward? The first point, I think, is to be aware of the possible limitations of comparative work such as this. How can we make valid comparisons across time (then, now, and in the future?), particularly if various nations are in various stages of the transition or consolidation process? As Shapiro correctly points out, if a nation is in some form of transition, it may be too late to study how it was and too early to study how it will be. The question of whether nations remain in the transition towards democracy or have already completed the journey requires conceptual clarification as well as empirical corroboration. The complex question of when a democracy has been consolidated depends upon justificatory theories of democracy and is intimately connected with the stability of a specific political system. All of these points raise complicated questions that depend for their explanations upon the peculiar circumstances of each nation and on certain predictions, particularly about the stability, development, and maturity of institutions. Analyzing these questions requires thorough research on the institutional structures of particular nations. Moreover, the transition or consolidation process is not always a progressive one. It is sometimes a process of loss and not of gain. Nations slip-slide back and forth between progress and disaster. Democratic development often depends on economic, social, and political factors that are beyond the control of courts (Argentina is a good example). But, of course, courts also have a role to play in resolving some of these issues.

A positive development in these nations seems to depend on the establishment of a deliberative democracy – one that allows for equal participation and rational discourse among all segments of society. This discourse, in turn, is essential for the creation of a moral consciousness of humanity that recognizes the value of human rights and abhors any notion that disregards them. Courts, of course, must play a role in this deliberative process, and help society resolve some of its major economic, political, and social problems. Indeed, this discourse is also essential for helping courts establish and maintain their legitimacy and independence. Moreover, as Gargarella makes clear, constitutional means and personal motives must also be added to the equation.

The contributions to this collection are all written from somewhat different visions of the good and the just and even of democracy itself. Comparative work in this field might benefit from well-developed theories that examine and explain the essential elements that make democracy so valuable and how legal institutions fit within such theories. Fortunately there is a plethora of such theories. What is needed is a marriage between the theory and the application to real life situations. As Sieder argues, there must be a thorough analysis of the historical context within which the law, justice, and rights are developed in various nations.

Assuming we are able to overcome some of these challenges, one way of pursuing these questions would be to classify nations and their judiciaries. We could do this by comparing whatever factors of accountability we conclude are necessary conditions for the effective operation of courts in democracies in similarly developed nations. Even if we do this, we may discover that court structures and constitutional adjudicative methods differ because of a number of factors related to the histories and cultures of nations. For example, while Chile has constitutional courts, Argentina does not. Would it make sense to sharpen the analytic tools by trying to have a clearer understanding of accountability, by comparing case studies on specific legal issues across cultures? Is this even possible? Certainly we need scholarly work to address such questions.

This volume raises at least one other significant concern regarding the role of law and courts in the democratic revolution – the tension between constitutionalism and democracy. These tensions arise when the expansion of democracy weakens constitutionalism, or when the strengthening of the constitutional ideal restrains the democratic process. In this writer's opinion, the relationship between democracy and constitutionalism depends most importantly on the interpretation of constitutionalism. Constitutionalism, like democracy, of course, has a range of meanings that vary in their conceptual thickness and lead to different interpretive schemes. Scholarly work is also needed on the issues raised by this observation.

In the past three decades of democratic transition, the judiciary has had rather limited success in promoting democratic reform. As the studies in this collection demonstrate, democratic change cannot be created in a vacuum. All parts of the public and private sectors must work together on these problems. So far that has not happened. But the promise and the hope for real democratic reform remain in the hearts and minds of the vast majority of the people in these nations. The judiciary, by living up to its democratic demands, must keep these hopes alive and help make them become a reality. Scholarly studies are crucial for suggesting ways for the courts to perform their proper democratic functions. The material here represents a wonderful beginning.

Abstracts

Judicial Review in Developed Democracies
MARTIN SHAPIRO

Defining successful judicial review as that which changes public policy in the direction desired by the court, federalism review is, in theory, the most likely to be successful, separation of powers less successful and rights review least successful of all. In fact the most successful review has been federalism review as exemplified by the United States and the European Union. The US record of rights review has been less successful than sometimes supposed, but the spread of rights review in Europe gives more cause for optimism. Both the inherent dangers of rights review in a democracy and the US record suggest that courts must be cautious and politically skilled if they are to succeed at rights review.

How Some Reflections on the United States' Experience May Inform African Efforts to Build Court Systems and the Rule of Law
JENNIFER WIDNER

This study examines how court systems capable of holding public officials accountable evolve. Although its main purpose is to inform the way we understand this process in Africa and other parts of the developing world, the account tries to make general points by way of a short, idiosyncratic excursion through United States' judicial history. The purpose is to examine more closely important aspects of explanations often not considered. Reform requires more than an incentive to seek change. Leadership, appropriate framing, a supply of ideas, and institutional capacity all matter too. Rarely do these things come together at the same moment, although happy conjunctions are more likely to occur in some political systems than in others. Change happens slowly, in fits and starts, with the benefits realized only after the ingredients are all assembled. Whether it is possible to sustain the impetus for reform while the pieces come together may depend heavily on the existence of organized civic groups and the links between the members of these groups and those in power.

The Constitutional Court and Control of Presidential Extraordinary Powers in Colombia
RODRIGO UPRIMNY

This study analyzes the attempts of Colombia's Constitutional Court to control the abuse of presidential emergency powers in the last decade. After describing the dilemmas that governmental emergency powers pose to constitutional regimes and explaining some particularities of Colombia as a democracy under permanent emergency, the account focuses on the efforts of the Constitutional Court to exercise a 'material' control of the declaration of a state of emergency by the President. According to this legal doctrine, it is the duty of the court to analyze if the facts invoked by the government constitute a crisis severe enough to justify the use of emergency powers. The analysis shows that the court has exercised this material control in a quite strict way and has nullified several declarations of a state of emergency by different presidents. The study goes on to show how this form of judicial review has been possible in a country like Colombia, with a precarious democracy and a cruel armed conflict. It describes also the impact of this form of judicial control in Colombian politics and offers some more general conclusions based on Colombian experience.

The Politics of Judicial Review in Chile in the Era of Democratic Transition, 1990–2002
JAVIER A. COUSO

The study addresses the politics and effects of judicial review in Chile. It concludes that by and large the Chilean courts have refused to exercise their constitutional review powers in defence of individual rights. Although this suggests that Chile represents a 'negative model' of judicial review in transitional democracies, the author argues that such an understanding would be simplistic. The Chilean courts' reluctance to exercise their review powers represents the continuation of a long-held strategic stance of avoiding politically controversial cases. This in turn has contributed to the preservation of the autonomy and political independence that has historically allowed the Chilean judiciary to play a crucial role in the promotion and maintenance of the legality that characterises this country. Merging the insights of two academic fields that rarely communicate – democratization studies and public law and courts – the author proposes that prematurely introducing judicial review of the constitution in non-consolidated democracies could actually make things worse. This, because it introduces irresistible incentives for government intervention in the work of the courts, thus destroying a *sine qua non* of the rule of law: judicial independence.

Legitimating Transformation: Political Resource Allocation in the South African Constitutional Court
THEUNIS ROUX

This study examines the performance of the South African Constitutional Court in four cases in which it was required to review the allocation of resources by the political branches. According to the conventional view, political resource allocation should be immune from judicial scrutiny because it involves decisions that courts are neither institutionally equipped nor mandated to make. In new democracies, the added reason for judicial self-restraint in this area is thought to be that courts should avoid potentially damaging confrontations with the political branches until they have established their legitimacy. And yet, in the cases examined here, the Constitutional Court has not only skillfully negotiated its review function, but actively sought out opportunities to subject political resource allocation to the standards set by the Constitution. In this way the Court has been able to build its legitimacy by endorsing the overall thrust of the political branches' transformation efforts. In turn, those efforts have been legitimated by their exposure to judicial scrutiny. This finding suggests that the conventional view may be wrong, and that constitutional courts in new democracies may need to involve themselves in controversial political questions if they are to play a meaningful role in the consolidation of democracy.

The Accountability Function of the Courts in Tanzania and Zambia
SIRI GLOPPEN

This comparative analysis of the judiciaries in Tanzania and Zambia finds that neither one has developed a strong accountability function vis-à-vis the government. It goes on to address *why* judges in the two countries rarely have restrained the government in politically significant cases, identifying three sets of factors that may explain why the judges perform as they do: the legal culture; the institutional structure; and the social legitimacy of the courts. The study concludes that there are signs in the Tanzanian judiciary of a certain willingness to hold the government accountable in politically salient cases, but that their opportunity to do so is limited, due to institutional, social and political factors restricting the flow of constitutional cases. The Zambian courts have more political cases and opportunities for fulfilling an accountability function vis-à-vis the executive, but are reluctant to assert such authority. This is attributed to the legal culture and to political pressure.

Renegotiating 'Law and Order': Judicial Reform and Citizen Responses in Post-war Guatemala
RACHEL SIEDER

This study examines reforms aimed at strengthening the rule of law in Guatemala implemented since the signing of the peace accords in December 1996. Despite nearly US$200 million in foreign aid to the justice sector, impunity remains the rule, the judicial process is subverted by military and criminal networks, citizen confidence in the judicial system remains low and recourse to non-judicial measures – the 'privatisation of justice'- is on the increase. It is argued that the institutionally-focused approach to rule of law reform currently predominating in donor thinking ignores the historical context within which understandings of 'law', 'justice' and 'rights' are shaped. Institutions do matter, but only by understanding the role of law in long-run processes of state formation and the dynamic, inter-subjective nature of legal interactions can we begin to understand the specificities of socio-legal change.

Economic Reform and Judicial Governance in Brazil: Balancing Independence with Accountability
CARLOS SANTISO

Conventional wisdom on judicial governance posits that an independent judiciary is the single most important prerequisite of the rule of law. However the case of Brazil demonstrates that this is not necessarily the case, as there exist tensions and trade-offs between independence and accountability. The democratic constitution of 1988 clearly succeeded in isolating the judiciary from political interference, thus enabling it to perform its role as an institution of horizontal accountability in particular through the judicial review of executive decrees. However, Brazil's unrestricted independence has progressively become a hindrance to effective economic governance, a policy area in which the judiciary has especially asserted itself. The central question is whether the judiciary is too autonomous, lacking effective mechanisms of democratic accountability and external control. The paradox is that excessive independence makes it particularly difficult to reform the judiciary. This study assesses the governance of the judiciary in Brazil and its impact on economic reform. It argues that the challenge of judicial reform resides in strengthening the countervailing mechanisms of accountability to enhance the judiciary's social responsiveness and political responsibility. Finding the right balance between independence and accountability is the defining challenge of judicial governance in Brazil.

In Search of Democratic Justice – What Courts Should Not Do: Argentina, 1983-2002
ROBERTO GARGARELLA

This study examines why, after so many years of economically costly judicial reforms in Latin America, the judicial system in most of the region is still working so poorly. The study assesses that part of the problem stems from a wrong theoretical analysis. Academics and leading reformers alike have placed too much emphasis on the politically dependent character of many Latin American judges, or the lack of basic resources both among judges and the people at large – such things as good salaries, administrative facilities, training, education and information. However, these serious problems are only part of the story. The case of Argentina shows that in order to reflect properly on future judicial reforms we should mainly concentrate our attention on the (questionable) constitutional 'means and motives' that have already been granted to the judges.

List of Contributors

Roberto Gargarella is Professor of Law and Constitutional Theory, Universidad Torcuato Di Tella, Buenos Aires, Argentina.

Siri Gloppen is Researcher at the University of Bergen, Department of Comparative Politics, and Head of the Courts in Transition Programme, Chr. Michelsen Institute, Bergen, Norway.

Elin Skaar is Senior Researcher and Head of the Human Rights Programme at the Chr. Michelsen Institute, Bergen, Norway.

Martin Shapiro is James W. and Isobel Coffroth Professor of Law, University of California, Berkeley, USA.

Jennifer Widner is Professor in the Department of Political Science, University of Michigan, USA.

Rodrigo Uprimny is Professor of Law, National University of Colombia and Deputy Judge at the Constitutional Court of Colombia.

Javier Couso is Professor of Law and Political Science, Universidad Diego Portales, Santiago, Chile.

Theunis Roux is Reader in Law and Society and Head of the Law & Transformation Programme, Centre for Applied Legal Studies, University of the Witwatersrand, South Africa.

Rachel Sieder is Senior Lecturer in Politics at the Institute of Latin American Studies, University of London, UK.

Carlos Santiso is a political economist at the Paul H Nitze School of Advanced International Studies of Johns Hopkins University, Washington DC, USA.

Irwin P. Stotzky is Professor of Law and Director of the Center for the Study of Human Rights, University of Miami School of Law, USA.

Index

For Product Safety Concerns and Information please contact our EU representative GPSR@taylorandfrancis.com
Taylor & Francis Verlag GmbH, Kaufingerstraße 24, 80331 München, Germany

www.ingramcontent.com/pod-product-compliance
Lightning Source LLC
LaVergne TN
LVHW011129300926
849160LV00008B/582

* 9 7 8 0 7 1 4 6 8 4 4 9 9 *